I0004015

Java Spring Boot

3 Books in 1 - "From Beginner to Pro: Navigating the Full Stack of Spring Boot for High-Performance Applications"

Henry Arias

© Copyright 2023 - All rights reserved.

The contents of this book may not be reproduced, duplicated or transmitted without direct written permission from the author.

Under no circumstances will any legal responsibility or blame be held against the publisher for any reparation, damages, or monetary loss due to the information herein, either directly or indirectly.

Legal Notice:

This book is copyright protected. This is only for personal use. You cannot amend, dis-tribute, sell, use, quote or paraphrase any part or the content within this book without the consent of the author.

Disclaimer Notice:

Please note the information contained within this document is for educational and entertainment purposes only. Every attempt has been made to provide accurate, up to date and reliable complete information. Readers acknowledge that the author is not engaging in the rendering of legal, financial, medical or professional advice. The content of this book has been derived from various sources. Please consult a licensed professional before attempting any techniques outlined in this book.

By reading this document, the reader agrees that under no circumstances is the author responsible for any losses, direct or indirect, which are incurred as a result of the use of information contained within this document.

Table of Contents

BOOK 1 - Java Spring Boot: *"A Beginner's Guide to Building Your First Web Applications with Java Spring Boot"*

BOOK 2 - Java Spring Boot: *"A Middle-Level Guide to Enhancing Microservices and RESTful APIs with Spring Boot"*

BOOK 3 - Java Spring Boot: *"A Pro-Level Guide to Expert Spring Boot Performance Tuning and Advanced Configuration"*

Introduction

The importance of web development in today's digital world

In our world that's increasingly ruled by digital interactions, the realm of web development claims a central role, intricately knitting the details of our daily lives. This domain, dedicated to forging, rolling out, and sustaining web platforms and applications, is pivotal in orchestrating the dialogue between people, enterprises, and cutting-edge tech trends. The indispensable nature of web development within our digital milieu is evident, serving as a catalyst for innovation, easing the flow of communication, and bolstering economic vitality.

Web development provides a critical platform for businesses to exhibit their offerings, enabling them to cast a wide net over an international audience with remarkable ease. Virtual spaces like websites and web apps stand as 24/7 showcases, erasing the boundaries set by geography and time. In the bustling marketplace of today, a firm's online persona is often viewed as a marker of its authenticity and breadth. Furthermore, web development grants businesses the ability to tailor their digital touchpoints to match the varied tastes of their audience, guaranteeing fluid interactions across an array of devices.

Yet, the significance of web development transcends its function as a mere digital veneer. It's fundamental to the internal machinations of organizations, infusing tasks from customer relations to stock management with efficiency and automation, thereby elevating productivity and trimming down costs. Consider, for instance, an advanced web-based system for inventory management capable of autonomously tracking inventory levels, refreshing data instantaneously, and alerting managers to looming shortages, effectively sidestepping typical inventory control hurdles.

Moreover, web development has transformed the way we communicate, reshaping the dynamics of how we forge and maintain relationships. Platforms such as social media sites, blogs, and discussion boards have given rise to dynamic forums where thoughts and information are exchanged without restraint. These platforms level the playing field for content generation, allowing anyone connected to the web to broadcast their perspectives, artistic expressions, and findings to a worldwide audience. This open exchange has galvanized social initiatives, sparked creativity, and facilitated the spread of knowledge.

In addition, web development stands at the leading edge of technological advancements. The advent of Web 3.0, highlighted by progress in blockchain, artificial intelligence, and machine learning, is set to redefine the web as a smarter, more distributed, and secure sphere. Developers are crucial in weaving these sophisticated technologies into web applications, amplifying their functionality and safeguarding features. For example, weaving AI into customer service interfaces can enable intricate, personalized interactions through chatbots, significantly boosting user engagement and contentment.

The impact of web development is particularly significant in the educational arena. E-learning platforms have democratized access to educational resources, empowering individuals from diverse backgrounds to tap into high-quality learning materials and partake in interactive educational experiences. These platforms employ web technologies to present a spectrum of content formats, accommodating a variety of learning preferences and needs.

On the technical front, web development is in a constant state of flux, embracing emerging technologies, frameworks, and methodologies. The emergence of Progressive Web Apps (PWAs), for instance, has muddied the waters between web and mobile applications, offering users a smooth, app-like experience through their web browsers. This is made possible by innovative web functionalities like service workers, which facilitate offline access, and web app manifests, which enable the 'installation' of web apps on user devices.

The incorporation of a service worker in JavaScript, facilitating offline functionality and resource caching for a web application, showcases how developers can bolster the resilience and user experience of web platforms. By initiating the service worker and leveraging `**install**` and `**fetch**` event listeners, the application can adeptly manage resource caching and retrieval.

To wrap up, web development stands as a vital element in the digital age, driving forward innovation across various sectors and communities. It not only guarantees the online visibility of businesses and individuals but also underpins the operational, communicative, and innovative aspects of modern society. As we continue to see the emergence of new technological breakthroughs, the relevance of web development is poised to escalate, sculpting the contours of our digital future.

Overview of Java Spring Boot and its role in modern web development

Java Spring Boot has established itself as a key player in the field of web development today, marking a significant advancement in the approach to creating and deploying applications for enterprises. This sophisticated iteration of the Spring framework is tailored to simplify the initialization and configuration of Spring-centric projects, proving to be a boon for developers striving for streamlined processes and reliability in their web ventures. Spring Boot is renowned for its approach that prioritizes conventions over configurations, complemented by an array of built-in functionalities that notably cut down the development and operational efforts typically required.

The foundational aim of Spring Boot is to demystify the development cycle. It sidesteps the traditional demands for extensive XML configurations and hands-on dependency management, freeing developers to invest their energies in the core functionalities rather than repetitive preparatory tasks. This lean approach does not compromise the strength or adaptability of applications; on the contrary, it enables developers to tailor applications with precision while ensuring the code base remains sleek and manageable.

One of the hallmark features of Spring Boot is its native support for embedded servers. This stands in contrast to the conventional method of Java web application deployment, which typically involves compiling the application into a WAR file for deployment on an external server such as Tomcat or Jetty. Spring Boot innovates by integrating these servers

12

directly into the application, facilitating the creation of standalone applications that can be easily executed and tested, embodying the 'just run' ethos of Spring Boot and simplifying the development and deployment of microservices and cloud-based applications considerably.

```
@SpringBootApplication
public class MyApp {

    public static void main(String[] args) {
        SpringApplication.run(MyApp.class, args);
    }

}
```

The simplicity of starting a Spring Boot application is exemplified in the code snippet above. The `@SpringBootApplication` annotation streamlines the setup by amalgamating essential features such as auto-configuration and component scanning, thus reducing the time needed for initial setup and encouraging a modular approach that resonates with contemporary software development practices.

Auto-configuration stands as a pillar of Spring Boot, offering intuitive setup options based on the project's dependencies, thus smoothing over both the initial and ongoing maintenance phases of application development. This intuitive feature ensures that while the framework offers a user-friendly experience, it also provides leeway for customized adjustments as needed.

In the domain of data handling, Spring Boot's integration with Spring Data JPA is seamless, simplifying the establishment of data access layers and reducing the typically encountered repetitive code in CRUD operations. This integration not only upholds best practices in data management but also guarantees consistency and efficiency throughout the application's data handling layers.

```java
@Entity
public class Customer {

    @Id
    @GeneratedValue(strategy = GenerationType.AUTO)
    private Long id;
    private String name;

    // Getters and setters
}

@Repository
public interface CustomerRepository extends JpaRepository<Customer, Long> {
}
```

The preceding example showcases how merely extending `JpaRepository` in a repository interface immediately endows it with a broad spectrum of standard CRUD functionalities without necessitating explicit implementations. This is reflective of Spring Boot's commitment to minimizing superfluous code, thereby allowing developers to dedicate their focus to the distinctive attributes of their application.

Web development inherently necessitates a strong focus on security, and Spring Boot tackles this head-on with a robust and versatile security framework. Out-of-the-box configurations provide a solid security base, which can be extensively customized to meet the specific security requirements of any application, covering aspects from authentication and authorization to session management.

Beyond simplifying coding and configuration, Spring Boot plays a pivotal role in encouraging the shift towards microservices architectures, thanks to its lightweight makeup and extensive support for a plethora of cloud deployment environments. It eases the development of modular, independently deployable services, perfectly aligning with the demands for scalable and resilient system architectures in the digital era.

The thriving ecosystem and the strong backing of the community surrounding Spring Boot significantly contribute to its popularity and broad adoption. A wide range of plugins, extensions, and third-party libraries extend its capabilities, addressing various needs from application monitoring and management to communication, ensuring Spring Boot remains a flexible and adaptable option for a wide spectrum of web development projects.

In essence, Spring Boot signifies a transformative development in the realm of Java web application creation and deployment. Its focus on simplifying configuration and enhancing built-in features makes it an essential tool for developers looking to develop robust, scalable, and easily maintainable web applications. Whether the goal is to construct straightforward CRUD applications or to architect complex microservices ecosystems, the significance of Spring Boot in the contemporary web development landscape is undeniable, cementing its status as an essential instrument in the toolkit of modern software developers.

What you will learn from this book

This volume is crafted as an in-depth exploration into Java Spring Boot, tailored to engage a diverse readership from beginners embarking on their Spring ecosystem journey to advanced developers looking to refine their skills in creating resilient, scalable web applications. Throughout this narrative, readers will be guided through a well-thought-out educational trajectory, delving into the complexities of Spring Boot and its indispensable role in contemporary web development. The goal extends beyond mere knowledge transfer to fostering a deep-seated understanding of the best practices and architectural principles essential for crafting high-caliber software.

A pivotal learning outcome from this text is a comprehensive grasp of Spring Boot's architecture and its integration within the larger Spring framework. The narrative will illuminate how Spring Boot eases the development process through its convention-over-configuration ethos, automating the tedious coding and configuration tasks typical in traditional Java development. This concept will be brought to life through practical examples, such as initiating a simple Spring Boot project:

```java
@SpringBootApplication
public class DemoApplication {

    public static void main(String[] args) {
        SpringApplication.run(DemoApplication.class, args);
    }

}
```

This code snippet underlines the streamlined procedure for launching a Spring Boot project, highlighting the framework's focus on developer efficiency and simplicity.

The discourse will extend to Spring Boot's robust capabilities in data management and access, a critical facet of modern web applications. Learners will be equipped to harness Spring Data JPA for effective database integration, enhancing the data access layer's readability and efficiency. Hands-on examples will illustrate the process of defining entities and repositories, showcasing the framework's ability to simplify complex data operations:

```
@Entity
public class User {

    @Id
    @GeneratedValue(strategy = GenerationType.IDENTITY)
    private Long id;
    private String name;
    // Getters and setters
}

public interface UserRepository extends JpaRepository<User, Long> {
}
```

Such examples will demonstrate the straightforward approach Spring Boot offers for abstracting and efficiently managing data operations.

Web development's intrinsic requirement for robust security is thoroughly addressed in this book. Through an in-depth look at Spring Security within the Spring Boot ecosystem, readers will learn about crafting secure authentication and authorization protocols, protecting REST APIs, and managing user sessions securely. These critical concepts will be rooted in tangible scenarios, showcasing how Spring Boot streamlines the implementation of strong security measures with ease.

The narrative also covers the microservices architectural style, which is paramount for developing systems that are both scalable and easy to maintain. This book will guide readers through the intricacies of designing and deploying microservices with Spring Boot, emphasizing the framework's capacity to facilitate the creation of modular, independently deployable services suited for complex, distributed environments. Discussions will cover aspects such as inter-service communication and effective service discovery, framed within the microservices built using Spring Boot.

```java
@RestController
public class OrderService {

    @GetMapping("/orders")
    public List<Order> getAllOrders() {
        // Implementation goes here
    }
}
```

This controller example lays the groundwork for discussions on crafting RESTful services and Spring Boot's contributions to microservices architecture.

Additionally, the book ventures into advanced topics like reactive programming with Spring WebFlux, cloud deployment strategies for Spring Boot applications, and leveraging Spring Boot Actuator for application monitoring and management. Each topic is thoroughly investigated, with code snippets and real-life scenarios ensuring a fluid transition from theoretical concepts to practical application.

Performance optimization is another critical theme addressed in this text. Readers will uncover methods to pinpoint and mitigate performance bottlenecks within Spring Boot applications, learning to apply caching, asynchronous processing, and database optimization strategies to enhance application performance significantly.

The text also recognizes the potential challenges and hurdles developers may encounter when navigating Spring Boot. It provides insightful troubleshooting tips and best practices for overcoming common obstacles, arming readers with the necessary tools to tackle issues head-on.

By the end of this book, readers will have attained a rounded perspective on Java Spring Boot and its application in real-world settings. They will be adept at constructing, securing, and deploying high-performance, scalable web applications, backed by an appreciation for the best practices and architectural paradigms vital for professional software development. Furthermore, the book encourages continuous exploration, prompting readers to delve deeper into the vast Spring Boot ecosystem, nurturing a culture of ongoing learning and innovation in their development pursuits

Chapter One

Getting Started with Spring Boot

Introduction to Spring Boot and its core features

Spring Boot emerges as a transformative element within the Spring framework constellation, presenting a streamlined avenue for developers to craft ready-for-production applications with reduced configuration demands. This framework is engineered to alleviate the complexities of the development process, enabling developers to pivot their focus toward the core functionality of their applications rather than wrestling with setup intricacies.

The foundational principle of Spring Boot revolves around "convention over configuration," promoting pre-established configurations that suffice for the majority of scenarios straight off the shelf, thereby diminishing the need for extensive custom configurations. Nonetheless, Spring Boot maintains a level of flexibility that allows for in-depth customization to meet specific project requirements.

One of the standout attributes of Spring Boot is its capability to support embedded servers. Unlike the conventional methodology that necessitates deploying Java web applications on external servers like Tomcat or Jetty, Spring Boot integrates these server functionalities directly within the application itself. This approach notably simplifies the development and deployment continuum, as demonstrated in the subsequent code snippet that kickstarts a Spring Boot application encompassing an embedded server:

```
@SpringBootApplication
public class SampleApp {

    public static void main(String[] args) {
        SpringApplication.run(SampleApp.class, args);
    }

}
```

This example accentuates the straightforward nature of initializing a Spring Boot application, leveraging the `@SpringBootApplication` annotation to streamline the setup process.

Auto-configuration stands as a pivotal feature within Spring Boot, intuitively tailoring the application's configuration based on the detected classpath libraries. For instance, detecting a database driver prompts Spring Boot to automatically configure an appropriate data source. This intelligent feature alleviates the developer from the cumbersome task of manually configuring numerous application components, thus optimizing the development workflow.

```
@RestController
public class WelcomeController {

    @GetMapping("/welcome")
    public String welcome() {
        return "Welcome to Spring Boot!";
    }
}
```

The REST controller depicted above is made operational without necessitating explicit configuration, illustrating Spring Boot's proficiency in auto-configuring web applications.

Furthermore, Spring Boot's starter dependencies epitomize its commitment to development efficiency. These pre-packaged sets of dependencies, tailored for specific development scenarios like web development or data access, encapsulate a harmonious collection of libraries that seamlessly work together.

```
<dependency>
    <groupId>org.springframework.boot</groupId>
    <artifactId>spring-boot-starter-web</artifactId>
</dependency>
```

The Maven dependency example for `**spring-boot-starter-web**` highlights how Spring Boot simplifies the orchestration of dependencies essential for web application development.

Application security, being an indispensable facet of development, is robustly catered to by Spring Boot. Through its integration with Spring Security, it simplifies the implementation of secure authentication and authorization protocols, ensuring that applications adhere to security best practices by default.

The provided code snippet establishes basic web security configurations, showcasing Spring Boot's seamless fusion with Spring Security to facilitate comprehensive security measures.

Moreover, Spring Boot is adept at underpinning microservices architectures, resonating with the current shift towards building systems that are scalable and maintainable. Its alignment with cloud infrastructures and container technologies like Docker underscores its suitability for modern development paradigms.

Spring Boot is also equipped with Actuator, a suite of tools dedicated to the post-deployment monitoring and management of applications. Actuator delivers essential insights into application metrics, health indicators, and operational features, empowering developers to efficiently oversee and troubleshoot applications within production environments.

To sum up, Spring Boot stands as a dynamic and versatile framework in the Spring family, devised to accelerate the application development journey with a focus on efficiency and ease of use. Its distinctive features, such as embedded server capabilities, smart auto-configuration, streamlined dependency management, and solid security setups, position it as an ideal tool for developers intent on delivering high-quality, production-ready applications. With its support for microservices, cloud compatibility, and operational tools like Actuator, Spring Boot is well-equipped to address the challenges of contemporary application development, establishing itself as an indispensable resource for developers across various project types.

Setting up your development environment

Initiating a development environment stands as the critical first maneuver for any software endeavor, especially for those involving Java and Spring Boot frameworks. This preparation involves outfiting one's technical workspace with the indispensable instruments, frameworks, and systems essential for seamless code development, testing, and deployment activities.

1. Java Development Kit (JDK) Deployment

The inauguration of the environment setup mandates the deployment of the Java Development Kit (JDK), fundamental for Java application crafting, inclusive of Spring Boot endeavors. The choice of JDK version is contingent upon the Spring Boot iteration in use—Spring Boot 2.x necessitates JDK 8 or later, whereas Spring Boot 3.x requires JDK 17 or upward. Procurement of the JDK from a credible source, like the official Oracle portal or OpenJDK, and the precise setting of the `**JAVA_HOME**` environment variable to denote the JDK installation locale, is imperative.

```
export JAVA_HOME=/usr/lib/jvm/java-8-oracle
export PATH=$JAVA_HOME/bin:$PATH
```

2. Integrated Development Environment (IDE) Selection

Identifying a suitable Integrated Development Environment (IDE) that aligns with Java and Spring Boot development is paramount. Esteemed IDEs such as IntelliJ IDEA, Eclipse, and Visual Studio Code, endowed with Spring Boot supportive functionalities like intelligent code completion, debugging tools, and automated code refactoring, substantially elevate development efficacy. It's paramount to ensure the selected IDE is adorned with the requisite Spring Boot plugins or extensions, exemplified by the Spring Boot Extension Pack in Visual Studio Code.

24

3. Incorporation of Build Tools

Leveraging build tools such as Maven or Gradle is quintessential in orchestrating Spring Boot projects, facilitating dependency management, build automation, and software packaging. The installation and configuration of the preferred build tool to ensure command-line accessibility pave the way for streamlined project orchestration via their respective configuration files (`pom.xml` for Maven, `build.gradle` for Gradle).

4. Spring Boot CLI Installation (Optional)

While not obligatory, embracing the Spring Boot Command Line Interface (CLI) can imbue the development process with added convenience, especially beneficial for swift prototyping through Groovy scripts. Electing to install the Spring Boot CLI can augment the development versatility for particular tasks.

5. Implementation of a Version Control System

Embedding a Version Control System (VCS) such as Git is elemental in contemporary software development paradigms, facilitating meticulous change documentation, collaborative efforts, and the management of divergent project versions. Ensuring the smooth integration of Git within the elected IDE lays the groundwork for a cohesive version control experience.

6. Database Configuration

Given the prevalent reliance on data persistence within many applications, early-stage database configuration is judicious. The project's specific requirements will dictate the adoption of either a relational database (such as MySQL or PostgreSQL) or an in-memory database (such as H2 for developmental phases). Early database configuration is crucial in enabling the application's subsequent data handling capabilities.

7. Preparation of Testing and Continuous Integration Tools

Establishing a foundation with testing frameworks (for instance, JUnit, Mockito, Spring Test) and continuous integration mechanisms (such as Jenkins or GitHub Actions) from the inception is beneficial, laying the infrastructure for a robust testing regimen and the automation of build and test processes, thereby enhancing code integrity and project sustainability.

8. Acquaintance with Containerization Technologies (Optional)

For projects with a trajectory towards containerized deployments, familiarity with containerization technologies such as Docker proves advantageous. Docker's installation and an understanding of containerization fundamentals are beneficial, especially for projects with a bent towards microservices architecture or those embracing cloud-native deployment methodologies.

9. Ensuring Accessibility to Web Browser and API Testing Tools

Possession of a reliable web browser is indispensable for the testing of web applications, while tools such as Postman or Swagger are invaluable for the efficient testing and interaction with RESTful APIs, simplifying the process of endpoint analysis and web service diagnostics.

10. Utilization of Spring Initializr

Albeit not a component of the local setup, Spring Initializr acts as a formidable online utility for the rapid initiation of new Spring Boot projects by generating project structures tailored to specific dependencies. Accessible through a web interface or directly within certain IDEs, it facilitates an expedited project commencement with a structured and orderly setup.

By diligently arranging each element of the development environment, developers carve out an efficient and harmonized workspace, establishing a robust platform for the lifecycle of Spring Boot application development. This encompassing setup transcends mere coding, embracing the full spectrum of development activities from testing and version control to deployment, thereby arming developers with the comprehensive arsenal required to tackle the multifaceted challenges presented by modern software development ventures.

Your first Spring Boot application: "Hello, World!"

Diving into Spring Boot development, crafting a "Hello, World!" application stands as a fundamental milestone for developers. This elementary yet pivotal project not only signifies the initiation into Spring Boot but also provides a foundational grasp of the framework's structure and operational dynamics.

Spring Boot is celebrated for its streamlined approach to initializing and developing Spring applications, emphasizing application functionality over configuration and setup. The "Hello, World!" project exemplifies this ethos, illustrating the framework's capacity for simplicity and efficiency in development.

Initial Setup

The adventure begins with the creation of a new Spring Boot project, a task seamlessly facilitated by the Spring Initializr web tool. This platform offers an intuitive interface for generating the basic scaffolding of a Spring Boot project by inputting project details and selecting preferences such as the Java version, Spring Boot version, and the build system (Maven or Gradle).

After downloading and unpacking the project archive, it can be imported into a preferred Integrated Development Environment (IDE) like IntelliJ IDEA, Eclipse, or Visual Studio Code, all of which provide robust support for Spring Boot development through various features and plugins.

Developing the Application

The crux of the "Hello, World!" application lies in its straightforwardness. A typical Spring Boot application is anchored by a main class, marked with the `@SpringBootApplication` annotation, which serves as the launchpad. This annotation amalgamates `@Configuration`, `@EnableAutoConfiguration`, and `@ComponentScan`, pivotal for the auto-configuration and component scanning that are hallmarks of Spring Boot.

```java
@SpringBootApplication
public class HelloWorldApp {

    public static void main(String[] args) {
        SpringApplication.run(HelloWorldApp.class, args);
    }

}
```

To actualize the "Hello, World!" output, a concise controller is constructed using the `@RestController` annotation, designating the class as a controller where each method's return value is directly rendered as a response body. Utilizing the `@GetMapping` annotation, one can craft a method dedicated to handling GET requests and delivering the classic greeting.

```java
@RestController
public class HelloWorldController {

    @GetMapping("/hello")
    public String helloWorld() {
        return "Hello, World!";
    }
}
```

Execution of the Application

Launching the Spring Boot application is an uncomplicated affair. Within the IDE, executing the main class as a regular Java application triggers the embedded web server (commonly Tomcat) to serve the application. The embedded server functionality of Spring Boot obviates the need for separate server setups, facilitating a more fluid development and testing phase.

The application can also be initiated from the command line by employing the build tool's specific run command (`**mvn spring-boot:run**` for Maven projects or `**gradle bootRun**` for Gradle projects), compiling and launching the embedded server.

Accessing the Application

With the application active, the "Hello, World!" output is accessible by directing a web browser to the defined endpoint or using a command-line tool like curl. For the instance delineated above, browsing to `**http://localhost:8080/hello**` should reveal the "Hello, World!" message, marking the successful execution of the inaugural Spring Boot application.

Conclusion

The endeavor to construct a "Hello, World!" application within Spring Boot transcends mere text output; it represents an immersion into the Spring Boot framework, revealing its potential to streamline application development. This elementary project lays the conceptual and practical groundwork for more intricate applications, acquainting developers with critical Spring Boot concepts such as auto-configuration, RESTful controllers, and the embedded server paradigm, which are integral to contemporary Spring Boot development projects.

Through this hands-on exploration, developers acquire valuable insights into Spring Boot's mechanisms, paving the way for the creation of complex, feature-rich applications. Thus, the "Hello, World!" application is not merely a starting point in Spring Boot exploration but a foundational step towards mastering the extensive and potent capabilities offered by the Spring Boot framework.

Chapter Two

Understanding Spring Boot Basics

Overview of the Spring Framework

The Spring Framework has firmly positioned itself as an essential toolkit for crafting enterprise-level applications in the Java ecosystem, tracing its origins back to Rod Johnson's initiative in the early 2000s to offer a more streamlined alternative to the complex Enterprise JavaBeans (EJB) framework. Since then, Spring has evolved into a comprehensive framework adept at navigating the intricate demands of enterprise application engineering, with a pronounced focus on fostering modularity and ease of testing through foundational principles like dependency injection and aspect-oriented programming.

Fundamental Elements

The essence of the Spring Framework is encapsulated in its Core Container, which is tasked with managing the lifecycle and configuration of application components, termed as beans. This container employs dependency injection (DI) to imbue beans with their dependencies, thereby encouraging a design that is both modular and conducive to testing.

```
@Configuration
public class BeanConfiguration {
    @Bean
    public MyService myService() {
        return new MyServiceImpl();
    }
}
```

Here, the `@Configuration` annotation signals a class containing bean definitions, and the `@Bean` annotation indicates that the method provides a bean for Spring's management.

Aspect-Oriented Features

Spring's embrace of Aspect-Oriented Programming (AOP) allows for the compartmentalization of ancillary concerns like logging or security into separate aspects, thereby decluttering the main business logic and enhancing the codebase's maintainability.

This code illustrates an aspect designed for logging, triggered before the invocation of any service method, leveraging `@Aspect` and `@Before` annotations.

Streamlined Data Operations

Within its Data Access/Integration layer, the Spring Framework offers a simplified approach to database engagement and transaction management, accommodating a slew of persistence technologies and ensuring a unified programming model for these operations.

```
@Aspect
public class MonitoringAspect {
    @Before("execution(* com.example.service.*.*(..))")
    public void logServiceInvocation(JoinPoint joinPoint) {
        System.out.println("Service call: " + joinPoint.getSignature().getName());
    }
}
```

The `@**Repository**` annotation here designates a class as a data repository, with the `**JdbcTemplate**` simplifying JDBC operations and thereby easing database interactions.

Web Development Infrastructure

The Spring Web module, particularly through Spring MVC, furnishes a robust framework for developing web applications, adhering to a Model-View-Controller architecture that advocates for a separation of concerns, thereby aiding in the applications' testability and maintenance.

```
@Repository
public class ProductRepository {
    @Autowired
    private JdbcTemplate jdbcTemplate;

    public Product findProductById(Long id) {
        return jdbcTemplate.queryForObject("SELECT * FROM products WHERE id = ?", new
            Object[]{id}, new ProductRowMapper());
    }
}
```

This controller is set to respond to GET requests on `/**account**`, dynamically populating the model with an `**accounted**` and pointing to the `**accountView**`.

Spring Boot Complement

While technically an extension, Spring Boot is integral to discussions on Spring for its contribution to streamlining

Spring application development. It introduces pre-configured setups, embedded servers, and auto-configuration to accelerate project kickoff and development.

```
@Controller
public class AccountController {
    @GetMapping("/account")
    public String viewAccount(@RequestParam(name="accountId", required=false) String
        accountId, Model model) {
        model.addAttribute("accountId", accountId);
        return "accountView";
    }
}
```

The `@SpringBootApplication` annotation consolidates various configurations, easing the initiation process of a Spring Boot application.

Comprehensive Suite

In addition, Spring broadens its capabilities with modules such as Spring Security, which strengthens applications with comprehensive authentication and authorization controls, and Spring Messaging, tailored for message-oriented applications.

Synopsis

With its extensive range of modules and features, the Spring Framework is adept at fulfilling the diverse requirements of enterprise application development. Its commitment to principles like dependency injection and aspect-oriented programming, coupled with its rich service abstractions, has redefined Java development paradigms. The ongoing evolution of Spring, especially with the introduction of Spring Boot, highlights the framework's perpetual relevance and adaptability, reaffirming its position as a fundamental part of the enterprise Java arsenal.

Inversion of Control (IoC) and Dependency Injection (DI) in Spring

Inversion of Control (IoC) and Dependency Injection (DI) are foundational elements within the Spring Framework, significantly influencing the architectural design and development practices of applications. Rooted deeply in Spring's philosophy, these concepts advocate for a structural blueprint that markedly improves software modularity, testability, and longevity.

Conceptualizing Inversion of Control (IoC)

IoC alters the conventional flow of control within program execution. Where typical applications directly oversee object creation and lifecycle within their codebase, IoC flips this paradigm, assigning these responsibilities to an external entity, known within Spring as the "IoC container." This container is tasked with object instantiation, configuration, and wiring, thereby abstracting the control flow from the primary application logic. This inversion not only augments the separation of concerns but also facilitates a declarative manner of outlining object interrelations, enhancing the system's overall modularity.

Fundamentals of Dependency Injection (DI)

DI, nested within the IoC principle, entails the external provision of an object's dependencies, as opposed to internal self-construction. Spring actualizes this through its IoC container, dynamically injecting necessary dependencies into the managed beans based on predefined configurations.

Spring delineates several DI methodologies, notably:

- Constructor Injection: Where dependencies are supplied via the constructor.

- Setter Injection: Where dependencies are injected post-construction through setter methods.

```
@Component
public class BillingService {
    private final BillingRepository billingRepository;

    @Autowired
    public BillingService(BillingRepository billingRepository) {
        this.billingRepository = billingRepository;
    }
}
```

This example demonstrates constructor injection, with `**BillingService**` receiving a `**BillingRepository**` dependency through its constructor, highlighted by the `**@Autowired**` annotation.

Merits of Integrating IoC and DI

1. Reduced Dependency Coupling: IoC and DI significantly curtail the interdependencies among classes, fostering a structure that is inherently more modular and adaptable.

2. Streamlined Testing: External dependency management simplifies component testing, particularly with the utilization of mock objects for unit tests.

3. Configurational and Scalable Efficiency: Centralizing dependency management and configurations simplifies

application administration and scalability, facilitating changes with minimal code impact.

4. Managed Object Lifecycle: The IoC container meticulously manages the lifecycle of beans, from creation to destruction, offering custom initialization and disposal mechanisms, thus optimizing resource management.

Spring's Approach to IoC and DI

Spring facilitates IoC and DI through a combination of annotations and XML configurations, enabling the declarative specification of beans and their interrelations. Annotations like `@Component`, `@Service`, `@Repository`, and `@Controller` assist in the automatic detection and registration of beans by Spring, with the `@Autowired` annotation designating injection points.

```java
@Repository
public class MembershipRepositoryImpl implements MembershipRepository {
    // Details of implementation
}

@Service
public class MembershipServiceImpl implements MembershipService {
    private final MembershipRepository membershipRepository;

    @Autowired
    public MembershipServiceImpl(MembershipRepository membershipRepository) {
        this.membershipRepository = membershipRepository;
    }

    // Details of implementation
}
```

In this configuration, `MembershipServiceImpl` is identified as a service bean and is provided with a

`MembershipRepository` dependency through constructor injection.

In Conclusion

IoC and DI play crucial roles in the development of applications that boast loose coupling, strong cohesion, and straightforward testability within the Spring framework. By entrusting the Spring container with the responsibility for managing object instantiation and dependency resolution, developers can concentrate on core business functionalities, ensuring that the architectural design remains in line with principles of clean, maintainable, and scalable software architecture.

Spring Boot auto-configuration explained

Spring Boot's auto-configuration mechanism is a cornerstone feature that streamlines the application setup process, embodying the framework's philosophy of convention over explicit configuration. This functionality facilitates the rapid development of Spring applications by intelligently applying default configurations.

Essence of Auto-Configuration

Auto-configuration in Spring Boot aims to simplify the initial setup and ongoing maintenance of Spring applications. It does so by automatically configuring Spring beans and various settings based on the application's context, the classes present on the classpath, and other factors. This feature enables developers to concentrate on the application's unique business logic and features, rather than on boilerplate configuration tasks.

When a Spring Boot application is initiated, its auto-configuration logic scans the classpath for any components and libraries that might require configuration and then applies appropriate defaults based on what it finds. This process is driven by conditions that check for the existence of certain classes, beans, or specific property settings before a particular auto-configuration is applied.

Auto-Configuration Mechanics

The auto-configuration process is triggered by the `@EnableAutoConfiguration` annotation, which prompts Spring Boot to look for auto-configuration candidates within `spring.factories` files across the classpath. These files enumerate the auto-configuration classes that Spring Boot considers for automatic application setup.

```
@SpringBootApplication
public class SampleApp {
    public static void main(String[] args) {
        SpringApplication.run(SampleApp.class, args);
    }
}
```

Embedded within the `@SpringBootApplication` annotation, `@EnableAutoConfiguration` activates the auto-configuration feature, making it a staple in Spring Boot applications.

Condition-Based Configuration

The smart aspect of auto-configuration is its reliance on conditional checks. Spring Boot employs various `@Conditional` annotations, such as `@ConditionalOnClass`, `@ConditionalOnBean`, `@ConditionalOnProperty`, among others, to decide whether a particular auto-configuration is appropriate. For instance, the presence of a specific database driver on the classpath might lead Spring Boot to automatically set up a corresponding data source.

```
@Configuration
@ConditionalOnClass({DataSource.class, EmbeddedDatabaseType.class})
public class DatabaseAutoConfiguration {
    // Configuration details
}
```

In this illustrative example, `DatabaseAutoConfiguration` is activated for auto-configuration only if the `DataSource` and `EmbeddedDatabaseType` classes are detected in the classpath.

Customizing Auto-Configuration

Spring Boot allows for the customization and overriding of default configurations. Developers can define their own bean configurations, specify properties in `application.properties` or `application.yml`, or exclude certain auto-configuration classes using the exclude attribute of the `@SpringBootApplication` annotation.

```
@SpringBootApplication(exclude = {DataSourceAutoConfiguration.class})
public class CustomApp {
    // Custom application logic
}
```

Here, the application explicitly excludes `DataSourceAutoConfiguration`, allowing for a custom data source configuration or scenarios where no data source is required.

Advantages of Auto-Configuration

1. Development Efficiency: Auto-configuration accelerates the development lifecycle by automating the configuration of Spring components and third-party libraries.

2. Default Optimizations: Spring Boot's default configurations are designed to be effective in most scenarios, minimizing the need for custom settings in typical applications.

3. Flexibility: Despite its automation, Spring Boot provides mechanisms for developers to override default configurations, ensuring that specific requirements can be met.

4. Contextual Configuration: Auto-configuration's reliance on conditional logic ensures that only relevant configurations are applied, optimizing the application's setup based on its unique context.

Conclusion

Spring Boot's auto-configuration feature simplifies the development and deployment process of Spring applications, offering a seamless blend of automated setup and the option for detailed customization. By providing intelligent default configurations and the flexibility to tailor settings, auto-configuration represents a harmonious balance that enhances the efficiency and robustness of enterprise-level application development with Spring Boot.

Chapter Three

Working with Spring Boot Projects

Structure of a Spring Boot project

The architecture of a Spring Boot project is meticulously crafted to foster simplicity and effectiveness, aligning with the framework's convention-over-configuration ethos. This architecture streamlines the development, upkeep, and deployment processes by presenting a clear and standardized project layout.

Principal Package

At the core of a Spring Boot project lies the principal package, which establishes the foundational package for the application. Positioned at this level, the main application class, marked with `@**SpringBootApplication**`, acts as the pivotal entry point for the Spring Boot application, enabling Spring's component scanning to automatically detect all sub-packages and classes.

```
package com.example.application;

import org.springframework.boot.SpringApplication;
import org.springframework.boot.autoconfigure.SpringBootApplication;

@SpringBootApplication
public class Application {

    public static void main(String[] args) {
        SpringApplication.run(Application.class, args);
    }
}
```

Layered Architecture

A structured Spring Boot project is typically segmented into distinct layers, each tasked with a specific role, adhering to the separation of concerns principle:

- Controller Layer (controller): Hosts `@RestController` or `@Controller` annotated classes that manage HTTP request and response handling. These controllers serve as gateways for external client interactions, directing requests to the appropriate services.

- Service Layer (service): Houses the core business logic of the application. Annotated with `@Service`, these classes contain methods that fulfill business operations, often liaising with the repository layer for data retrieval and persistence.

- Repository Layer (repository): Dedicated to data access and manipulation tasks, typically involving database interactions. Repository interfaces extend Spring Data's repositories, like `JpaRepository`, to utilize its comprehensive data handling capabilities.

- Model Layer (model or domain): Comprises the domain model entities and data transfer objects (DTOs), which articulate the persistent data structure of the application, often corresponding to database table structures.

Configuration Management

Configurations for a Spring Boot project are consolidated in `application.properties` or `application.yml` files located in the `src/main/resources` directory. These files accommodate settings for database connections, server configurations, and other application-specific properties, facilitating environment-specific configuration management.

Resources and Templates

The `src/main/resources` directory also accommodates `static` and `templates` sub-directories for storing static web resources (CSS, JS, images) and view templates (Thymeleaf, FreeMarker), respectively, which are integral to rendering web application views.

Database Versioning

For projects employing database migrations and versioning, a `db/migration` sub-directory under `src/main/resources` can host migration scripts, with tools like Flyway or Liquibase orchestrating these scripts to ensure systematic schema evolution.

Testing Structure

Adhering to standard Maven or Gradle layouts, tests, including unit and integration tests, are situated in the `src/test/java` directory. Spring Boot's testing support, exemplified by annotations such as `@SpringBootTest`, simplifies integration testing by loading the complete application context for tests.

```
package com.example.application;

import org.junit.jupiter.api.Test;
import org.springframework.boot.test.context.SpringBootTest;

@SpringBootTest
class ApplicationTests {

    @Test
    void contextLoads() {
    }
}
```

Build Configuration

The project's root houses the `pom.xml` (for Maven) or `build.gradle` (for Gradle) file, detailing the project's dependencies, plugins, and build instructions, which are vital for dependency management and build processes.

Synopsis

The structured design of a Spring Boot project encourages development best practices, ensuring applications remain scalable, maintainable, and consistent across various scales and complexities. This design, coupled with Spring Boot's auto-configuration features, empowers developers to concentrate on crafting unique business functionalities, minimizing the burdens associated with initial project setups and configurations.

Using Spring Initializr for project setup

Spring Initializr serves as an essential facilitator within the Spring framework ecosystem, offering a streamlined approach to initializing Spring Boot projects through a web-based interface. This tool simplifies the project setup phase, enabling developers to dive directly into building the core functionalities of their applications.

Overview of Spring Initializr

Available via a web portal and directly integrated into popular IDEs such as IntelliJ IDEA, Eclipse, and Visual Studio Code, Spring Initializr provides a straightforward method for configuring project attributes like Group, Artifact, chosen Spring Boot version, programming language, and necessary dependencies. Upon completion, it compiles a downloadable zip file containing a structured project ready for immediate development.

Crafting a Project with Spring Initializr

To initiate a Spring Boot project using Spring Initializr, one would:

1. Navigate to Spring Initializr: This can be done through its web page or via an IDE's integrated feature.

2. Detail Project Specifications:

   - Opt for Maven or Gradle as the build tool.

   - Select the programming language (Java, Kotlin, or Groovy).

   - Choose the Spring Boot version, typically the default for optimal compatibility.

   - Provide the Group, Artifact, and other details like Name, Description, and Package name.

3. Incorporate Dependencies: Spring Initializr permits the selection of various starter dependencies relevant to different development needs, such as web services, data handling, or security, automatically integrating the necessary libraries into the project.

4. Generate and Download Project: With all options specified, the project is generated and presented as a zip file for download, encapsulating the initial project scaffold.

Exploring the Generated Project Scaffold

The project structure crafted by Spring Initializr adheres to the conventional Maven/Gradle project layouts, comprising:

- `src/main/java` Directory: Hosts the primary application class, generally named after the project and marked with the `@SpringBootApplication` annotation, signifying the springboard for the Spring Boot application.

- `src/main/resources` Directory: This directory is the repository for application configuration files (`application.properties` or `application.yml`), and possibly static resources and templates if corresponding dependencies are included.

- `src/test/java` Directory: Reserved for test cases, this directory supports the adoption of Test-Driven Development (TDD) from the outset of the project.

Personalizing and Augmenting the Initial Scaffold

While the scaffold provided by Spring Initializr lays down a foundational structure, it's intended to be the starting point from which further personalization and expansion can occur:

- Dependency Augmentation: Additional dependencies required by the evolving project can be appended to the build file (`**pom.xml**` for Maven, `**build.gradle**` for Gradle).

- Configuration Tailoring: The `**application.properties**` or `**application.yml**` files are amenable to modifications to suit specific application configurations like server settings, database connections, and more.

- Structural Enhancements: Depending on the project's domain-specific needs and architectural preferences, further packages and modules can be integrated into the initial structure.

IDE Integration Benefits

The integration of Spring Initializr within leading IDEs amplifies its utility, enabling the generation and importation of projects directly within the development environment, thus enhancing the overall development workflow.

Spring Initializr's Merits

Spring Initializr offers numerous advantages, solidifying its status as a vital instrument for Spring Boot developers:

- Efficient Project Initialization: It dramatically lessens the time and complexity involved in setting up a new Spring Boot project, providing a project structure primed for development with minimal setup.

- Adherence to Best Practices: The project structure and default configurations generated adhere to Spring Boot's recommended practices, ensuring a robust foundation for application development.

- Adaptable and Customizable: Spring Initializr allows for tailored project configurations, offering flexibility in the choice of build tool, programming language, and dependencies.

- Widespread Accessibility: With its availability as a web service and through IDE integration, Spring Initializr is readily accessible for developers across various environments.

In Summary

Spring Initializr epitomizes the principles of efficiency and productivity that are central to the Spring Boot philosophy. By facilitating rapid and customizable project generation, it empowers developers to transition smoothly from project conception to actual development, equipped with a well-structured foundation that aligns with industry best practices. Whether accessed online or through an IDE, Spring Initializr streamlines the preparatory phase of project development, enabling a swift progression to implementation and feature development.

Understanding the POM file and Maven dependencies

The Project Object Model (POM) file, commonly referred to as `pom.xml`, together with Maven's dependency management framework, plays a crucial role in Java project setup and maintenance. This POM file is instrumental in conveying comprehensive details about a project to Maven, outlining its configuration, dependencies, and the specifics of its build process. Gaining a deep understanding of the POM file's structure and how Maven handles dependencies is vital for the efficient management and development of Java projects.

Significance of the POM File

The POM file, formatted in XML, provides Maven with exhaustive information regarding a project, encompassing its unique identifiers, the external libraries it depends upon, plugins for the build phase, and the objectives of those builds. Essentially, it serves as the blueprint of the project, delineating its components, dependencies, and the order of build tasks.

Within the typical layout of a POM file, you'll find:

- Project Identifiers: The groupId, artifactId, and version fields that uniquely identify the project within Maven, critical for the deployment of artifacts.

- Dependency Listings: This segment lists out the external libraries essential for the project's build and runtime, each identified by unique coordinates to assist Maven in their retrieval and incorporation during the build process.

- Plugin Declarations: This section details the additional tasks Maven is tasked with during the build process, covering code compilation, packaging, and documentation.

- Variable Definitions: This part of the file is used for defining variables to ensure consistency across the POM file and ease in making updates.

```xml
<project xmlns="http://maven.apache.org/POM/4.0.0"
         xmlns:xsi="http://www.w3.org/2001/XMLSchema-instance"
         xsi:schemaLocation="http://maven.apache.org/POM/4.0.0 http://maven.apache.org/xsd
         /maven-4.0.0.xsd">
    <modelVersion>4.0.0</modelVersion>

    <groupId>com.example</groupId>
    <artifactId>my-app</artifactId>
    <version>1.0-SNAPSHOT</version>

    <dependencies>
        <dependency>
            <groupId>org.springframework.boot</groupId>
            <artifactId>spring-boot-starter</artifactId>
            <version>2.3.1.RELEASE</version>
        </dependency>
    </dependencies>
</project>
```

Maven Dependency Framework

In Maven, dependencies are the cornerstone, representing the necessary external Java libraries a project requires. Maven simplifies this aspect by centrally managing these dependencies, automating their resolution and incorporation from a central repository.

Maven's transitive dependency resolution ensures the inclusion of not just the directly specified libraries but also their dependencies, creating a full suite of required libraries for the project.

```
<dependency>
    <groupId>org.springframework</groupId>
    <artifactId>spring-webmvc</artifactId>
    <version>5.2.7.RELEASE</version>
</dependency>
```

Maven's Dependency Management Approaches

Maven offers various mechanisms for effective dependency management:

- Dependency Lifecycle Phases: Maven allows the specification of the stage in a project's lifecycle when a dependency is necessary, such as compile, test, or runtime phases.

- Dependency Exclusions: Maven enables the exclusion of certain dependencies that might be unnecessary or potentially cause conflicts within the project.

- Consolidated Dependency Management: For projects with multiple modules, Maven supports the centralization of dependency information to ensure uniformity in versioning and configuration across the project's modules.

Overview

The POM file, alongside Maven's efficient dependency management capabilities, forms the foundation for managing Java projects within the Maven framework, providing a structured approach to project configuration and facilitating the seamless integration of necessary external libraries. Mastery of the POM file's functionality and Maven's approach to dependencies is indispensable for Java developers, ensuring streamlined project builds, coherent dependency management, and a well-organized project structure.

Chapter Four

Introduction to Spring MVC

Basics of the Model-View-Controller (MVC) pattern

The Model-View-Controller (MVC) paradigm is a critical architectural framework that partitions software applications into three interconnected elements: Model, View, and Controller. This stratification enhances the clear demarcation of responsibilities, simplifying application governance, scalability, and testing by enabling segregated development, assessment, and management of each component. Originally conceived for desktop graphical interfaces, MVC has become indispensable in web development, adeptly addressing the complexities of advanced application structures.

Model Component

At its core, the Model encapsulates the application's fundamental data and operational logic. It contains the business rules and the application's state, operating autonomously from the user interface. The Model's principal function is to manage the data, subsequently altered by the Controller based on the View's input.

For instance, in Java-based applications, the Model may encompass domain entities that articulate the application's data schema and service classes that embody business logic, orchestrating database interactions or external services for data operations.

```java
public class Profile {
    private String name;
    private String email;

    // Getter and setter methods not shown for brevity
}
```

View Element

The View is tasked with rendering the Model's data for the user, effectively constituting the application's user interface. Its sole concern is the presentation of information, facilitating a distinct separation between the graphical interface and the application's business logic.

Within web applications, the View can be crafted using HTML, CSS, and JavaScript or through templating engines like Thymeleaf or FreeMarker, and may also utilize dynamic frameworks such as React or Angular for enriched user interfaces.

```html
<!DOCTYPE html>
<html>
<head>
    <title>Profile Page</title>
</head>
<body>
    <h1>Profile Page</h1>
    <p>Name: ${profile.name}</p>
    <p>Email: ${profile.email}</p>
</body>
</html>
```

Controller Role

Functioning as the bridge between the Model and the View, the Controller interprets user inputs from the View, engages with the Model for data fetching or updates, and then revitalizes the View with new information. It manages the exchange of data, orchestrating user interactions and delegating Model operations, subsequently updating the View.

In frameworks such as Spring MVC, Controllers are delineated as Java classes marked with `@Controller` or `@RestController`, with methods that align with specific HTTP request paths.

```java
@Controller
public class ProfileController {

    @GetMapping("/profile/{id}")
    public String displayProfile(@PathVariable String id, Model model) {
        Profile profile = profileService.fetchProfileById(id);
        model.addAttribute("profile", profile);
        return "profilePage";
    }
}
```

Advantages of MVC Framework

1. Defined Role Separation: The MVC framework's compartmentalized architecture permits isolated progression, evaluation, and maintenance of each facet, augmenting the system's modularity and intelligibility.

2. Facilitated Application Expansion: The framework's component-based architecture eases application expansion and modification, allowing for updates in one sector without disturbing the others.

3. Autonomy in UI Design: The disconnection of the View from the Model and Controller allows for dedicated focus on UI design, circumventing the intricacies of the business logic.

4. Promotion of Collaborative Work: The MVC architecture's clear distinction of roles supports effective collaboration among developers, designers, and testers, encouraging concurrent development activities.

5. Efficient Testing Protocols: The isolation of components within the MVC framework streamlines unit testing and troubleshooting, particularly for the Model and Controller, ensuring more dependable applications.

Synopsis

The Model-View-Controller architectural design provides a coherent framework for crafting and evolving applications, particularly within the web development sphere. By segregating an application into three separate yet interrelated components, MVC not only clarifies the architectural design but also elevates the system's maintainability, scalability, and testability. This structured approach encourages a collaborative development environment, enabling specialized teams to simultaneously work on various aspects of the application, thus enhancing productivity and spurring innovation in software development ventures.

Configuring a Spring MVC application

Configuring a Spring MVC application is a crucial step in developing dynamic web applications rooted in the Model-View-Controller (MVC) framework. Spring MVC, an integral module within the extensive Spring Framework, equips developers with a rich set of functionalities for managing web requests, fine-tuning application configurations, and dynamically rendering views. Grasping the configuration process of a Spring MVC application is essential to fully utilize the myriad features offered by Spring, such as efficient dependency injection and comprehensive data binding.

Starting Configuration

Launching a Spring MVC project typically involves crafting a structured project framework. Utilizing Spring Initializr, developers can effortlessly generate a project blueprint complete with essential dependencies and a standardized layout.

DispatcherServlet Setup

At the forefront of a Spring MVC application is the `DispatcherServlet`, which serves as the primary gateway, intercepting and routing HTTP requests to appropriate handlers. For Spring Boot projects, this configuration is automated. However, traditional setups may necessitate manual configuration in the `web.xml` descriptor or via Java configuration classes.

```
public class WebInitializer implements WebApplicationInitializer {

    @Override
    public void onStartup(ServletContext servletContext) {
        AnnotationConfigWebApplicationContext applicationContext = new
            AnnotationConfigWebApplicationContext();
        applicationContext.register(AppConfig.class);
        applicationContext.setServletContext(servletContext);

        ServletRegistration.Dynamic servlet = servletContext.addServlet("dispatcher", new
            DispatcherServlet(applicationContext));
        servlet.setLoadOnStartup(1);
        servlet.addMapping("/");
    }
}
```

Setting up Application Context

Establishing the application context is vital for declaring components such as controllers, service layers, and data repositories. This setup can be achieved through XML configuration or more commonly through `@Configuration` annotated Java classes.

```
@Configuration
@EnableWebMvc
@ComponentScan("com.example.project")
public class AppConfig {
    // Bean configuration goes here
}
```

Here, `@EnableWebMvc` triggers Spring MVC-specific configurations, while `@ComponentScan` guides Spring to the component-containing packages.

Configuring View Resolvers

View resolvers play a critical role in determining the correct views based on the controller's directives. Commonly, the `InternalResourceViewResolver` is employed for JSP views, though other technologies like Thymeleaf are also viable options.

```
@Bean
public InternalResourceViewResolver viewResolver() {
    InternalResourceViewResolver resolver = new InternalResourceViewResolver();
    resolver.setViewClass(JstlView.class);
    resolver.setPrefix("/WEB-INF/views/");
    resolver.setSuffix(".jsp");
    return resolver;
}
```

Managing Static Assets

Proper management of static resources such as CSS files, JavaScript, and images is crucial. This is typically handled by overriding the `addResourceHandlers` method to define resource locations.

```
@Override
public void addResourceHandlers(ResourceHandlerRegistry registry) {
    registry.addResourceHandler("/static/**").addResourceLocations("/static/");
}
```

Exception Handling

Spring MVC allows for flexible exception handling through `@ExceptionHandler` annotations within controllers or by employing `@ControllerAdvice` classes for application-wide exception management.

```
@ControllerAdvice
public class GlobalExceptionHandler {

    @ExceptionHandler(Exception.class)
    public ModelAndView handleGlobalExceptions(Exception ex) {
        ModelAndView mav = new ModelAndView("errorView");
        mav.addObject("errorMessage", "Global exception message");
        return mav;
    }
}
```

Implementing Internationalization

Incorporating support for multiple languages and locales involves configuring a `LocaleResolver` and, optionally, a `LocaleChangeInterceptor` to facilitate locale changes via request parameters.

```
@Bean
public LocaleResolver localeResolver() {
    SessionLocaleResolver resolver = new SessionLocaleResolver();
    resolver.setDefaultLocale(Locale.ENGLISH);
    return resolver;
}

@Bean
public LocaleChangeInterceptor localeInterceptor() {
    LocaleChangeInterceptor interceptor = new LocaleChangeInterceptor();
    interceptor.setParamName("language");
    return interceptor;
}
```

Summary

The process of configuring a Spring MVC application involves a meticulous arrangement of several key components that collectively ensure the seamless handling of web requests, efficient data binding, and dynamic view rendering. From initializing the `DispatcherServlet` and defining the application context to integrating view resolvers and organizing static resources, each configuration step significantly impacts the application's functionality. Skillful configuration of a Spring MVC application empowers developers to construct interactive, high-performance web applications that conform to the MVC architecture, leveraging the full spectrum of capabilities provided by the Spring Framework.

Building a simple web application using Spring MVC

Embarking on crafting a basic web application with Spring MVC involves harnessing the Spring Framework's web module capabilities, enabling the development of lively and robust web applications that adhere to the Model-View-Controller (MVC) design philosophy. This structured approach partitions the application into three key segments, simplifying the management of its complexities. The seamless melding of Spring MVC with the foundational elements of the Spring Framework, such as Dependency Injection and Inversion of Control, establishes a solid base for constructing scalable applications suited for the enterprise domain.

Preparing the Development Landscape

The journey begins with setting up the development environment, typically involving the selection of a build tool like Maven or Gradle to streamline dependency management, the build workflow, and the handling of project artifacts. Spring Initializr offers a quick start by generating a project structure equipped with essential dependencies.

Structuring the Project

A Spring MVC project is characterized by a specific directory layout:

- `src/main/java` - Hosts Java source files, including controllers, service implementations, and models.

- `src/main/resources` - Reserved for application properties and other resource files.

- `src/main/webapp` - Allocated for web-specific assets, including JSP files and static elements like CSS and JavaScript.

Configuring Spring MVC

Configuring Spring MVC is essential for defining how the application handles requests, resolves views, and deals with static assets. This setup can be achieved via Java or XML configurations. Using Java configuration, a class adorned with `@Configuration` and `@EnableWebMvc` activates Spring MVC's capabilities, with `@ComponentScan` indicating to Spring the components to be included.

```
@Configuration
@EnableWebMvc
@ComponentScan("com.example.myapp")
public class WebAppConfig implements WebMvcConfigurer {
    // Configuration specifics
}
```

Controller Deployment

Controllers play a pivotal role in intercepting web requests, directing them to the relevant service layer, or responding with a view. They are marked with the `@Controller` annotation and use annotations like `@RequestMapping` or its variants to map web requests.

```
@Controller
public class PageController {

    @GetMapping("/page")
    public String page(@RequestParam(name="userId", defaultValue="User") String userId, Model model) {
        model.addAttribute("userId", userId);
        return "pageView";
    }
}
```

This controller manages GET requests to `/page`, adding a `userId` to the model and routing to the `pageView`.

Crafting the View

The view layer in Spring MVC, which can be built using JSP, Thymeleaf, or other technologies, relies on controller-supplied data to produce HTML output for the client.

```
<!DOCTYPE html>
<html>
<head>
    <title>User Page</title>
</head>
<body>
    <h1>Welcome, ${userId}!</h1>
</body>
</html>
```

Typically found in `src/main/webapp/WEB-INF/views/`, this JSP file dynamically injects the `userId` using Expression Language (EL).

Implementing ViewResolver

In Spring MVC, a `ViewResolver` transforms the string-based view names into actual view objects. The

66

`InternalResourceViewResolver` is frequently utilized for JSPs:

```
@Bean
public ViewResolver viewResolver() {
    InternalResourceViewResolver resolver = new InternalResourceViewResolver();
    resolver.setPrefix("/WEB-INF/views/");
    resolver.setSuffix(".jsp");
    return resolver;
}
```

Static Resource Handling

Proper configuration for serving static resources like CSS and JavaScript is crucial. This is often achieved by extending the `addResourceHandlers` method to specify locations for static content.

```
@Override
public void addResourceHandlers(ResourceHandlerRegistry registry) {
    registry.addResourceHandler("/img/**").addResourceLocations("/img/");
}
```

Application Deployment

Spring MVC applications can be deployed on servlet containers or application servers such as Tomcat or Jetty. Spring Boot further simplifies deployment by embedding a servlet container, enabling the application to run independently.

Summary

Building a simple web application using Spring MVC encompasses several critical steps, from initializing the project with the necessary configurations to deploying controllers, creating views, and ultimately launching the application.

Following the MVC design principle allows for organized and maintainable web application development, fully exploiting the Spring Framework's vast capabilities. This methodical approach ensures focused attention on the application's specific business logic and UI design, promoting a streamlined development process and a clear division of responsibilities.

Chapter Five

Handling Data with Spring Boot

Introduction to Spring Data JPA

Spring Data JPA is a significant element of the extensive Spring Data ecosystem, aimed at enhancing the creation of data access layers by diminishing the need for routine database interaction code. Its chief purpose is to streamline the linkage between the domain model and data access layers, capitalizing on the Java Persistence API (JPA) to adeptly handle relational data within Java frameworks.

Insights into JPA

The Java Persistence API (JPA) stands as a Java specification that facilitates the interaction, persistence, and management of data between Java objects and relational databases. It introduces a set of guidelines for ORM (Object-Relational Mapping) implementations, enabling developers to map Java objects to database entities using annotations or XML configurations. JPA's main objective is to offer a uniform ORM framework that eases data persistence in Java applications while ensuring compatibility across various ORM solutions.

The Role of Spring Data JPA

Spring Data JPA extends JPA's functionalities, offering a more efficient methodology for developing data access layers. It introduces a repository abstraction layer that automatically handles typical CRUD operations, freeing developers to focus on the application's core logic rather than database access details.

Highlighted Features of Spring Data JPA

1. Repository Abstraction: Spring Data JPA offers repository interfaces, such as `**CrudRepository**` and `**PagingAndSortingRepository**`, predefining essential CRUD functionalities. By extending these interfaces, custom repositories gain these operations without manual implementation.

2. Method-based Query Generation: A notable capability of Spring Data JPA is its ability to generate SQL queries from repository interface method names, streamlining the process of defining query methods by just specifying method signatures.

```
public interface ClientRepository extends JpaRepository<Client, Long> {
    List<Client> findByLastName(String lastName);
}
```

3. Annotation-driven Custom Queries: For more intricate queries beyond simple method naming conventions, Spring Data JPA enables the use of the `**@Query**` annotation to specify custom JPQL (Java Persistence Query Language) or native SQL queries.

```
public interface ClientRepository extends JpaRepository<Client, Long> {
    @Query("SELECT c FROM Client c WHERE c.email = ?1")
    Client findByEmail(String email);
}
```

4. Seamless Transaction Management: Spring Data JPA is designed to integrate with Spring's transaction management system, ensuring that database operations are conducted within transactional contexts.

5. Flexibility with JPA Providers: Spring Data JPA supports a range of JPA providers, such as Hibernate, EclipseLink, and OpenJPA, offering the flexibility to choose the underlying ORM framework.

Spring Data JPA Integration

Integrating Spring Data JPA into a project involves adding the Spring Data JPA dependency along with a chosen JPA provider, like Hibernate, to the build configuration. For projects managed with Maven, this means updating the pom.xml file with the appropriate dependencies.

Setting up application properties is also crucial for defining the database connection, selecting the JPA provider, and adjusting other relevant settings.

Application in Practice

Employing Spring Data JPA in practice usually entails defining an entity class that maps to a database table and a repository interface that extends one of Spring Data JPA's repository interfaces. Spring Data JPA then dynamically generates the repository implementation at runtime, equipping it with CRUD operations and any custom query methods declared in the interface.

```java
@Entity
public class Member {
    @Id
    @GeneratedValue(strategy = GenerationType.IDENTITY)
    private Long id;

    private String name;
    private String email;

    // Accessors and mutators are not included for brevity
}

public interface MemberRepository extends JpaRepository<Member, Long> {
    List<Member> findByEmailLike(String email);
}
```

Concluding Thoughts on Spring Data JPA

Spring Data JPA is an indispensable resource for Java developers, significantly simplifying the incorporation of data persistence into applications by automating common data access tasks. Its repository abstraction, combined with sophisticated query formulation capabilities and seamless integration with the Spring framework, enables developers to efficiently manage relational data, focusing their efforts on the application's primary functionalities. With its extensive set of features, Spring Data JPA is a critical tool for developers navigating the intricacies of relational database management in contemporary Java applications.

Configuring a database in Spring Boot

Initiating a database setup within a Spring Boot framework is engineered for ease and effectiveness, mirroring the framework's intent to simplify database integration and configurations. Spring Boot adopts a principle of providing sensible defaults to minimize manual setup efforts, while still offering the flexibility for detailed customizations to cater to diverse project requirements.

Streamlined Database Setup with Spring Boot

Spring Boot intelligently prepares your database configuration by recognizing a database driver in your project's classpath, which significantly eases the initial setup. It accommodates a broad spectrum of databases, including SQL types like MySQL and PostgreSQL, as well as NoSQL varieties such as MongoDB and Cassandra, simply by adding the respective database drivers to your project dependencies.

Dependency Inclusion

Connecting to a database necessitates including the appropriate database driver in your project's build configuration file. For Maven-based projects, this means inserting the dependency in the `pom.xml`:

```
<dependency>
    <groupId>com.mysql.cj.jdbc</groupId>
    <artifactId>mysql-connector-java</artifactId>
</dependency>
```

And for those using Gradle, the dependency is added to the `build.gradle` file:

```
implementation 'com.mysql.cj.jdbc:mysql-connector-java'
```

Database Connection Details

Spring Boot's `application.properties` or `application.yml` file is where you articulate your database connection specifics. These configurations instruct Spring Boot on how to auto-configure a DataSource bean, which is essential for database operations.

For instance, a MySQL database configuration in the `application.properties` file would resemble:

```
spring.datasource.url=jdbc:mysql://localhost:3306/mydatabase
spring.datasource.username=dbuser
spring.datasource.password=dbpass
spring.datasource.driver-class-name=com.mysql.cj.jdbc.Driver
```

Or, in a YAML format:

```yaml
spring:
  datasource:
    url: jdbc:mysql://localhost:3306/mydatabase
    username: dbuser
    password: dbpass
    driver-class-name: com.mysql.cj.jdbc.Driver
```

Integrating Spring Data

Incorporating Spring Data JPA into your project eases the implementation of the data access layer, especially when paired with Hibernate, Spring Boot's default JPA provider. Alternative JPA providers can also be utilized if preferred.

```xml
<dependency>
    <groupId>org.springframework.boot</groupId>
    <artifactId>spring-boot-starter-data-jpa</artifactId>
</dependency>
```

For MongoDB engagements, adding the Spring Data MongoDB starter dependency configures the necessary beans for MongoDB interactions:

```xml
<dependency>
    <groupId>org.springframework.boot</groupId>
    <artifactId>spring-boot-starter-data-mongodb</artifactId>
</dependency>
```

Configuring Connection Pools

HikariCP is Spring Boot's default choice for database connection pooling, known for its stellar performance and dependability. The connection pool settings can be customized in the `application.properties` file:

```
spring.datasource.hikari.maximum-pool-size=5
spring.datasource.hikari.minimum-idle=2
```

Database Migration Tools

Spring Boot offers seamless integration with migration tools like Flyway and Liquibase, facilitating schema versioning. Adding the relevant dependency activates the chosen migration tool:

For Flyway:

```xml
<dependency>
    <groupId>org.flywaydb</groupId>
    <artifactId>flyway-core</artifactId>
</dependency>
```

And for Liquibase:

```xml
<dependency>
    <groupId>org.liquibase</groupId>
    <artifactId>liquibase-core</artifactId>
</dependency>
```

Migration scripts should be placed in standard locations (`db/migration` for Flyway and `db/changelog` for Liquibase), and Spring Boot will automatically execute them upon application startup.

Testing Database Configurations

Spring Boot simplifies testing setups with embedded databases such as H2, HSQLDB, or Derby. By incorporating an embedded database dependency, Spring Boot configures it for testing purposes:

```xml
<dependency>
    <groupId>com.h2database</groupId>
    <artifactId>h2</artifactId>
    <scope>test</scope>
</dependency>
```

Overview

Configuring a database in Spring Boot is designed to be straightforward and efficient, aligning with the framework's goals of ease of use and rapid development. By automatically setting up the database based on classpath dependencies and providing easy customization options through the `application.properties`, Spring Boot ensures a smooth development process without losing sight of configurability. Whether the application requires a conventional SQL database, a contemporary NoSQL database, or an in-memory database for testing purposes, Spring Boot's database configuration features are crafted to quickly set up the data layer, allowing developers to focus on building the application's primary functionalities.

Creating and using repositories

In modern software development, particularly within the Spring Framework's ecosystem, repositories serve as crucial components for abstracting the data access layer. These constructs essentially act as in-memory collections of domain entities, facilitating seamless interactions with the underlying data storage mechanisms. The concept is rooted in the Repository Design Pattern, which aims to decouple the business logic from the data access logic.

Fundamentals of Repositories

Repositories function as gateways to domain objects, offering an abstraction over the complexities involved in data access technologies such as JDBC, JPA, Hibernate, or various NoSQL databases. This abstraction allows developers to concentrate on the business logic, abstracted from the complexities of the data storage and retrieval processes.

Spring's Approach to Repositories

Within the Spring ecosystem, specifically through Spring Data, the process of implementing repositories is greatly simplified. Spring Data provides predefined interfaces that encapsulate common data operations, enabling developers to focus on their domain-specific needs without worrying about the underlying data access code.

Crafting a Repository Interface

In Spring Data JPA, creating a repository starts with defining an interface. This interface typically extends Spring Data's predefined interfaces like **`CrudRepository`** or **`JpaRepository`**, each tailored to different requirements.

```
public interface PersonRepository extends JpaRepository<Person, Long> {
}
```

This snippet illustrates a **`PersonRepository`** extending **`JpaRepository`**, automatically inheriting a comprehensive set of data operations for the **`Person`** entity.

Deriving Queries from Method Names

A standout feature of Spring Data repositories is their ability to construct SQL or JPQL queries directly from the method names defined in the repository interface, translating intuitive method names into actual database queries.

```
public interface PersonRepository extends JpaRepository<Person, Long> {
    List<Person> findByFirstName(String firstName);
}
```

In this example, the **`findByFirstName`** method is automatically interpreted by Spring Data into a query to retrieve persons by their first name.

Employing Custom Queries with Annotations

For scenarios where method names are insufficient to express complex queries, Spring Data repositories allow for custom JPQL or SQL queries through the **`@Query`** annotation.

```java
public interface PersonRepository extends JpaRepository<Person, Long> {
    @Query("SELECT p FROM Person p WHERE p.email = :email")
    Person findByEmail(@Param("email") String email);
}
```

This method defines a JPQL query to find a person by their email address, demonstrating the flexibility of Spring Data repositories in handling complex queries.

Utilizing Repositories

Spring Data automates the generation of the repository implementation, enabling its injection into service classes for direct use in application logic.

```java
@Service
public class PersonService {

    @Autowired
    private PersonRepository personRepository;

    public Person findPersonById(Long id) {
        return personRepository.findById(id).orElse(null);
    }
}
```

Here, the `personRepository` is seamlessly integrated into the service class, simplifying database interactions within the business logic.

Benefits of Employing Repositories

1. Data Access Layer Simplification: Repositories abstract away the intricacies of direct data access, presenting a streamlined, object-oriented interface for persistence layer interactions.

2. Boilerplate Reduction: Spring Data's repository interfaces significantly reduce the need for repetitive data access code, allowing developers to channel their efforts into the core business logic.

3. Enhanced Testability: The decoupling of data access into repositories improves the testability of applications, facilitating the use of mock frameworks or in-memory databases for testing purposes.

4. Consistency Across the Application: Repositories ensure a uniform methodology for data access and manipulation, promoting consistency throughout the application.

Conclusion

In the landscape of application development, particularly with Spring and Spring Data, repositories embody an efficient pattern for managing data persistence. They simplify the data access layer's implementation, bolstering application maintainability, testability, and consistency. By defining interfaces for repositories and harnessing Spring Data's capability to auto-generate implementations, developers can adeptly manage the persistence of domain entities, focusing primarily on the application's business logic.

Chapter Six

Developing Web Applications

Thymeleaf and template engines

Thymeleaf is recognized as a comprehensive Java template engine, proficient in processing a myriad of content forms such as HTML, XML, JavaScript, CSS, and even raw text. It excels notably in the realm of HTML5, enabling the utilization of templates for both static prototypes and interactive web pages, thus fostering a well-defined separation between the visual layers and the core business logic.

The Vital Role of Template Engines

Template engines are indispensable in the realm of web development, facilitating the dynamic generation of web pages. They meld predefined templates with a data model to produce HTML documents, enabling a design-once, populate-dynamically approach to web page creation.

Thymeleaf's Unique Proposition

Thymeleaf distinguishes itself within the template engine domain through several key attributes:

- Natural Templating Ability: Thymeleaf's templates can be directly viewed in browsers as static documents, enhancing the collaborative dynamics between developers and designers.

- Robust Integration with Spring: Thymeleaf is particularly tailored for Spring-based applications, thanks to its extensive integration capabilities with the framework.

- Expandable Dialects: Beyond accommodating standard dialects, Thymeleaf allows for the crafting of custom dialects, extending its versatility.

- Globalization Support: Thymeleaf is equipped to handle the development of applications intended for an international audience, with inherent support for internationalization.

Practical Application of Thymeleaf

Incorporating Thymeleaf into a Spring Boot project is initiated by adding the Thymeleaf starter dependency to the project's `pom.xml`:

```xml
<dependency>
    <groupId>org.springframework.boot</groupId>
    <artifactId>spring-boot-starter-thymeleaf</artifactId>
</dependency>
```

With Thymeleaf set up, the next step involves crafting templates, typically HTML files, located within the `src/main/resources/templates` directory. An illustrative example is shown below:

```
<!DOCTYPE html>
<html xmlns:th="http://www.thymeleaf.org">
<head>
    <title>Basic Thymeleaf Example</title>
</head>
<body>
    <h1 th:text="'Salutations, ' + ${user} + '!'"></h1>
</body>
</html>
```

This sample template showcases how the `th:text` attribute is used for dynamically integrating the `user` variable into the page content.

Controller Connectivity

A controller is essential for channeling data towards a Thymeleaf template for rendering purposes:

```
@Controller
public class WelcomeUserController {

    @GetMapping("/welcome/user")
    public String welcomeUser(@RequestParam(name="user", defaultValue="Visitor") String
        user, Model model) {
        model.addAttribute("user", user);
        return "welcomeUser"; // Relates to welcomeUser.html Thymeleaf template
    }
}
```

This controller sets up the `welcomeUser` view by linking the `user` parameter with the model, pointing to the `welcomeUser.html` Thymeleaf template.

Template Fragment Reusability

The Layout Dialect in Thymeleaf enables the repurposing of template segments across different pages, promoting consistency and minimizing code duplication.

Form Handling Efficiency

Thymeleaf is adept at managing form operations, providing comprehensive support for inputs, bindings, and error displays, and it integrates flawlessly with Spring MVC's validation framework.

Security Enhancements

When integrated with Spring Security, Thymeleaf introduces specialized attributes aimed at fortifying the security within the application's presentation layer.

Summarizing Thymeleaf

Thymeleaf is a potent and adaptable tool for dynamically generating web content, especially within environments powered by the Spring framework. Its natural templating capabilities, deep Spring integration, and internationalization features position Thymeleaf as an optimal choice for development teams. By promoting a distinct delineation between the visual components and the business logic, Thymeleaf not only boosts developer productivity but also fosters a synergistic collaboration between developers and designers, culminating in the development of web applications that are both highly maintainable and secure.

Creating dynamic web pages with Spring Boot and Thymeleaf

Blending Spring Boot's capabilities with Thymeleaf facilitates the creation of vibrant web interfaces. Known for making Spring application development straightforward, Spring Boot pairs well with Thymeleaf's capacity for dynamic template rendering, optimizing the workflow for crafting web applications replete with sophisticated features while curtailing the need for extensive manual coding.

Enhancing Development Efficiency with Spring Boot

Spring Boot is lauded for its "convention over configuration" ethos, propelling rapid development cycles by offering pre-configured setups for initiating projects and handling dependencies. It excels in tailoring the expansive suite of Spring's components to align with the project's specific dependency needs, markedly trimming the development timeline.

Thymeleaf's Templating Proficiency

Thymeleaf is celebrated for its 'natural templating' feature, allowing templates to be directly viewed in browsers as static mockups, thus smoothing the prototyping stage and bolstering teamwork between developers and design personnel. With its capability to process diverse content forms such as HTML, XML, JavaScript, CSS, and plaintext, Thymeleaf stands as a versatile tool for web development endeavors.

Integrating Thymeleaf into Spring Boot Projects

Incorporating Thymeleaf into Spring Boot projects entails adding the Thymeleaf starter dependency to the Maven or Gradle build configuration. For Maven-based projects:

```xml
<dependency>
    <groupId>org.springframework.boot</groupId>
    <artifactId>spring-boot-starter-thymeleaf</artifactId>
</dependency>
```

85

And for those utilizing Gradle:

```
implementation 'org.springframework.boot:spring-boot-starter-thymeleaf'
```

Although Spring Boot configures Thymeleaf with defaults suitable for a wide range of projects, these can be customized in the application's properties files to cater to specific project needs.

Developing Interactive Web Interfaces

The journey to constructing an interactive web interface with Spring Boot and Thymeleaf encompasses a few essential steps:

1. Configuring a Controller: Launch a Spring MVC controller tasked with handling web requests and augmenting the model with pertinent data, using annotations like `@Controller` and `@GetMapping`.

```
@Controller
public class UserWelcomeController {

    @GetMapping("/welcome-user")
    public String welcomeUser(@RequestParam(name="username", defaultValue="Companion")
        String username, Model model) {
        model.addAttribute("username", username);
        return "welcomeUser"; // Connects to the 'welcomeUser' Thymeleaf template
    }
}
```

This controller caters to `/welcome-user` requests, embedding a `username` attribute within the model.

2. Designing Thymeleaf Templates: Construct a Thymeleaf template within the `src/main/resources/templates` directory,

utilizing Thymeleaf's dynamic attributes to infuse content dynamically.

```html
<!DOCTYPE html>
<html xmlns:th="http://www.thymeleaf.org">
<head>
    <title>Welcome User</title>
</head>
<body>
    <h1 th:text="'Hello, ' + ${username} + '!'">Hello, Companion!</h1>
</body>
</html>
```

Here, the `th:text` attribute dynamically incorporates the `username` variable from the model into the webpage content.

Harnessing Thymeleaf's Broad Feature Spectrum

Thymeleaf's extensive range of features further enriches the creation of dynamic web pages:

- Expression Flexibility: Thymeleaf supports a variety of expressions that allow for the dynamic evaluation and manipulation of data within templates.

- Reusable Components: The Layout Dialect enables the recycling of common layout elements across various pages, ensuring design uniformity and reducing repetitive coding.

- Streamlined Form Management: Thymeleaf excels in handling user input forms, offering comprehensive support that meshes seamlessly with Spring MVC's data binding and validation frameworks.

Final Thoughts

The fusion of Spring Boot with Thymeleaf offers an efficient pathway to developing dynamic web applications. This blend not only streamlines the development process by combining Spring Boot's auto-configuration capabilities with Thymeleaf's intuitive templating system but also fosters a collaborative atmosphere between development and design teams. The result is the production of engaging, well-structured, and easily maintainable web applications.

Form handling and validation

Managing forms and ensuring data integrity through validation are fundamental elements in crafting interactive web applications. Within the Spring ecosystem, specifically through the utilization of Spring MVC and Spring Boot, the process of handling forms is made efficient and robust, granting developers a comprehensive toolkit for processing user inputs with precision and security.

Leveraging Spring MVC for Form Management

Spring MVC, a component of the extensive Spring Framework, facilitates form management via its model-view-controller architecture. It employs annotations such as `@Controller` and `@RequestMapping` to direct web requests and render the corresponding views. For form data, Spring MVC uses the `@ModelAttribute` annotation to bind incoming form fields to Java objects, streamlining data handling.

Consider a basic user registration form. The form data can be mapped to a **User** entity like so:

```java
public class User {
    private String username;
    private String email;
    // Accessors and mutators are not shown for brevity
}
```

A controller can then bind this form data to the `User` entity, facilitating access within the controller method:

```java
@Controller
public class UserRegistrationController {

    @GetMapping("/signup")
    public String displaySignupForm(Model model) {
        model.addAttribute("user", new User());
        return "signupForm";
    }

    @PostMapping("/signup")
    public String processSignup(@ModelAttribute User user) {
        // Implementation of user signup logic
        return "signupSuccess";
    }
}
```

The `displaySignupForm` method presents the signup form, whereas the `processSignup` method deals with the submitted form data.

Implementing Validation in Spring

Spring MVC embraces form validation via the `@Valid` annotation in tandem with the Bean Validation API (`javax.validation`). By applying validation constraints like `@NotNull`, `@Size`, or `@Email` to the `User` class fields, specific validation rules are enforced:

```
public class User {
    @NotNull
    @Size(min = 3, max = 50)
    private String username;

    @NotNull
    @Email
    private String email;

    // Accessors and mutators are omitted for brevity
}
```

The controller, adorned with the `@Valid` annotation, activates the validation process, capturing any errors in a `BindingResult` object:

```
@PostMapping("/signup")
public String processSignup(@Valid @ModelAttribute User user, BindingResult bindingResult)
    {
    if (bindingResult.hasErrors()) {
        return "signupForm";
    }
    // User signup logic implementation
    return "signupSuccess";
}
```

Crafting Custom Validators

For validation scenarios that extend beyond the scope of standard constraints, Spring facilitates the creation of tailor-made validators. By implementing the `Validator` interface and defining custom validation logic in the `validate` method, bespoke validation routines can be established:

```java
public class UserCustomValidator implements Validator {

    @Override
    public boolean supports(Class<?> clazz) {
        return User.class.isAssignableFrom(clazz);
    }

    @Override
    public void validate(Object obj, Errors errors) {
        User user = (User) obj;
        // Insert custom validation logic here
    }
}
```

This custom validator can subsequently be applied within the controller or configured globally for the entire application.

Form Rendering and Validation Feedback with Thymeleaf

Thymeleaf's integration with Spring enhances form rendering and error messaging. Its form-binding attributes align smoothly with Spring's model attributes, enabling effortless form rendering:

```html
<form action="#" th:action="@{/signup}" th:object="${user}" method="post">
    <input type="text" th:field="*{username}" />
    <input type="email" th:field="*{email}" />
    <button type="submit">Sign Up</button>
</form>
```

Thymeleaf also offers mechanisms for displaying validation messages adjacent to the relevant form fields, improving the feedback loop for users:

```html
<div th:if="${#fields.hasErrors('username')}">
    <p th:each="err : ${#fields.errors('username')}" th:text="${err}"></p>
</div>
```

Conclusion

Form handling and validation stand as pivotal components in the development of secure and interactive web applications. The Spring Framework, particularly through Spring MVC and Spring Boot, coupled with Thymeleaf, provides a robust set of tools for efficient form management and user input validation. Utilizing Spring's annotations, the Bean Validation API, and Thymeleaf's seamless integration, developers can devise effective form handling and validation strategies, ensuring data integrity and enhancing user experience.

Chapter Seven

Spring Boot Security Essentials

Basic concepts of web security

Navigating the complexities of digital security to fortify web applications against diverse cyber threats exploiting online vulnerabilities is imperative in the current digital era. Web security, comprising a gamut of defensive measures, protocols, and technological safeguards, aims to shield internet-based services, websites, and their users from harmful incursions. For tech aficionados and corporate entities, a deep-rooted knowledge of web security's foundational aspects is paramount to preserving the integrity, privacy, and accessibility of web-centric data and functionalities.

Key Pillars: Authentication and Authorization

At the nucleus of web security are the critical notions of authentication and authorization, pivotal in ensuring that access to digital resources is confined to authenticated individuals.

- Authentication refers to the procedure of confirming an individual's identity, typically through methods like passwords, biometric checks, or sophisticated multi-factor authentication techniques, serving as the gateway to verifying a user's identity claim.

- Authorization follows the authentication trail, specifying the range of resources and activities accessible to a verified user. It encompasses granting or limiting permissions to users based on their verified identities.

The deployment of exhaustive authentication and authorization frameworks is essential for facilitating secure user transactions and safeguarding sensitive information.

The Imperative of Encryption

Encryption, a linchpin in web security, involves the transformation of readable data into a secure encoded variant (ciphertext), decipherable only with the appropriate decryption mechanism. It guarantees the confidentiality and integrity of information relayed over the internet.

The prevalence of HTTPS (Hypertext Transfer Protocol Secure) in encrypting communications between a user's browser and web servers accentuates the importance of encryption. HTTPS employs SSL/TLS (Secure Sockets Layer/Transport Layer Security) protocols to encrypt the data flow, ensuring the secure transmission of sensitive data.

Mitigating XSS and CSRF Risks

Cross-Site Scripting (XSS) entails the injection of malicious scripts into reputable web entities, targeting web applications that inadequately validate or sanitize user inputs. Remedial measures typically include output encoding and stringent user input validation or cleansing.

Cross-Site Request Forgery (CSRF) involves deceiving a user into executing unintended actions within a web application where they are authenticated, leveraging anti-CSRF tokens to authenticate user requests, affirming their intentional nature.

Safeguarding Against SQL Injection

SQL Injection allows intruders to alter an application's database queries, especially menacing for web applications reliant on SQL databases. Preventive measures include the employment of parameterized queries with prepared statements, the use of stored procedures, and the meticulous sanitization of user inputs.

Fortifying Session Management

Robust session management is pivotal in warding off session hijacking and fixation threats. Optimal session management practices encompass:

- Crafting secure session identifiers with substantial entropy.

- Ensuring the protected conveyance of session identifiers (e.g., via HTTPS).

- Diligently overseeing session durations, including setting timeouts and invalidating sessions post-logout.

Leveraging Security Headers

Enhancing security through the implementation of HTTP response headers directs browsers on securely handling a site's content. These headers can activate security protocols like the Content Security Policy (CSP) to diminish XSS risks, HTTP Strict Transport Security (HSTS) to mandate secure connections, and X-Content-Type-Options to thwart MIME sniffing.

Prioritizing Timely Software Updates and Patch Management

Frequently updating software components constitutes a straightforward yet effective security strategy. Ensuring that systems like web servers, content management platforms, plugins, and libraries are up-to-date shields against known vulnerabilities. An efficient patch management infrastructure is indispensable for the prompt deployment of security enhancements.

Integrating Security from the Outset

Embracing a security-centric perspective involves embedding security considerations from the initial phases of web development, ingraining security into the development lifecycle from the get-go. This approach inherently results in more secure web applications.

The Significance of Awareness

Educating both users and developers about prevailing security threats and preventive tactics is crucial. Users should be aware of phishing hazards, the significance of robust passwords, and the necessity of software updates, while developers need continuous training in secure coding methodologies, awareness of new threats, and familiarity with modern defensive strategies.

Synopsis

The domain of web security is vast and perpetually evolving, unveiling new challenges as technology advances. Thoroughly understanding the basic elements of web security, including authentication, encryption, countermeasures against prevalent threats, and secure coding principles, is crucial for those involved in creating, managing, or utilizing web applications. Adhering to established security norms and staying informed about novel threats and vulnerabilities can significantly reduce the likelihood of security incidents, ensuring the protection of valuable online resources and data.

Configuring Spring Security in your application

Integrating Spring Security into an application markedly enhances its defense mechanisms. Esteemed for its robust authentication and control features, Spring Security equips Spring-based applications with an array of security functionalities such as user validation, access control, safeguarding against vulnerabilities, and managing user sessions efficiently.

Spring Security Essentials

Spring Security is designed to offer a comprehensive suite of security features, including authenticating users, granting permissions, securing against common threats, and controlling sessions, making it adaptable and scalable to meet varied application security demands.

Initializing Spring Security

Incorporating Spring Security starts with adding the necessary dependencies to your project's build system. For Maven configurations, the dependencies are specified in the `pom.xml`:

```xml
<dependency>
    <groupId>org.springframework.boot</groupId>
    <artifactId>spring-boot-starter-security</artifactId>
</dependency>
```

In Gradle configurations, the dependencies are included in the `build.gradle`:

```
implementation 'org.springframework.boot:spring-boot-starter-security'
```

Adding these dependencies triggers Spring Security's default settings to be applied, introducing form-based login and basic authentication by default.

Security Configuration Overview

Customizing Spring Security involves creating a configuration class that extends **`WebSecurityConfigurerAdapter`**. This setup allows for overriding certain methods to tailor security settings. A typical configuration might appear as:

```java
@EnableWebSecurity
public class AppSecurityConfig extends WebSecurityConfigurerAdapter {

    @Override
    protected void configure(HttpSecurity http) throws Exception {
        http
            .authorizeRequests()
                .antMatchers("/", "/welcome").permitAll()
                .anyRequest().authenticated()
                .and()
            .formLogin()
                .loginPage("/userLogin")
                .permitAll()
                .and()
            .logout()
                .permitAll();
    }
}
```

This setup indicates that paths `/` and `/**welcome**` are publicly accessible, while all other paths require user authentication. It also activates form-based authentication with a designated login page.

Developing a Custom UserDetailsService

For authentication, Spring Security may need to retrieve user-specific data. Typically, it defaults to an in-memory user store. However, custom implementations usually fetch user details from a database or other repositories. An example custom `**UserDetailsService**` is illustrated below:

```java
@Service
public class ApplicationUserService implements UserDetailsService {

    private final UserRepository userRepository;

    @Autowired
    public ApplicationUserService(UserRepository userRepository) {
        this.userRepository = userRepository;
    }

    @Override
    public UserDetails loadUserByUsername(String username) throws UsernameNotFoundException
    {
        User user = userRepository.findByUsername(username)
                .orElseThrow(() -> new UsernameNotFoundException("Username not located: " +
                    username));
        return new org.springframework.security.core.userdetails.User(user.getUsername(),
            user.getPassword(), Collections.emptyList());
    }
}
```

Secure Password Strategies

Securely managing passwords is essential, and storing them in plaintext is not advisable. Spring Security encourages using various password encoding strategies, with `**DelegatingPasswordEncoder**` being preferred for its flexibility. A sample password encoder configuration is:

```
@Bean
public PasswordEncoder passwordEncoder() {
    return PasswordEncoderFactories.createDelegatingPasswordEncoder();
}
```

Adjust the `**configure(AuthenticationManagerBuilder auth)**` method to leverage this encoder:

```
@Autowired
public void configureGlobal(AuthenticationManagerBuilder auth) throws Exception {
    auth
        .userDetailsService(userDetailsService)
        .passwordEncoder(passwordEncoder());
}
```

Adjusting Authorization Protocols

Authorization in Spring Security is managed by intercepting and inspecting HTTP requests, applying pre-defined rules to grant or deny access. The authorization rules are set in the `**configure(HttpSecurity http)**` method:

```
@Override
protected void configure(HttpSecurity http) throws Exception {
    http
        .authorizeRequests()
            .antMatchers("/admin/**").hasRole("ADMIN")
            .antMatchers("/user/**").hasAnyRole("USER", "ADMIN")
            .anyRequest().authenticated()
            .and()
        .formLogin()
            .and()
        .httpBasic();
}
```

This configuration restricts `**/admin/**`** paths to users with an "ADMIN" role, permits `**/user/**`** paths to "USER" or "ADMIN" roles, and enforces authentication for other paths.

Summarizing the Configuration

Setting up Spring Security within an application involves customizing authentication, refining authorization rules, handling passwords securely, and more, tailored to the specific security needs of the application. The adaptability of Spring Security supports a variety of security setups, from simple configurations with minimal customizations to intricate, customized security frameworks for extensive systems. Grasping the security requirements of your application and utilizing Spring Security's rich feature set is vital for adequately securing your application.

Adding authentication and authorization

Embedding robust authentication and authorization frameworks is essential in safeguarding web applications, ensuring that access to certain areas is restricted to verified users. Authentication serves to validate a user's credentials against a trusted source, using methods such as password checks, token-based systems, or multifactor authentication to maintain security integrity.

Authentication Essentials

Authentication functions as the initial checkpoint for application security, examining credentials like usernames and passwords against authenticated entities such as databases or external services. In the context of Spring Security, a basic form-based authentication setup might resemble:

```
@Configuration
@EnableWebSecurity
public class SecurityConfigurations extends WebSecurityConfigurerAdapter {

    @Override
    protected void configure(HttpSecurity http) throws Exception {
        http
            .authorizeRequests()
            .antMatchers("/public/**").permitAll()
            .anyRequest().authenticated()
            .and()
            .formLogin()
            .loginPage("/auth")
            .permitAll();
    }
}
```

This setup dictates that paths under `/public/**` are accessible to all, whereas other areas demand authentication, redirecting unauthorized access to a specific login page.

Authorization Techniques

Post-authentication, authorization determines the level of access an authenticated individual has, essentially deciding what actions the user can perform within the application.

Configuring authorization within Spring Security to restrict access based on roles could be depicted as:

```
@Override
protected void configure(HttpSecurity http) throws Exception {
    http
        .authorizeRequests()
        .antMatchers("/management/**").hasRole("MANAGER")
        .antMatchers("/profile/**").hasAnyRole("USER", "MANAGER")
        .anyRequest().authenticated();
}
```

Here, access to `/**management/\*\***` is reserved for users with the "MANAGER" role, while `/**profile/\*\***` is accessible to those with "USER" or "MANAGER" roles.

Secure Handling of Passwords

In authentication processes, the secure management of passwords is of utmost importance, ensuring they're not stored or transmitted in plaintext. Utilizing Spring Security's `**PasswordEncoder**` interface, particularly `**BCryptPasswordEncoder**`, aids in the encryption of passwords:

```
@Bean
public PasswordEncoder encoder() {
    return new BCryptPasswordEncoder();
}
```

This `**PasswordEncoder**` can then be utilized within a `**UserDetailsService**` implementation to encrypt and authenticate passwords:

```
@Autowired
private PasswordEncoder encoder;

@Override
public UserDetails loadUserByUsername(String username) throws UsernameNotFoundException {
    User user = findUserByUsername(username);
    if (user != null) {
        return new org.springframework.security.core.userdetails.User(user.getUsername(),
            encoder.encode(user.getPassword()), user.getAuthorities());
    }
    throw new UsernameNotFoundException("Username could not be found");
}
```

Token-Based Authentication

Token-based authentication, such as JWT, is preferable for stateless applications like RESTful services. JWT tokens, issued after authentication, are used in subsequent HTTP request headers for accessing protected resources.

Incorporating JWT within Spring Security could involve crafting a custom `**AuthenticationFilter**` to assess the JWT token in every request:

```java
public class JwtVerificationFilter extends OncePerRequestFilter {

    @Override
    protected void doFilterInternal(HttpServletRequest request, HttpServletResponse
        response, FilterChain filterChain) throws ServletException, IOException {
        String token = retrieveToken(request);
        if (token != null && tokenIsValid(token)) {
            Authentication auth = createAuthentication(token);
            SecurityContextHolder.getContext().setAuthentication(auth);
        }
        filterChain.doFilter(request, response);
    }

    // Implementation details for retrieveToken, tokenIsValid, and createAuthentication are
    //    excluded for brevity
}
```

Guarding RESTful Services

Protecting RESTful services involves securing endpoints based on user roles or permissions, achievable with Spring Security's `**@PreAuthorize**` for method-level constraints:

```java
@RestController
@RequestMapping("/service")
public class ServiceController {

    @PreAuthorize("hasRole('MANAGER')")
    @GetMapping("/manager-data")
    public ResponseEntity<?> getManagerData() {
        // Endpoint functionality
    }

    @PreAuthorize("hasAnyRole('USER', 'MANAGER')")
    @GetMapping("/user-data")
    public ResponseEntity<?> getUserData() {
        // Endpoint functionality
    }
}
```

Wrap-Up

Integrating authentication and authorization into web applications involves a spectrum of activities from securely managing credentials to setting permissions and ensuring seamless integration of these security aspects. Leveraging Spring Security allows for effective application protection, data security, and a fortified user experience. Proficiency in implementing these security measures is crucial for developing secure and reliable web applications in the current cybersecurity landscape.

Chapter Eight

RESTful Web Services with Spring Boot

Understanding REST principles

Gaining proficiency in REST (Representational State Transfer) principles is indispensable for engineering web services that excel in scalability, performance, and maintainability. Originated by Roy Fielding in his academic dissertation, REST is an architectural framework rather than a stringent protocol, cleverly capitalizing on the web's inherent protocols and conventions, with HTTP being central, rendering it an excellent framework for developing web APIs.

Foundational Pillars of REST

The robustness and flexibility of REST are built upon six fundamental principles:

1. Separation of Client and Server: REST is founded on a clear demarcation between the client and server, segregating the concerns of user interface from data storage, which enhances the system's adaptability and scalability.

2. Stateless Exchanges: In a RESTful architecture, each interaction between the client and server is self-contained, necessitating that every client request carries all the necessary information for the server to fulfill the request, thus promoting reliability and scalability.

3. Caching Capabilities: Responses in REST should be explicitly marked as cacheable or non-cacheable to improve network efficiency and client-side responsiveness.

4. Standardized Interface: REST advocates for a uniform interface that simplifies the overall system architecture by decoupling the service's functionalities from their usage. This uniformity is maintained through the consistent use of HTTP verbs, standardized URI patterns, and response codes.

5. Hierarchical Architecture: REST supports the construction of applications with a multi-layered architecture, enabling intermediate layers that can offer additional functionalities like load balancing or security, thereby augmenting scalability and security.

6. Code on Demand (optional): Though less frequently applied, this principle enables servers to dynamically extend client functionalities by sending executable code.

Utilizing HTTP Methods in REST

In RESTful services, standard HTTP methods are employed to conduct CRUD operations on resources:

- GET: Retrieves either a single resource or a set of resources. For example, `GET` `/books` might list all available books, while `GET /books/123` would retrieve details of a specific book.

- POST: Used to create a new resource. For instance, `POST /books` with relevant data could introduce a new book to the system.

- PUT: Updates an existing resource. For instance, `PUT /books/123` with updated information could modify the details of a particular book.

- DELETE: Removes a resource, such as `DELETE /books/123` to eliminate a specific book from the system.

Stateless Operations Example

Consider a RESTful service for managing a library's inventory. A `GET` request to `/books` displays a catalog of books, while a `POST` request to `/books` with details about a book adds it to the inventory. Each request operates independently, without the server retaining session data.

Resource Identification and Representation

In REST, resources are uniquely identified through URIs, like `/books/1` for a specific book. The representation of these resources, such as JSON or XML, is generally determined based on client needs and specified through HTTP headers.

Sample RESTful API Response

A successful `POST` request to add a book might return a `201 Created` status, with the `Location` header pointing to the URI of the newly created resource:

```
POST /books HTTP/1.1
Host: examplelibrary.org
Content-Type: application/json

{
  "title": "Microservices Patterns",
  "author": "Chris Richardson"
}
```

```
HTTP/1.1 201 Created
Location: /books/101
```

Conclusion

Adhering to REST principles enables the creation of web services that are not only intuitive and streamlined but also highly adaptable. By following standardized HTTP methods, ensuring stateless interactions, and upholding a uniform interface, RESTful APIs facilitate efficient and effective communication between clients and servers. As web technologies continue to advance, REST remains a cornerstone methodology for devising interoperable, scalable, and high-performing web applications.

Developing RESTful APIs with Spring Boot

Building RESTful APIs utilizing Spring Boot harnesses the framework's robust auto-configuration and extensive RESTful web services support. Spring Boot facilitates the development of scalable and easily maintainable web services by eliminating much of the customary manual configuration, providing a plethora of annotations and tools designed expressly for crafting RESTful services.

Essential Steps for Creating RESTful APIs with Spring Boot

Spring Boot's preference for convention over configuration greatly simplifies the process of initiating RESTful API projects. Tools like Spring Initializr allow for quick project setup with key dependencies such as `**spring-boot-starter-web**` for web functionalities and `**spring-boot-starter-data-jpa**` for data persistence integration.

```xml
<dependency>
    <groupId>org.springframework.boot</groupId>
    <artifactId>spring-boot-starter-web</artifactId>
</dependency>
<dependency>
    <groupId>org.springframework.boot</groupId>
    <artifactId>spring-boot-starter-data-jpa</artifactId>
</dependency>
```

Defining Domain Models

At the heart of a RESTful API in Spring Boot are the domain models that represent the application's data structures. These models, often entity classes, are marked with JPA annotations to outline their database table mappings. A straightforward `**Book**` entity might be depicted as follows:

```java
@Entity
public class Book {
    @Id
    @GeneratedValue(strategy = GenerationType.AUTO)
    private Long id;
    private String title;
    private String author;
    // Getters and setters are simplified for clarity
}
```

Establishing the Repository Layer

Data access is streamlined in Spring Data JPA, which offers built-in CRUD functionality through simple repository interfaces. Extending `JpaRepository` grants access to an array of database operations with minimal coding.

```java
public interface BookRepository extends JpaRepository<Book, Long> {
}
```

Crafting the Service Layer

The service layer in a Spring Boot application is where business logic resides, acting as an intermediary between the controller and the data access layers. This layer is tasked with executing business operations and repository interactions.

```java
@Service
public class BookService {
    private final BookRepository bookRepository;

    @Autowired
    public BookService(BookRepository bookRepository) {
        this.bookRepository = bookRepository;
    }

    public List<Book> fetchAllBooks() {
        return bookRepository.findAll();
    }
    // Additional functionalities are not shown for simplicity
}
```

Constructing REST Controllers

Controllers in Spring Boot, designated by the `@RestController` annotation, manage HTTP requests and responses. These controllers rely on services to process business logic and communicate with the database.

```java
@RestController
@RequestMapping("/api/books")
public class BookController {
    private final BookService bookService;

    @Autowired
    public BookController(BookService bookService) {
        this.bookService = bookService;
    }

    @GetMapping
    public List<Book> getAllBooks() {
        return bookService.fetchAllBooks();
    }

    // Further endpoints are omitted for brevity
}
```

Managing Exceptions and Validating Requests

Spring Boot offers `@ControllerAdvice` for comprehensive exception handling and `@Valid`, coupled with JSR-303 annotations, for enforcing request body validation, ensuring the API's integrity.

Documenting, Securing, and Testing the API

API documentation, facilitated by tools like Swagger, is crucial for understanding and testing API functionalities interactively. Security, integral to API design, is bolstered in Spring Boot through Spring Security integration, safeguarding API endpoints.

Testing stages are well-supported in Spring Boot, offering libraries for both unit and integration tests to confirm API reliability and performance.

```
@SpringBootTest(webEnvironment = SpringBootTest.WebEnvironment.RANDOM_PORT)
public class BookControllerTestSuite {
    @Autowired
    private TestRestTemplate restTemplate;

    @Test
    public void testRetrieveBooks() {
        ResponseEntity<List<Book>> response = restTemplate.exchange("/api/books",
            HttpMethod.GET, null, new ParameterizedTypeReference<List<Book>>() {});
        assertEquals(HttpStatus.OK, response.getStatusCode());
        // More assertions follow
    }
}
```

In Summary

The process of developing RESTful APIs with Spring Boot is streamlined, capitalizing on Spring Boot's rich ecosystem and auto-configuration features. From project initialization and domain model definition to business logic implementation and endpoint security, Spring Boot offers a coherent pathway for creating scalable, maintainable, and secure web services. Familiarity with the key components and workflow of Spring Boot applications is essential to leverage its comprehensive capabilities in RESTful API development.

Testing APIs with Postman

Assessing APIs through the lens of Postman is a pivotal aspect of the software engineering process, ensuring APIs adhere to expected behaviors across various scenarios. Renowned for its streamlined functionality, Postman presents a comprehensive suite for API assessment, facilitating effortless interactions with web services and thorough analysis of their responses, thus accommodating both hands-on and automated testing paradigms.

Introduction to Postman for API Assessment

Postman serves as a dynamic API tool, enabling the dispatch of HTTP requests to web services, thereby empowering developers and quality assurance specialists to construct, evaluate, and modify APIs within its accessible interface, rendering it suitable for an array of users due to its simplicity.

Kickstarting API Assessment with Postman

To embark on API assessment using Postman, one must first install the Postman application, compatible with various operating systems. Postman simplifies the creation of new requests by allowing the specification of the HTTP method, the endpoint URL, and pertinent headers or body information.

Crafting Requests in Postman

Postman's capabilities extend to intricate request configurations:

- HTTP Method: The method selection (e.g., GET, POST) hinges on the intended interaction with the API.

- Endpoint URL: This field is designated for the API endpoint's URL that is under scrutiny.

- Headers: Vital HTTP headers such as `**Content-Type**` or authentication details can be set up.

- Request Body: For methods akin to POST, the request's body content can be specified, offering format choices such as raw JSON or form data.

Delving into Responses

Upon executing a request, Postman elucidates the API's response, showcasing crucial elements like the status code, response timing, headers, and body, vital for assessing the API's operational integrity and efficiency.

- Status Code: Denotes the request's outcome (e.g., 200 OK, 404 Not Found).

- Response Timing: Illustrates the server's response interval, pivotal for evaluating API latency.

- Response Headers: Convey supplementary data about the response, like content type or caching directives.

- Response Body: Encompasses the actual data relayed by the API, usually in JSON or XML formats.

Leveraging Postman Collections

Postman Collections provide a methodical way to aggregate related API requests, assisting in the orchestration of complex APIs, fostering team collaboration, or scripting automated test sequences.

Utilizing Environment Variables

Postman champions the use of environment variables for encapsulating mutable data such as API keys or server addresses, boosting test flexibility and easing transitions across distinct testing phases.

Test Automation within Postman

Postman's forte lies in its test automation potential, permitting the scripting of tests in JavaScript with a broad spectrum of assertions to scrutinize API responses.

For instance, to validate a response's 200 status code, one could employ a script like:

```
pm.test("Status code is 200", function () {
    pm.response.to.have.status(200);
});
```

These scripts are autonomously executed post-request, with results promptly visualized within Postman, offering immediate feedback.

Continuous Integration Compatibility with Postman

Postman tests can be seamlessly woven into Continuous Integration (CI) cycles through Newman, Postman's command-line counterpart, ensuring API modifications do not inadvertently introduce regressions.

Promoting Collaborative Dynamics

Postman excels in facilitating collaborative dynamics via the sharing of collections and configurations, bolstering teamwork. Its cloud-based service guarantees that collaborative efforts remain synchronized, keeping all participants aligned with the most current tests and documentation.

Synopsis

The Postman toolkit for API testing simplifies the verification process for web services, establishing itself as an essential instrument for development teams. With its intuitive interface coupled with robust testing and automation capabilities, it provides a comprehensive approach to API testing. Employing Postman ensures APIs are precise, perform optimally, and integrate seamlessly, contributing to the development of reliable and high-quality software solutions.

Chapter Nine

Error Handling and Logging

Exception handling in Spring Boot

Exception management is a crucial component in crafting resilient and user-centric applications. Within the Spring Boot ecosystem, renowned for facilitating the development of enterprise-grade Spring applications, effective strategies for addressing exceptions are paramount for sustaining application robustness and ensuring a smooth user journey. Spring Boot enhances the experience of managing errors, offering diverse methodologies to elegantly tackle and communicate exceptions.

Spring Boot's Default Approach to Exceptions

Spring Boot inherently provides a rudimentary mechanism for addressing exceptions encountered in Spring MVC applications. Upon an exception occurrence, Spring Boot renders a basic error page detailing the status code alongside a concise message. While this default setup is beneficial during development phases, production-ready applications often necessitate a more elaborate strategy to gracefully manage exceptions and relay more informative error messages.

Advanced Exception Management with @ControllerAdvice

The `@ControllerAdvice` annotation stands out in Spring Boot as a formidable tool for global error handling. It enables the crafting of a centralized error handling class that intercepts exceptions thrown across various controllers, enhancing error management coherence.

```
@ControllerAdvice
public class ApplicationExceptionHandler {

    @ExceptionHandler(ResourceNotFoundException.class)
    public ResponseEntity<Object> handleResourceNotFound(ResourceNotFoundException
        exception, WebRequest request) {
        ErrorDetails details = new ErrorDetails(new Date(), exception.getMessage(), request
            .getDescription(false));
        return new ResponseEntity<>(details, HttpStatus.NOT_FOUND);
    }

    // Additional exception handlers can be included here
}
```

This snippet demonstrates handling a custom `ResourceNotFoundException`, constructing a detailed error response through an `ErrorDetails` object.

Utilizing @ExceptionHandler for Specific Errors

Within a `@ControllerAdvice`-annotated class, the `@ExceptionHandler` annotation permits defining methods to tackle specific exceptions. This enables precise error response tailoring for various exception types.

```
@ExceptionHandler(Exception.class)
public ResponseEntity<Object> handleAllExceptions(Exception exception, WebRequest request) {
    ErrorDetails details = new ErrorDetails(new Date(), exception.getMessage(), request
        .getDescription(false));
    return new ResponseEntity<>(details, HttpStatus.INTERNAL_SERVER_ERROR);
}
```

Here, a general exception handler is depicted, catching all exceptions not explicitly managed by other `@ExceptionHandler`-annotated methods.

Structuring Custom Error Responses

For conveying meaningful error data to clients, adopting a custom error response structure is advisable. An `ErrorDetails` class can encapsulate essential error information like timestamp, message, and other pertinent details.

```java
public class ErrorDetails {
    private Date timestamp;
    private String message;
    private String details;

    public ErrorDetails(Date timestamp, String message, String details) {
        this.timestamp = timestamp;
        this.message = message;
        this.details = details;
    }

    // Getters and setters are omitted for conciseness
}
```

Exception Handling in RESTful Services

For RESTful applications, Spring Boot introduces `@RestControllerAdvice`, akin to `@ControllerAdvice` but specifically tailored for REST APIs. It streamlines exception handling in REST services, enabling the serialization of error data into JSON or XML formats.

```java
@RestControllerAdvice
public class ApiExceptionHandler {

    @ExceptionHandler(ResourceNotFoundException.class)
    public ResponseEntity<?> resourceNotFoundHandler(ResourceNotFoundException exception) {
        ErrorDetails details = new ErrorDetails(new Date(), exception.getMessage(),
            "Resource not found");
        return new ResponseEntity<>(details, HttpStatus.NOT_FOUND);
    }
}
```

Complex Exception Handling Approaches

For intricate scenarios, Spring Boot facilitates customizing responses based on the client type (e.g., web browser, REST client) by implementing the `ErrorController` and assessing request specifics to deliver the appropriate response type.

Moreover, extending Spring Boot's `ResponseEntityExceptionHandler` offers a streamlined avenue to customize responses for standard Spring MVC exceptions, allowing for the overriding of its methods to tailor exception handling.

In Closing

Navigating exceptions in Spring Boot is fundamental for developing applications that are not only robust but also informative when discrepancies arise. By employing annotations such as `@ControllerAdvice`, `@ExceptionHandler`, and `@RestControllerAdvice`, developers are equipped to institute a comprehensive and centralized exception handling framework. Tailoring error responses and presenting them in a structured manner enhances transparency with clients, facilitating improved user experiences and simplifying troubleshooting. Spring Boot's versatile exception handling capabilities empower developers to construct applications that are resilient and communicative in the face of errors, contributing significantly to application stability and dependability.

Custom error pages

Creating personalized error pages is essential for enhancing the overall user interaction and preserving the uniform appearance of web applications, even during error occurrences. Custom error pages effectively turn potential negative encounters with standard, impersonal error messages into chances for constructive user engagement, offering helpful information while upholding the application's visual and communicative consistency.

Significance of Personalized Error Pages

Custom error pages are beneficial for several reasons:

- Elevating User Interaction: They prevent users from being met with stark, standard, or complex error messages, which can be unsettling or bewildering.

- Upholding Brand Unity: They ensure that error scenarios are addressed in a manner that aligns visually and tonally with the rest of the application.

- Assisting Users: They can offer links or advice to help users navigate from the error page, possibly resolving their issue or directing them back to main content.

- Logging Errors: They enable the capturing of error details on the server side for debugging purposes, while presenting a more approachable interface to the user.

Implementing Personalized Error Pages Across Platforms

The method for setting up custom error pages can vary depending on the underlying technology. In dynamic frameworks such as Spring Boot or ASP.NET, built-in functionalities exist for custom error handling, whereas in static environments or with traditional web servers, configurations might be required at the server level.

Custom Error Handling in Spring Boot

Spring Boot facilitates custom error responses by allowing developers to define a controller that handles the `/error` endpoint, which Spring Boot defaults to when unhandled exceptions occur:

```java
@Controller
public class ErrorControllerCustom implements ErrorController {

    @RequestMapping("/error")
    public String handleError(HttpServletRequest request) {
        // Extract and potentially log error information from the request
        // Determine the appropriate view based on the error or other criteria
        return "errorCustomView";
    }

    @Override
    public String getErrorPath() {
        return "/error";
    }
}
```

In this instance, `errorCustomView` would be a user-friendly template that relays the error information in a digestible format.

Server Configuration for Static Sites and Web Servers

In scenarios involving static sites or web servers like Apache or Nginx, error page configurations are generally handled through server configuration files. In Apache, for example, one might use the `.htaccess` file to direct specific error statuses to dedicated HTML pages:

```
ErrorDocument 404 /errors/404-custom.html
ErrorDocument 500 /errors/500-custom.html
```

This configuration guides the server to display `/errors/404-custom.html` for 404 errors and `/errors/500-custom.html` for 500 errors.

Design Principles for Custom Error Pages

When designing custom error pages, adhering to certain best practices can enhance their effectiveness:

- Comforting the User: Use a calm and reassuring tone, avoiding technical terminology that could confuse the layman.

- Providing Direction: Embed links to the homepage, search functionality, or support sections to aid users in finding a way forward.

- Maintaining Design Cohesion: Ensure the error page's design is consistent with the site's overall branding and aesthetic.

- Detailing Errors for Debugging: While offering a simplified error message to the user, detailed error information should be logged on the server for troubleshooting purposes.

- Thorough Testing: Regular testing should be conducted to ensure custom error pages are displayed correctly across various error conditions.

Considerations for Security and Legal Compliance

It's imperative to construct error pages that don't divulge sensitive details potentially exploitable by adversaries. Opt for general messages that conceal the specific nature of the error. Moreover, the error handling approach should comply with relevant legal standards, especially for applications with wide public exposure.

Conclusion

Personalized error pages are a critical facet of web application design, mirroring the application's dedication to quality and positive user experience, even in moments of failure. By devising error pages that are informative, aesthetically harmonious, and user-friendly, developers can significantly uplift the user experience, transforming potential points of frustration into opportunities for positive user interaction and brand reinforcement.

Introduction to logging with Logback

Logging plays a pivotal role in software development, offering critical insights into how applications perform, identifying errors, and monitoring efficiency. Logback, renowned in the Java community for its robustness, adaptability, and superior performance, is a logging framework that has gained traction. It's conceived as the evolutionary successor to the log4j project by Ceki Gülcü, who aimed to enhance its architecture and customization capabilities.

Logback at a Glance

Logback is segmented into three core modules: Logback-core, Logback-classic, and Logback-access. The core module lays the foundation of the framework, upon which Logback-classic builds to serve as SLF4J's native implementation, effectively replacing log4j and offering a sophisticated logging solution for Java applications. Logback-access facilitates logging of HTTP access within Servlet environments.

Setting Up Logback

Logback offers the flexibility of being configured either through code or via configuration files, supporting XML and Groovy formats. The XML configuration method is prevalently used for its ease of comprehension and flexibility. An exemplary `logback.xml` configuration might resemble:

```xml
<configuration>
    <appender name="CONSOLE" class="ch.qos.logback.core.ConsoleAppender">
        <encoder>
            <pattern>%date{ISO8601} [%thread] %-5level %logger - %msg%n</pattern>
        </encoder>
    </appender>

    <root level="info">
        <appender-ref ref="CONSOLE" />
    </root>
</configuration>
```

This configuration delineates a console appender named `CONSOLE` that outputs log messages adorned with timestamps, thread identifiers, log levels, logger names, and the messages themselves. The root logger is configured at the `info` level, thereby filtering out debug messages but including info, warn, error, and critical messages.

Distinctive Features of Logback

Logback introduces several innovative features that contribute to its preference as a logging framework:

- Conditional Configuration: Logback's configuration files can include conditions, allowing dynamic adjustments based on environmental variables or specific conditions.

- Config Reloadability: It supports the real-time reloading of configuration files upon modification, negating the need for application restarts and boosting developer efficiency.

- Fine-grained Filtering: Logback offers precise control over which log entries are processed by an appender through the use of filters.

- Mapped Diagnostic Context (MDC): It provides MDC support, enabling the enrichment of log messages with contextual data, invaluable in scenarios involving concurrent operations or multiple users.

- Time and Size-based Log Rotation: The RollingFileAppender facilitates the rotation of log files based on time or size constraints, ensuring logs remain manageable and disk usage is optimized.

Logback Logging Best Practices

Employing Logback effectively involves adhering to certain best practices:

- Judicious Use of Log Levels: It's crucial to categorize log messages accurately using the appropriate log levels (TRACE, DEBUG, INFO, WARN, ERROR) to reflect their urgency and significance.

- Context Enrichment with MDC: Augmenting log messages with relevant contextual information (such as user or transaction identifiers) can significantly aid in debugging and monitoring.

- Preventing Log Duplication: Proper logger configuration is essential to avoid the redundancy of log messages across various appenders.

- Guarding Sensitive Data: Care should be taken not to inadvertently log sensitive or personal information, maintaining compliance with security standards.

- Performance Consideration: The impact of logging, especially at verbose levels like DEBUG or TRACE, on application performance should be considered, with asynchronous logging being a viable option for high-demand scenarios.

Conclusion

Logback emerges as an exemplary logging framework for Java, distinguished by its comprehensive feature set and configurability, catering to a wide array of logging requirements. Its thoughtful design, emphasizing efficiency and customization, coupled with advanced functionalities such as conditional configuration, MDC support, and log rotation, renders it an exceptional choice for developers seeking an all-encompassing logging solution. By embracing best practices and harnessing Logback's full spectrum of capabilities, developers can implement efficient logging strategies that elevate application transparency and maintainability.

Chapter Ten

Testing Your Spring Boot Application

The importance of testing

Testing in software development transcends being a mere step in the development process—it's an essential element that guarantees software functions effectively, meets user expectations, and withstands various operational stresses. It significantly influences the software's quality, its ability to meet business goals, and its reliability under actual usage conditions.

A Detailed Look at Software Testing

Software testing encompasses several approaches, each aimed at examining different aspects of the software:

- Unit Testing: At this fundamental level, individual units or components of the software are tested to ensure they function correctly. Here's how a basic unit test might look in Java using JUnit:

```java
import static org.junit.Assert.*;
import org.junit.Test;

public class ArithmeticOperationsTest {
    @Test
    public void testAddition() {
        assertEquals("Addition result did not match expected output", 3, Arithmetic.add(1,
            2));
    }
}
```

- Integration Testing: This type tests interactions between integrated units to expose problems that might not be detectable during unit testing.

- System Testing: Here, the entire software system is tested to verify that it complies with the specified requirements.

- Acceptance Testing: Typically the last phase before the software is released, where actual users test the software to ensure it can perform required tasks in real-world scenarios.

The Importance of a Comprehensive Testing Strategy

Developing a comprehensive testing strategy is critical for several reasons:

- Improving Software Quality: Meticulous testing helps uncover and resolve defects early in the development cycle, enhancing the overall quality of the software.

- Enhancing User Satisfaction: Software that is intuitive and free from significant disruptions leads to higher user satisfaction and trust.

- Reducing Costs: Early detection of defects through detailed testing reduces the costs associated with later fixes, which tend to be significantly higher.

- Ensuring Regulatory Compliance: For software in regulated industries, thorough testing is necessary to ensure compliance and avoid potential legal issues.

Automated versus Manual Testing

The decision between automated and manual testing is crucial. Automation offers speed and efficiency, ideal for extensive regression, load, and performance testing. Conversely, manual testing is indispensable for evaluating usability and detailed user interactions. Employing a blend of both approaches often provides the best results.

Integration with Continuous Integration Systems

In Agile and DevOps methodologies, continuous integration (CI) and continuous testing play pivotal roles. These practices involve running automated tests immediately following each code integration, promptly identifying and addressing issues:

```
# Script example for a CI pipeline that executes tests
echo "Initiating unit tests"
run_tests.sh --unit

echo "Conducting integration tests"
run_tests.sh --integration
```

This example highlights how automated tests in CI/CD pipelines provide immediate insights, enhancing code quality and deployment readiness.

Testing as a Vital Investment

Given the critical role of software in business and daily life, investing in robust testing procedures is not just beneficial; it's imperative. The potential consequences of insufficient testing—such as financial losses and reputational harm—are too significant to ignore. Thus, robust testing should be viewed not just as an expense but as an essential investment in the software's success and longevity.

Conclusion

The role of testing in software development is foundational, ensuring that the software is not only operational and sturdy but also maximizes user satisfaction and efficiency in maintenance costs. Integrating both automated and manual testing into the development lifecycle enables organizations to create products that are durable and adaptable to future technological advances.

Unit testing with JUnit

Unit testing is an essential aspect of software development, focusing on individual units or components to ensure they function correctly. JUnit is a highly regarded framework in the Java ecosystem, pivotal for facilitating efficient and effective unit testing. Originating from the collaborative efforts of Erich Gamma and Kent Beck, JUnit has evolved through its iterations, with JUnit 5 being the latest version, integrating modern Java features and enhancing the testing experience.

The Structure of JUnit

JUnit 5 is organized into various modules under three main sub-projects:

- JUnit Platform: This serves as the foundation, launching testing frameworks on the JVM and providing the TestEngine API for developing new testing frameworks.

- JUnit Jupiter: This module is where testers write tests using the new functionalities provided by JUnit 5.

- JUnit Vintage: This ensures backward compatibility by enabling the running of JUnit 3 and JUnit 4 tests on the new platform.

This modular approach makes JUnit adaptable for testing in comprehensive project environments.

Crafting a Simple Unit Test with JUnit

To demonstrate JUnit's utility, consider a basic scenario where you need to test an arithmetic function. Here's how you might implement a test for an addition method in a Java class:

```java
public class Arithmetic {
    public static int add(int numberOne, int numberTwo) {
        return numberOne + numberTwo;
    }
}
```

A JUnit test class to verify this might look like:

```java
import static org.junit.jupiter.api.Assertions.assertEquals;
import org.junit.jupiter.api.Test;

public class ArithmeticTest {

    @Test
    void testAddition() {
        assertEquals(5, Arithmetic.add(2, 3), "Should return the sum of two numbers");
    }
}
```

Here, `@Test` identifies that `testAddition()` is a test method. `assertEquals` checks if the expected outcome matches the actual result, and it flags an error if there is a mismatch.

JUnit 5 Enhancements

JUnit 5 introduces several enhancements that improve its functionality:

- Advanced Annotations: New annotations like `@BeforeEach`, `@AfterEach`, `@BeforeAll`, `@AfterAll`, and `@Disabled` facilitate better test organization and execution control.

- Robust Assertions: JUnit 5 expands its assertion capabilities with methods like `assertThrows`, `assertNotNull`, `assertTrue`, and `assertAll` for comprehensive testing needs.

- Assumptions: Assumptions such as `assumeTrue` and `assumeFalse` allow tests to be conditionally ignored based on specific criteria.

- Tagging and Filtering: Tests can be tagged for selective execution, useful in different contexts like integration testing or targeted environment testing.

- Nested Testing: Support for nested tests enables a more structured approach to writing tests, allowing for logical grouping and hierarchy.

Best Practices in Unit Testing with JUnit

To maximize the effectiveness of JUnit testing, consider these best practices:

1. Maintain Test Independence: Ensure each test can run independently and does not depend on the outcome of others.

2. Clear Test Naming: Use descriptive names for test methods to clearly state what they verify.

3. Mock External Dependencies: Use tools like Mockito to mock external classes and focus on the unit being tested.

4. Consider Edge Cases: Include tests for potential edge cases to guarantee comprehensive coverage.

5. Integrate with Build Systems: Incorporate JUnit tests into your build process and continuous integration systems to automatically check each integration for issues.

Conclusion

JUnit stands as a vital tool for developers aiming to ensure the reliability and quality of their Java applications. By providing an environment that supports detailed and repeatable tests, JUnit aids in verifying that all software components perform as expected before being integrated into larger systems. Mastery of JUnit is therefore indispensable for developers committed to creating robust, high-quality software.

Integration testing with Spring Boot Test

Integration testing is a critical aspect of software development, ensuring that individual modules work together seamlessly within a complete system. Spring Boot Test, a component of the broader Spring Boot ecosystem, greatly facilitates integration testing for Spring applications. It offers tools and annotations tailored for a Spring context, integrating effortlessly with established testing frameworks like JUnit.

Core Features of Spring Boot Test

Spring Boot Test is designed to make the testing process straightforward and effective by providing utilities that support the automatic or selective loading of application contexts. This is vital for integration testing, where simulating a production-like environment is necessary to verify the system's integrated behavior. Here are some prominent features:

- @SpringBootTest: This annotation configures a Spring application context for tests, simulating the full application for comprehensive integration testing.

- Test Configuration: Developers can define specific configurations with `@TestConfiguration` to customize the application context during tests, tailoring beans or settings for the testing environment.

- Mocking Support: Spring Boot Test seamlessly integrates with mocking frameworks such as Mockito, offering annotations like `@MockBean` and `@SpyBean` to replace or spy on beans within the application context.

- Web Environment Testing: It allows for testing in a real or mocked web environment through the `webEnvironment` attribute of `@SpringBootTest`, which is crucial for RESTful service testing.

- Database Interaction: It can be combined with annotations like `@DataJpaTest`, `@JdbcTest`, and `@DataMongoTest` to focus on testing the data access layers with respective configurations for JPA, JDBC, and MongoDB.

Implementing an Integration Test in Spring Boot

To illustrate the application of Spring Boot Test, consider testing a scenario involving a Spring MVC controller, service, and repository. Below is a sample integration test using JUnit 5:

```java
import org.junit.jupiter.api.Test;
import org.springframework.beans.factory.annotation.Autowired;
import org.springframework.boot.test.context.SpringBootTest;
import org.springframework.boot.test.mock.mockito.MockBean;
import org.springframework.boot.test.web.client.TestRestTemplate;
import org.springframework.http.HttpStatus;
import org.springframework.http.ResponseEntity;

import static org.assertj.core.api.Assertions.assertThat;
import static org.mockito.Mockito.when;

@SpringBootTest(webEnvironment = SpringBootTest.WebEnvironment.RANDOM_PORT)
public class ProductIntegrationTest {

    @Autowired
    private TestRestTemplate restTemplate;

    @MockBean
    private ProductService productService;
```

```
@Test
  void testProductFetch() {
      // Setup mock response
      Product mockProduct = new Product("1", "High-Performance Spring Tee");
      when(productService.findProductById("1")).thenReturn(mockProduct);

      // Execute HTTP request
      ResponseEntity<Product> response = restTemplate.getForEntity("/products/1", Product
          .class);

      // Assert response details
      assertThat(response.getStatusCode()).isEqualTo(HttpStatus.OK);
      assertThat(response.getBody()).isNotNull().isEqualToComparingFieldByField
          (mockProduct);
  }
}
```

In this test, `@SpringBootTest` sets up a test environment resembling the production setup, while `TestRestTemplate` is used for making real HTTP requests. The `@MockBean` allows the isolation of the test from the service layer by providing mock behavior for the `ProductService`.

Best Practices for Spring Boot Integration Testing

- Selective Mocking: Use `@MockBean` judiciously to maintain the integrity of the integration perspective. Prefer real interactions where feasible.

- Focused Tests: Each integration test should target specific interactions or integrations to keep tests manageable and meaningful.

- Data Management: Ensure any data manipulation in tests is properly managed or isolated using transactional behavior or test-specific database setups.

- Profile-specific Properties: Use Spring profiles to configure properties exclusive to the testing environment.

- Transactional Rollback: Apply `@**Transactional**` on tests that change database state to rollback changes post-test, preserving database integrity.

Conclusion

Spring Boot Test equips developers with an array of tools to efficiently conduct integration testing, ensuring that all components of a Spring application work cohesively. By adhering to best practices and leveraging the full spectrum of features provided by Spring Boot Test, developers can enhance the robustness, reliability, and maintainability of their applications.

Chapter Eleven

Spring Boot Actuator: Monitoring and Management

Introduction to Spring Boot Actuator

Spring Boot Actuator stands as a fundamental part of the Spring Boot framework, offering crucial tools for real-time monitoring and management of applications. This module is particularly vital for tracking application performance and behavior, proving indispensable for effective maintenance and operation in microservices architectures.

Overview of Spring Boot Actuator

Spring Boot Actuator arms developers with production-grade features through various endpoints that reveal operational details about the application. This includes data on health, metrics, configurations, and more, accessible via JMX or HTTP endpoints. Actuator's design is to assist developers in monitoring their applications and identifying issues directly from the production environment.

Key Functionalities of Spring Boot Actuator

- Health Monitoring: Actuator's health endpoint offers an immediate look at the application's health, extendable to include detailed checks on subsystems like databases and disk space.

- Metrics Collection: It captures essential performance metrics such as memory usage, HTTP traffic, and database operations, aiding in the evaluation of application performance.

- Audit Trails: Capable of logging significant actions within the application, such as logins and data access, crucial for maintaining security.

- HTTP Trace: This functionality provides detailed tracing of HTTP request and response data, useful for debugging purposes.

- Dynamic Logging Levels: Allows for the adjustment of logging levels dynamically, providing a versatile approach to debugging without restarting the application.

- Thread Diagnostics: Offers thread dump insights, helping diagnose performance issues or deadlocks.

- Custom Application Information: Enables developers to add specific application information that can be exposed through Actuator endpoints, like version details or additional metadata.

Integrating Spring Boot Actuator

To incorporate Spring Boot Actuator into a Spring Boot application, you must add the Spring Boot Starter Actuator dependency. Here's how to include it in a Maven build:

```xml
<dependency>
    <groupId>org.springframework.boot</groupId>
    <artifactId>spring-boot-starter-actuator</artifactId>
</dependency>
```

Once added, the exposure of Actuator endpoints can be managed through the application's configuration settings. For example:

```
management.endpoints.web.exposure.include=health,info,metrics
```

Accessing Actuator Endpoints

If Spring Security is configured, access to Actuator endpoints may be restricted, requiring proper authorization. Typical endpoints might include:

```
http://localhost:8080/actuator/health
http://localhost:8080/actuator/info
```

These endpoints return data such as:

```
{
    "status": "UP"
}
```

from the `/health` endpoint, and configuration-specific information from the **/info** endpoint as defined in the application properties:

```
info.app.name=Example App
info.app.version=1.0.0
```

Best Practices with Spring Boot Actuator

- Secure Sensitive Endpoints: Crucial endpoints should be secured, restricting access to necessary personnel and protecting them via Spring Security.

- Regular Review of Exposed Data: It's important to continually audit the data exposed through Actuator to ensure that no sensitive information is inadvertently disclosed.

- Extend Default Metrics: Enhance the default metrics with custom metrics that provide deeper insights specific to the application.

- System Integration: Leverage Actuator metrics within a larger monitoring and alerting framework to maintain a continuous check on application health and performance indicators.

Conclusion

Spring Boot Actuator is an essential tool for any organization deploying Spring Boot applications in production. It offers comprehensive insights into application health and performance, facilitates troubleshooting, and enhances the manageability of applications. With proper configuration and careful management of its endpoints, Spring Boot Actuator can significantly boost operational efficiency and ensure robust application performance.

Configuring actuator endpoints

Spring Boot Actuator is a vital module within the Spring Boot framework that enriches the ability to oversee and manage applications through its diverse range of endpoints, offering real-time operational insights. Optimizing the configuration of these endpoints is key to utilizing Actuator's full potential, enabling detailed monitoring of application health and performance.

Introduction to Actuator Endpoints

Actuator endpoints provide essential operational data from your application, such as health status, metrics, logs, and HTTP trace information. These endpoints can be customized and secured to prevent the exposure of sensitive information while still delivering valuable insights.

Integrating Actuator in Your Project

To incorporate Spring Boot Actuator, you must first add the necessary dependency to your project's build configuration, here's how you can do it for Maven and Gradle:

For Maven:

```xml
<dependency>
    <groupId>org.springframework.boot</groupId>
    <artifactId>spring-boot-starter-actuator</artifactId>
</dependency>
```

For Gradle:

```gradle
implementation 'org.springframework.boot:spring-boot-starter-actuator'
```

Post-installation, activation or deactivation of specific endpoints can be managed through your application's properties or YAML configurations.

Configuring Endpoint Exposure

By default, critical endpoints such as `**health**` and `**info**` are exposed. To control the exposure of additional endpoints, adjust your application's configuration:

```
management.endpoints.web.exposure.include=health, info, metrics, env
```

To limit access to particular endpoints:

```
management.endpoints.web.exposure.exclude=loggers, httptrace
```

Securing Actuator Endpoints

Since Actuator endpoints can reveal comprehensive and sensitive application data, securing these endpoints is essential. If Spring Security is in use, it will automatically secure these endpoints. You can specify custom security settings to further control access:

```java
import org.springframework.security.config.annotation.web.builders.HttpSecurity;
import org.springframework.security.config.annotation.web.configuration
    .WebSecurityConfigurerAdapter;

public class AppSecurityConfig extends WebSecurityConfigurerAdapter {

    @Override
    protected void configure(HttpSecurity http) throws Exception {
        http
            .authorizeRequests()
            .requestMatchers(EndpointRequest.toAnyEndpoint()).hasRole("ADMIN")
            .and()
            .httpBasic();
    }
}
```

This configuration limits Actuator endpoint access to users with the `ADMIN` role.

Enhancing Actuator with Customizations

You can also configure Actuator to show detailed information based on user roles:

```
management.endpoint.health.show-details=when-authorized
management.endpoint.health.roles=ADMIN
```

Furthermore, Spring Boot Actuator allows for the creation of custom endpoints to surface bespoke functionalities or data relevant to your application:

```java
import org.springframework.boot.actuate.endpoint.annotation.Endpoint;
import org.springframework.boot.actuate.endpoint.annotation.ReadOperation;

@Endpoint(id = "customEndpoint")
public class CustomEndpoint {

    @ReadOperation
    public MyCustomData provideCustomData() {
        return new MyCustomData("value");
    }

    static class MyCustomData {
        private String data;

        MyCustomData(String data) {
            this.data = data;
        }

        // getters and setters
    }
}
```

Conclusion

Effectively configuring Spring Boot Actuator endpoints is imperative for robust monitoring and managing of applications within production environments. By fine-tuning endpoint exposure, ensuring thorough security measures, and augmenting functionality with custom endpoints, developers can significantly bolster their operational strategies, ensuring their applications are efficient and resilient.

Monitoring your application's health and metrics

In the complex field of software development, effectively monitoring the health and metrics of applications is critical. It ensures that applications are not only performing optimally but also remain resilient across different operational environments. Proper monitoring can preemptively identify potential issues and provide essential data to enhance application performance and inform capacity expansion strategies.

Importance of Health Monitoring

Health monitoring involves assessing key aspects of an application to confirm their operational integrity. This usually covers checking database connections, disk space utilization, external service dependencies, and vital system metrics like CPU load and memory usage. The aim is to maintain a current view of the application's health to ensure continuous uptime and consistent user access.

Spring Boot Actuator enriches this facet by allowing developers to integrate health endpoints that report on various aspects of the system. Here's an illustration of how a health indicator might be implemented using Spring Boot:

```
import org.springframework.boot.actuate.health.Health;
import org.springframework.boot.actuate.health.HealthIndicator;
import org.springframework.stereotype.Component;

@Component
public class ApplicationHealthIndicator implements HealthIndicator {

    @Override
    public Health health() {
        int errorCode = systemHealthCheck(); // Implement your health check logic here
        if (errorCode != 0) {
            return Health.down().withDetail("Error Code", errorCode).build();
        }
        return Health.up().build();
    }

    private int systemHealthCheck() {
        // Method that performs the system health check
        return 0; // 0 indicates the system is healthy
    }
}
```

This health indicator adds to an overall health status accessible through an endpoint such as `/actuator/health`, showing JSON formatted health status data.

Metrics Monitoring

Beyond health checks, metrics monitoring offers a detailed quantitative review of an application's performance, tracking elements such as the number of requests, latency, CPU usage, and memory consumption. These metrics are crucial for analyzing how an application handles varying loads.

For metrics collection, tools like Prometheus are typically paired with Grafana for effective visualization. Here's a basic setup for Prometheus in a Spring Boot application:

```java
import io.micrometer.core.instrument.Counter;
import io.micrometer.core.instrument.MeterRegistry;
import org.springframework.context.annotation.Bean;
import org.springframework.context.annotation.Configuration;

@Configuration
public class ApplicationMetricsConfiguration {

    @Bean
    public Counter httpRequestCounter(MeterRegistry registry) {
        return Counter.builder("http_requests_total")
                .description("Counter for total HTTP requests received.")
                .register(registry);
    }
}
```

This counter monitors HTTP requests, made available via the /actuator/prometheus endpoint for Prometheus scraping.

Visualization and Alerting

Effective visualization of these metrics is essential for spotting operational trends or anomalies. Grafana offers robust tools for creating dynamic dashboards based on Prometheus data, and it can trigger alerts if metrics exceed set thresholds, alerting teams to potential issues promptly.

Best Practices for Monitoring

1. Comprehensive Monitoring: Ensure that both the application and its infrastructure components are thoroughly monitored.

2. Alerts for Anomalies: Configure proactive alerts for any metrics that deviate from established norms to detect issues before they escalate.

3. Update Monitoring Tools Regularly: Adapt and update monitoring configurations to accommodate new

features or changes in the application or its environment.

4. Benchmarking Performance: Regularly analyze performance metrics to establish benchmarks that help identify when operational parameters deviate from the norm.

Conclusion

Monitoring the health and metrics of your application is indispensable for maintaining optimal performance and reliability. Using tools like Spring Boot Actuator for health assessments and integrating Prometheus with Grafana for metrics monitoring provides comprehensive insights into operational health, enabling quick responses to maintain exceptional service quality. Effective monitoring is not merely about ensuring an application runs smoothly; it's about optimizing functionality and improving overall user experiences.

Chapter Twelve

Deploying Your Spring Boot Application

Overview of deployment options

In today's rapidly advancing tech landscape, selecting the right deployment strategy is crucial for ensuring that applications remain scalable, accessible, and manageable. The evolution of deployment technologies, especially with the advent of cloud services and containerization, has broadened the spectrum of available deployment methods. This discussion delves into the various deployment options, ranging from traditional setups to contemporary cloud-based and serverless models.

Traditional Deployment

Traditional or "on-premise" deployment requires hosting applications on physical servers within an organization's own infrastructure. This approach affords total control over the computing environment but demands significant capital for infrastructure and its maintenance. Key challenges include scalability issues and the necessity for in-house IT staff to handle server upkeep, security updates, and potential hardware failures.

Example:

```
# Setting up a web application using a traditional LAMP stack.
sudo apt-get install apache2 mysql-server php libapache2-mod-php php-mysql
sudo systemctl start apache2
sudo systemctl enable apache2
# Transfer your PHP application files to the server's web directory.
cp -r my_php_app/* /var/www/html/
```

Cloud-Based Deployment

Cloud deployment uses the infrastructure of cloud service providers such as AWS, Microsoft Azure, or Google Cloud Platform, eliminating the need for physical hardware maintenance and enhancing scalability and flexibility. This method is divided into several service models:

- Infrastructure as a Service (IaaS): Offers virtual computing resources via the internet. Users manage operating systems and applications but not the underlying hardware.

- Platform as a Service (PaaS): Provides cloud components to certain software while being used mainly for applications. PaaS offers a development and hosting environment in the cloud.

- Software as a Service (SaaS): Software is available over the internet on a subscription basis, managed by the service provider.

Example:

```
# Launching an application on an AWS EC2 instance
aws ec2 run-instances --image-id ami-0abcdef1234567890 --count 1 --instance-type t2.micro
    --key-name MyKeyPair --security-group-ids sg-903004f8 --subnet-id subnet-6e7f829e
```

Containerized Deployment

Containerization involves isolating an application and its dependencies into a container that ensures consistent operation across any computing environment. Docker is widely used for containerization, while Kubernetes is the standard for orchestrating these containers, managing their lifecycle, and scaling them as needed.

Example:

```
# Running a Docker container with an Nginx web server
docker run -d -p 80:80 nginx
```

Serverless Deployment

Serverless frameworks enable developers to build and deploy applications without directly managing the underlying servers. The server and infrastructure management are handled by cloud providers, who automatically scale and allocate resources as needed. This setup is ideal for applications with variable workloads.

Example:

```
# Deploying a function on AWS Lambda
aws lambda create-function --function-name my-function --runtime nodejs12.x --role arn:aws
    :iam::123456789012:role/service-role/MyLambdaRole --handler index.handler --zip-file
    fileb://function.zip
```

Microservices Deployment

Deploying an application as microservices means breaking it down into smaller, independent services that communicate over light protocols, often HTTP. This strategy fits well with containerized and serverless frameworks due to its inherent need for distributed architecture and scalability.

Conclusion

Choosing an effective deployment strategy is vital for aligning with an organization's technical needs and operational goals. Whether through traditional on-premise servers, versatile cloud platforms, containerized environments, or agile serverless architectures, each option presents unique benefits. Understanding these can help developers and organizations make informed decisions that optimize application performance and simplify lifecycle management.

Deploying to an external Tomcat server

Deploying web applications on an external Tomcat server is common in organizational environments where development and operational stages are distinctly separated. Apache Tomcat, celebrated for its robust Java servlet capabilities, is chosen for its dependable performance, extensive Java EE support, and stable functionality.

Key Aspects of Tomcat Deployment

Tomcat streamlines the deployment process via WAR (Web Application Archive) files. These archives, which house all necessary elements of a web application, are simply placed in Tomcat's `webapps` directory. Tomcat automatically activates these applications on startup or when it recognizes new files during operation.

Preparing Your Application for Deployment

To deploy your application to an external Tomcat server, it must first be compiled into a WAR file. This can typically be accomplished using an IDE like Eclipse or IntelliJ, or through a build system such as Maven or Gradle.

Here's a brief rundown on preparing a WAR file with Maven:

1. Structure Your Project: Typically, a Maven project has its Java source files in `src/main/java` and web

assets like JSPs and HTML in `src/main/webapp`, which should include the `WEB-INF` directory.

2. Configure the pom.xml: Make sure your `pom.xml` includes all necessary dependencies and specifies the packaging type as `war`:

```
<packaging>war</packaging>
```

3. Generate the WAR file: Compile and package your application into a WAR file located in the `target` directory by running:

```
mvn package
```

Deploying the WAR File

Once the WAR file is prepared, deploy it to Tomcat using these steps:

1. Transferring the File: Upload the WAR file to the `webapps` directory on your Tomcat server via a suitable file transfer method, such as FTP or SCP.

2. Using Tomcat Manager (Optional): The Tomcat Manager web application facilitates easier deployment. It allows for deploying, undeploying, and managing applications through a browser. Ensure proper access by configuring users in `conf/tomcat-users.xml`:

```
<role rolename="manager-gui"/>
<user username="admin" password="password" roles="manager-gui"/>
```

Access the Manager by going to `**http://<your-tomcat-server>:8080/manager/html**`.

Optimizing Tomcat Settings

Enhance Tomcat's performance and reliability by adjusting a few configurations:

1. JVM Settings: Tailor the JVM settings for memory management in the `**setenv.sh**` (Linux/Mac) or `**setenv.bat**` (Windows) files located in the `**bin**` directory:

```
export JAVA_OPTS="-Xms512M -Xmx1024M -server"
```

2. Adjust Server Configurations: Modify settings like ports and SSL in the conf/server.xml.

3. Manage Logging: Configure log settings in `**conf/logging.properties**` to adjust log levels and specify log file destinations.

4. Secure Your Setup: Enhance security by limiting access to the Tomcat Manager, implementing HTTPS, and establishing security protocols in `**web.xml**`.

Best Practices for Effective Deployment

- Regular Updates: Consistently update Tomcat to benefit from the latest security enhancements and functional improvements.

157

- Monitor Server Health: Continuously monitor performance metrics like memory and thread usage to fine-tune server operations.

- Ensure Robust Security: Apply stringent security protocols, especially for applications managing sensitive data.

Conclusion

Efficient deployment of applications on an external Tomcat server involves preparing a WAR file, transferring it, and fine-tuning Tomcat configurations for optimal performance and security. Understanding these steps and adhering to best practices will ensure that your Java web applications are deployed effectively, making the most of Tomcat's robust server environment

Introduction to deploying with Docker

Docker has revolutionized deployment practices by facilitating a standardized, portable environment that ensures applications perform consistently across various computing platforms. This introduction to deploying with Docker will cover how this technology streamlines deployment processes and ensures uniform application behavior from development to production.

Overview of Docker

Docker is an innovative open-source platform that uses software containers to automate application deployment. These containers wrap an application with all its dependencies into a compact, executable package that runs uniformly on any system supporting Docker. This standardization solves common issues where applications behave differently in various environments.

Key Concepts in Docker

Images and Containers: Docker operates on a system of images and containers. An image is a static template that includes the application code and its dependencies, while a container is a runtime instance of an image, where the application actually executes.

Dockerfile: A Dockerfile is a script consisting of commands that Docker uses to build images. It outlines how to assemble an image containing the application and its runtime environment.

Docker Hub and Registries: Docker Hub is a service that allows users to find and share Docker images. It provides a centralized repository for Docker images, facilitating easy sharing and distribution of containerized applications. Docker also supports private registries for storing images securely.

Starting With Docker

To initiate Docker deployment, Docker Desktop must be installed on your system. Running a basic Docker container can be achieved with the following command:

```
docker run hello-world
```

This command pulls the `hello-world` image from Docker Hub if it's not available locally and runs it in a container, which will output a welcome message and then terminate.

Deploying Your Application Using Docker

Deploying an application using Docker typically involves creating a Docker image and then running this image as a container. Here's how to deploy a Node.js application:

1. Develop a Dockerfile: This file is crucial for building your Docker image. Below is an example of a Dockerfile for a Node.js application:

```
# Use the official Node.js image as a base
FROM node:14

# Set the working directory inside the container
WORKDIR /usr/src/app

# Copy all files from the current directory to the container
COPY . .

# Install any necessary dependencies
RUN npm install

# Make port 80 available to the world outside this container
EXPOSE 80

# Define the command to run on container start
CMD ["node", "app.js"]
```

2. Build the Docker image:

```
docker build -t my-node-app .
```

This command creates an image labeled `**my-node-app**` using the Dockerfile located in the current directory.

3. Start the container:

```
docker run -p 4000:80 my-node-app
```

This runs the `my-node-app` container, mapping port 80 inside the container to port 4000 on your host machine, allowing access through `http://localhost:4000`.

Best Practices for Docker Deployment

- Optimize image size: Strive for smaller Docker images to enhance deployment speed and efficiency. Utilize multi-stage builds and avoid including unnecessary files.

- Use specific version tags: Define explicit version tags in your image specifications to ensure consistency and reliability, rather than relying on `latest`.

- Secure handling of secrets: Avoid embedding sensitive information, like passwords, directly in Docker images or Dockerfiles. Prefer environment variables or Docker's secret management features for better security.

Conclusion

Deploying with Docker provides significant advantages by encapsulating the necessary environment to run an application into a single, coherent unit. This approach reduces discrepancies across environments, simplifies the deployment process, and reduces overhead, allowing developers to focus more on development and less on deployment specifics. Docker's method improves deployment strategies by providing a reliable and consistent framework for application lifecycles.

Chapter Thirteen

Best Practices and Tips

Project structure and packaging best practices

In the realm of software development, adhering to effective project structuring and packaging methodologies is pivotal for enhancing maintainability, scalability, and collaboration. Proper organization facilitates seamless navigation and understanding of the codebase, crucial in large-scale or multi-developer projects. This article explores the best practices for structuring and packaging software projects efficiently.

Significance of Project Structure

A well-defined project structure aids developers in locating resources quickly, managing changes effectively, and grasping the overall architecture of the software. This organizational clarity is essential in projects with multiple contributors to prevent disarray and manageability issues.

Recommended Practices for Project Structure

1. Adhere to Language and Framework Guidelines: Different programming languages and frameworks have their preferred organizational structures. For instance, Java projects often utilize Maven or Gradle, which suggest specific directories for source code (`src/main/java`), resources (`src/main/resources`), and tests (`src/test`).

2. Organize Code by Functionality: Code should be organized following the Separation of Concerns principle, ideally separating application layers (e.g., controllers, services, repositories) into distinct packages:

```
com.example.myapp
├── controller     // Classes handling HTTP requests
├── service        // Business logic classes
├── repository     // Data access layer classes
├── model          // Domain objects
```

3. Centralize Configuration Files: Keep configuration files in a dedicated directory or package to facilitate easy adjustments without altering the codebase.

4. Mirror Test Structure: Test directories should mirror the structure of the application code to simplify the location of corresponding test cases:

```
src/
├── main/
│   ├── java/
│   └── resources/
└── test/
    ├── java/
    └── resources/
```

5. Employ Descriptive Naming: File and directory names should clearly reflect their content or function to avoid confusion.

Best Practices for Packaging

Packaging involves compiling software components into a distributable format, which includes all necessary compilations and configurations.

1. Limit Dependencies: Restrict your project's dependencies to essential ones to reduce build time and mitigate potential conflicts.

2. Define Dependency Scope: Appropriately scope your dependencies. For example, dependencies used only for testing should not be included in the production build:

```
<dependency>
  <groupId>junit</groupId>
  <artifactId>junit</artifactId>
  <version>4.13.2</version>
  <scope>test</scope>
</dependency>
```

3. Implement Semantic Versioning: Follow semantic versioning rules (`major.minor.patch`) to indicate breaking changes, new features, and bug fixes respectively.

4. Utilize Build Automation: Employ tools like Maven, Gradle, or npm to manage dependencies, automate builds, and streamline testing processes.

5. Incorporate Continuous Integration (CI): Set up CI practices to automate building, testing, and packaging processes, which enhances code quality and early detection of potential issues.

Example: Maven Project Structure

Below is an example of how a simple Maven project might be organized, demonstrating a clear separation of responsibilities and concerns:

```
my-application/
├── pom.xml          // Maven configuration file
├── src/
│   ├── main/
│   │   ├── java/
│   │   │   └── com/
│   │   │       └── example/
│   │   │           ├── Application.java    // Entry point
│   │   │           ├── controller/
│   │   │           ├── service/
│   │   │           └── repository/
│   │   └── resources/
│   │       ├── application.properties       // Configuration file
│   │       └── logback.xml                  // Logging configuration
│   └── test/
│       ├── java/
│       └── resources/
└── target/          // Target directory where outputs are placed
```

Conclusion

A logical and well-maintained project structure along with sensible packaging practices form the backbone of successful software development projects. By adopting these best practices, developers ensure that their applications are robust, maintainable, and ready for efficient collaboration and future growth. These methods not only boost productivity but also enhance the overall software lifecycle management.

Performance optimization tips

Performance optimization is a fundamental aspect of software development and system management, aimed at enhancing the speed and efficiency of operations. Proper optimization practices can significantly reduce the consumption of resources, improve user experiences, and bolster overall system durability. This guide delves into key strategies for optimizing performance, covering everything from code refinement to system adjustments.

Strategic Selection of Algorithms and Data Structures

The core of effective performance optimization lies in the judicious selection of algorithms and data structures, which can greatly impact how applications perform.

- Opt for Effective Data Structures: Selecting the appropriate data structures tailored to specific functions can dramatically improve performance, such as employing hash tables for expedited data retrieval operations, which can access data in $O(1)$ time.

- Refine Algorithms: Evaluating and improving algorithms for better time and space efficiency is crucial. For example, implementing complex sorting algorithms like quicksort or mergesort can handle large data sets more efficiently than simpler methods such as bubble sort.

Consider this Java example utilizing a hash map for rapid data retrieval:

```java
import java.util.HashMap;
Map<String, Integer> map = new HashMap<>();
map.put("one", 1);
map.put("two", 2);
map.put("three", 3);

// Accessing a value swiftly
int value = map.get("two");
```

Profiling and Enhancing Code

Identifying and addressing code bottlenecks through profiling is essential for targeted performance enhancements. Profiling reveals specific code segments where resource usage is excessively high.

- Deploy Profiling Tools: Using tools like VisualVM, JProfiler, or GProf can pinpoint areas that consume excessive CPU or memory, allowing for precise optimization efforts.

- Streamline Code: Modify and optimize code based on profiling data, eliminating redundant operations and simplifying complex functions to enhance performance.

Database Interaction Optimization

Optimizing the way applications interact with databases is critical for improving performance, given the pivotal role databases often play.

- Utilize Indexing: Creating indexes on database tables can considerably speed up query times.

- Optimize SQL Queries: Craft SQL queries to be more efficient by selecting only necessary columns, using joins effectively, and applying filters early.

Here's an example of a streamlined SQL query:

```
SELECT name, age FROM users WHERE age > 20 AND active = 1;
```

This SQL statement is optimized to perform filtering directly, minimizing the processing burden.

Implementing Effective Caching

Caching reduces the load on databases, cuts down latency, and enhances response times by temporarily storing frequently accessed data.

- Advanced Caching Techniques: Implement caching mechanisms like Redis or Memcached to cache data such as user sessions or dynamic web pages, significantly improving access times.

- Enable Browser Caching: Configure HTTP headers to facilitate browser caching of static resources such as images, CSS, and JavaScript, which reduces server requests and speeds up page loads.

Upgrading Hardware and Adjusting Systems

Addressing performance issues may sometimes require hardware upgrades or system configuration tweaks.

- Enhance Hardware: Upgrading components like RAM, switching to SSDs, or enhancing CPUs can immediately boost performance.

- Optimize System Configurations: Fine-tune system settings to tailor the environment to the specific demands of your applications.

Network Optimization

In environments where components are spread across multiple networks, enhancing network performance is key to reducing latency and improving data throughput.

- Refine Network Settings: Modify network configurations and employ Content Delivery Networks (CDNs) to distribute content effectively and reduce latency.

- Apply Data Compression: Use compression techniques to decrease the size of data being transferred, enhancing transmission speed and efficiency.

Conclusion

Performance optimization encompasses a comprehensive approach that includes refining algorithms, adjusting code, improving database interactions, and optimizing network and system settings. By focusing on these areas through systematic analysis and targeted enhancements, developers can significantly elevate the performance and reliability of their applications. Continuous performance monitoring and iterative adjustments based on feedback are crucial for sustaining optimal operations.

Keeping your Spring Boot application secure

Maintaining security in Spring Boot applications is crucial due to the framework's widespread use and inherent vulnerabilities associated with its popularity. Effective security strategies encompass several layers, including safe management of dependencies, secure coding practices, precise configuration settings, and proactive system monitoring. Below are vital techniques to ensure robust security in Spring Boot applications.

Strategic Dependency Management

Careful management of software dependencies is essential as external libraries can introduce security risks:

- Continually Update Dependencies: Ensure that all dependencies are regularly updated to incorporate the latest security patches. Automation tools like Maven or Gradle can facilitate this by enforcing security protocols within project builds.

- Conduct Regular Vulnerability Scans: Use tools such as OWASP Dependency-Check, Snyk, or Spring's `spring-boot-starter-security` to periodically assess vulnerabilities in project dependencies.

Example setup for OWASP Dependency-Check in a Maven project:

```xml
<plugin>
    <groupId>org.owasp</groupId>
    <artifactId>dependency-check-maven</artifactId>
    <version>RELEASE</version>
    <executions>
        <execution>
            <goals>
                <goal>check</goal>
            </goals>
        </execution>
    </executions>
</plugin>
```

Enhancing Security Configurations

Adjusting default security configurations in Spring Boot is necessary to enhance the security level of applications:

- Implement HTTPS: Secure communication is fundamental, and implementing SSL/TLS to encrypt client-server communication is essential. Configure this in Spring Boot through the `application.properties`:

```
server.port=8443
server.ssl.key-store=classpath:keystore.jks
server.ssl.key-store-password=yourpassword
server.ssl.keyStoreType=JKS
server.ssl.keyAlias=tomcat
```

- Enable CSRF Protection: CSRF protection is crucial for session-based applications and is readily provided by Spring Security.

Secure Authentication and Authorization

Spring Security facilitates robust authentication mechanisms and authorization controls essential for securing applications:

- Adopt JWT Authentication: For REST APIs, using JSON Web Tokens (JWT) provides a secure, stateless authentication mechanism, easily integrated into Spring Boot via the `**spring-security-oauth2-resource-server**`.

- Define Access Permissions: Use Spring Security to manage detailed access permissions within your application. Employ annotations such as `**@PreAuthorize**` to control access based on user roles:

```
@PreAuthorize("hasRole('ADMIN')")
public void deleteCustomer(String id) {
    repository.deleteById(id);
}
```

Logging and Monitoring

Effective logging and monitoring are crucial for identifying and responding to security threats:

- Implement Detailed Logging: Log all critical security-related events, leveraging Spring Boot's compatibility with log management frameworks such as Logback or Log4j2.

- Monitor with Spring Boot Actuator: Actuator offers features to monitor and manage application health and metrics securely:

```
management.endpoints.web.exposure.include=health,info
management.endpoint.health.show-details=when_authorized
```

Upholding Best Security Practices

- Thorough Input Validation: Protect against common vulnerabilities like SQL injection and XSS by rigorously validating all user inputs. Spring frameworks support JSR-303/JSR-380 validations for robust input checking.

- Secure Error Handling: Design error handling to avoid revealing sensitive information or details about the system's internals.

Example of handling errors in Spring Boot:

```
@ControllerAdvice
public class CustomGlobalExceptionHandler extends ResponseEntityExceptionHandler {

    @ExceptionHandler(Exception.class)
    public final ResponseEntity<ErrorDetails> handleAllExceptions(Exception ex, WebRequest
        request) {
        ErrorDetails errorDetails = new ErrorDetails(new Date(), ex.getMessage(),
            request.getDescription(false));
        return new ResponseEntity<>(errorDetails, HttpStatus.INTERNAL_SERVER_ERROR);
    }
}
```

By implementing these security measures, developers can significantly minimize the risks associated with deploying Spring Boot applications. Keeping dependencies up to date, securing configurations, enforcing strict authentication and authorization protocols, along with vigilant monitoring and logging, are fundamental for maintaining a secure operational environment.

173

Conclusion

Recap of what we've covered

Throughout our discussions, we've navigated through an extensive array of critical topics tailored for software developers at all levels, focusing on foundational programming skills, advanced software architecture, and stringent security measures. This summary aims to encapsulate and reinforce the key ideas and methods we've explored, underscoring the essential strategies integral to proficient software development and operational security.

Fundamental Programming Techniques and Guidelines

We started with the basics, emphasizing the importance of writing clear and maintainable code. We covered core programming concepts such as variables, control structures, data types, and introductory algorithms, which are fundamental for any developer. Additionally, we advocated for adherence to best practices like the DRY (Don't Repeat Yourself) and KISS (Keep It Simple, Stupid) principles to promote code efficiency and clarity.

Here's an example illustrating the DRY principle:

```
public int sum(int[] numbers) {
    int total = 0;
    for (int number : numbers) {
        total += number;
    }
    return total;
}
```

This code snippet demonstrates encapsulating the logic for summing numbers within a single, reusable method, thus avoiding the redundancy of repeating logic throughout the codebase.

Advanced Programming Concepts and Software Architecture

We delved deeper into advanced topics like object-oriented programming (OOP), design patterns, and the Model-View-Controller (MVC) framework. These areas are crucial for constructing scalable and robust applications. OOP helps organize code around real-world models, design patterns address common software issues efficiently, and MVC aids in separating the concerns of data handling, user interface, and input/output processes.

Web Development Technologies and Frameworks

Our exploration extended to encompass both front-end and back-end web development technologies. We discussed essential web technologies such as HTML, CSS, and JavaScript, and evaluated dynamic frameworks like React and Angular. On the back-end, we concentrated on Java and its Spring Boot framework, which simplifies building complex server-side applications.

Example of a Spring Boot REST controller:

```
@RestController
public class GreetingController {

    @RequestMapping("/greeting")
    public Greeting greet(@RequestParam(value = "name", defaultValue = "World") String name
        ) {
        return new Greeting(counter.incrementAndGet(), String.format("Hello, %s!", name));
    }
}
```

This snippet illustrates how Spring Boot facilitates the development of RESTful services, showcasing the framework's capability to handle server-side logic efficiently.

Security Practices

Security was a recurring theme, given its critical importance in development. We discussed how to secure applications effectively, focusing on regular security audits, implementing HTTPS, robust authentication protocols, and defense mechanisms against common threats such as SQL injection.

Optimization Strategies

Finally, we covered performance optimization, emphasizing the necessity of writing efficient code, optimizing database interactions, and implementing effective caching strategies. We suggested using profiling tools to pinpoint performance bottlenecks, discussing various techniques to enhance system responsiveness and efficiency.

Conclusion

This recap synthesizes a broad spectrum of fundamental and complex topics in software development—from elementary programming skills to intricate software architecture, from basic user interface design to complex backend system optimizations. This comprehensive overview not only aims to enrich technical knowledge but also to illustrate how these diverse elements coalesce in larger software development projects.

This synthesis highlights how interconnected and crucial these topics are for developing efficient, robust, and secure applications in our rapidly advancing technological landscape.

Moving forward, these foundational insights will assist in addressing more complex challenges and embracing emerging technologies.

The journey ahead: transitioning to intermediate and advanced topics

As software developers progress from foundational to more advanced stages, their journey becomes enriched with a broader scope of intricate concepts, state-of-the-art tools, and complex problem-solving tasks. This advancement deepens their core programming acumen and equips them with the sophisticated capabilities necessary to address the dynamic challenges of modern software development. Such growth is essential for developers who aim to thrive in a rapidly evolving tech landscape.

Expanding Core Technical Proficiency

Transitioning to intermediate and advanced stages involves a significant enhancement of basic programming skills. Developers might deepen their understanding of familiar languages or explore new ones that cater to specific project needs.

For example, Java developers looking to expand their skill set might delve into more complex areas such as concurrency and multithreading, essential for crafting efficient, high-performance applications. Here's a basic example of implementing a thread in Java:

```
public class HelloThread extends Thread {
    public void run() {
        System.out.println("Hello from a thread!");
    }

    public static void main(String[] args) {
        (new HelloThread()).start();
    }
}
```

This code snippet demonstrates the creation and execution of a thread, introducing developers to the concept of concurrent operations within an application.

Advancing in Software Architecture and Design Patterns

As developers advance, a deeper appreciation for software architecture and design patterns becomes crucial. These patterns solve common software challenges efficiently and enhance the scalability and maintainability of applications.

An example is the Singleton pattern, which ensures a class only has one instance and provides a global point of access to it:

```
public class Singleton {
    private static Singleton instance;

    private Singleton() {}

    public static Singleton getInstance() {
        if (instance == null) {
            instance = new Singleton();
        }
        return instance;
    }
}
```

This implementation restricts the instantiation of a class to one object, providing a controlled access point throughout the application.

Employing Advanced Frameworks and Technologies

Moving forward, developers often begin to harness more complex frameworks and technologies that provide robust solutions to specific development needs. For instance, exploring deeper functionalities within Spring Boot, like utilizing Spring Security for detailed authentication and Spring Data for efficient data handling, becomes prevalent.

```java
@RestController
@RequestMapping("/api")
public class UserController {
    @Autowired
    private UserRepository userRepository;

    @GetMapping("/users")
    public List<User> getUsers() {
        return userRepository.findAll();
    }
}
```

This example uses Spring Data's `JpaRepository` to facilitate database interactions, illustrating how advanced frameworks can simplify complex backend development tasks.

Mastering Sophisticated Development Tools

Achieving proficiency in advanced development tools and environments also marks this transitional phase. Tools like Docker for containerization, Kubernetes for orchestration, and Jenkins for continuous integration play crucial roles as project complexities increase.

```
# Example Docker command to run a Java application
docker run -it --rm --name my-java-app java:11 java -jar /usr/myapp/my-java-app.jar
```

This Docker command showcases how to run a Java application in a container, emphasizing the streamlined management of application deployments.

Engaging in Advanced Problem Solving

Finally, advanced developers tackle more sophisticated problem-solving activities, focusing on algorithm optimization, system scalability, or effective memory management to boost application performance and enhance user experiences.

Conclusion

The path from beginner to advanced development is marked not just by learning complex programming techniques but by gaining a comprehensive understanding of integrating various technologies to build sophisticated and efficient software solutions. It entails becoming adept at navigating and innovating within a constantly evolving technological field. As developers progress along this path, they arm themselves with the vital expertise needed to tackle innovative projects and push the boundaries of current technology.

Resources for further learning

In the dynamic world of software development, staying updated through continuous education and engaging with a variety of learning resources are crucial for developers aiming to keep pace with technological innovations and industry standards. This enhancement is vital for both newcomers and seasoned professionals who strive to polish their skills and remain at the forefront of the competitive tech landscape. This guide provides an overview of diverse resources that enable further learning in software development, including foundational literature, interactive online platforms, professional networks, and essential development tools to boost career growth.

Seminal Books

Books offer profound insights and are foundational for deepening understanding across diverse software development domains, from programming basics to complex architectural frameworks.

- "Clean Code" by Robert C. Martin: Renowned for its clear guidance, this book addresses the essentials of writing maintainable code, complete with practical examples that underline the importance of coding best practices.

- "Design Patterns: Elements of Reusable Object-Oriented Software" by Erich Gamma, Richard Helm, Ralph Johnson, John Vlissides: Often referred to as the "Gang of Four" book, this resource is indispensable for developers seeking to master the art of using reusable software design patterns.

- "You Don't Know JS" (series) by Kyle Simpson: This comprehensive series provides an exhaustive exploration of JavaScript, making it a valuable resource for developers focusing on frontend or full-stack development.

Digital Platforms for Learning

These platforms provide current, interactive educational experiences that cater to developers seeking to apply the latest technological advances in practical scenarios.

- Coursera: Featuring a wide range of courses from prestigious universities and leading tech firms, Coursera offers topics from basic programming to complex fields like artificial intelligence, often leading to certification.

- Udemy: Known for its vast array of learning topics, Udemy allows individuals to learn at their own pace, covering a broad spectrum of software development areas.

- Pluralsight: Specializing in technology and creative content, Pluralsight offers in-depth courses tailored to enhance technical skills or knowledge of specific tools and technologies.

Professional Communities and Networks

Involvement in professional communities provides essential support, mentorship, and access to the latest trends, helping developers stay informed and connected.

- Stack Overflow: Beyond being a resource for coding queries, Stack Overflow fosters a collaborative community where developers can exchange expertise, tackle complex problems, and refine their coding skills.

- GitHub: Central to the developer community, GitHub supports not only project version control but also collaboration on open-source projects, enhancing learning through community engagement.

- Meetup: This platform enables developers to find and join local tech communities, offering access to workshops, technical talks, and networking events that can significantly enhance professional growth.

Advanced Tools and Technologies

Expertise in sophisticated tools and software environments is crucial for applying learned theories to real-world tasks, streamlining workflows, and improving project outcomes.

- Visual Studio Code: This powerful code editor supports a variety of programming languages and comes equipped with integrated Git commands, optimizing coding and version control processes.

- Docker: Mastery of Docker is essential for those looking to understand containerization, which is fundamental for consistent development environments and effective microservices architectures.

- Jenkins: Familiarity with Jenkins and its capabilities for continuous integration and continuous delivery (CI/CD) can automate significant portions of the development process, enhancing efficiency and ensuring higher quality in deliverables.

Conclusion

A plethora of resources exists for developers eager to advance their knowledge and skills in software development. From detailed academic texts and engaging online courses to active community participation and robust development tools, these resources are crucial in shaping a developer's ability to navigate and contribute to complex software projects effectively. Engaging with these educational resources not only sharpens technical skills but also prepares professionals to adeptly handle the evolving challenges of modern software development, ensuring they are well-equipped to contribute to industry progress and innovation.

Introduction

The evolving landscape of web application development

The arena of web application development has undergone significant transformation, evolving from rudimentary, static web pages to complex, dynamic applications that accommodate intricate user interactions and sophisticated aesthetics. This shift has been driven by rapid advancements in technology and shifting user demands, challenging developers to keep pace with a landscape marked by cutting-edge technological innovations, an imperative for mobile-optimized designs, and the need for applications that perform robustly and integrate fluidly with a variety of external systems.

Technological Progress in Web Development

Significant technological strides have been central to the evolution of web application development. The rollout of HTML5, CSS3, and advanced JavaScript versions has greatly expanded the capabilities of web applications, allowing for enhanced interactivity and visual appeal without sacrificing performance.

For instance, HTML5 eliminated the need for external plugins for media playback by supporting audio and video content natively. CSS3 introduced advanced styling options like animations and transitions, enabling developers to create more engaging and responsive designs. JavaScript has evolved into a robust language capable of supporting extensive functionalities, powered by frameworks and libraries such as React, Angular, and Vue.js.

```javascript
// Simple React component example
import React from 'react';

const UserWelcome = () => {
  return <h1>Welcome to our service!</h1>;
}

export default UserWelcome;
```

This example shows a basic React component, highlighting how contemporary JavaScript frameworks streamline the creation of dynamic and modular user interfaces.

Emphasis on Mobile-First and Adaptive Designs

With the dominance of mobile devices in internet access, adopting mobile-first and responsive design principles is increasingly critical. Applications must be designed to perform seamlessly across various devices, tailoring their layout and functionality to different screen sizes and user conditions.

Responsive design, utilizing CSS media queries, adjusts the application's layout dynamically based on the device's screen size, ensuring optimal usability and consistency across devices.

```css
/* CSS for responsive design */
@media (max-width: 600px) {
  .sidebar {
    display: none;
  }
}
```

This CSS code demonstrates the use of media queries to alter layout elements for optimal display on mobile devices, enhancing usability by adapting the interface to smaller screens.

Optimizing Application Performance

Given the high expectations for quick loading times and fluid interactions, enhancing the performance of web applications is imperative. Developers leverage strategies such as lazy loading, code splitting, and advanced caching to improve responsiveness and operational efficiency.

Frameworks and tools like Webpack facilitate these optimizations by automating tasks like code splitting, allowing for selective loading of application parts, thereby reducing initial load times.

```
// React code splitting with lazy loading
import React, { Suspense, lazy } from 'react';

const OptionalComponent = lazy(() => import('./OptionalComponent'));

function EnhancedApp() {
  return (
    <Suspense fallback={<div>Loading component...</div>}>
      <OptionalComponent />
    </Suspense>
  );
}

export default EnhancedApp;
```

This React example showcases lazy loading alongside Suspense for code splitting, effectively minimizing initial load times by only fetching components as they are required.

Integration with Diverse External Systems

Modern web applications often integrate with multiple external services and APIs—from financial transaction platforms to social media interfaces—necessitating robust API management and seamless integration capabilities. Additionally, the shift towards microservices architectures and technologies like Docker and Kubernetes has redefined application development, deployment, and scalability.

Conclusion

The landscape of web application development is continually evolving, presenting both challenges and opportunities. Developers must remain committed to continuous learning to master new technologies and methods. With anticipated further integrations with AI, machine learning, and immersive experiences, developers must be ready to continuously innovate and adapt their skills. Staying agile and informed enables developers to create applications that not only respond to current technological demands but also shape future trends in the tech landscape.

Transitioning from monolithic to microservices architecture

Migrating from a monolithic to a microservices architecture marks a crucial evolution in the way organizations develop software, aiming to boost scalability, flexibility, and ease of maintenance. This strategic shift involves extensive preparation, significant architectural redesign, and a transformative shift in team dynamics. Below is a comprehensive discussion on how to navigate this transition, detailing the challenges faced and effective strategies to overcome them.

Key Architectural Concepts

Monolithic Architecture: Initially, applications are often built as monolithic systems where all functionalities, from input handling to database management and output delivery, are tightly integrated into a single, indivisible unit. While this model simplifies initial deployment and operations, it becomes problematic as the application scales up, complicating updates and maintenance due to its tightly coupled nature.

Microservices Architecture: In contrast, microservices architecture decomposes an application into a suite of smaller, independent services, each designed to execute a specific business function. These services operate autonomously and can be developed, deployed, and scaled independently of one another. This separation enhances the agility of development processes, simplifies updates, and improves fault isolation.

Strategic Transition Planning

The shift to microservices requires thoughtful planning and execution:

1. Business Capability Analysis: Begin by delineating the business functionalities of the existing application to identify logical service boundaries based on business roles rather than technological layers.

2. Incremental Transition: Target specific components of the monolith that stand to gain the most from microservices, such as those needing more frequent updates or independent scaling capabilities.

3. Technological Considerations: Select the appropriate technology stack for each service considering factors like compatibility and performance needs. Decide on the methods for services to communicate, whether through REST APIs, messaging systems, etc.

Overcoming Technical Challenges

Monolith Decomposition: Breaking down a monolithic application into microservices involves defining clear service boundaries and managing the dependencies that were previously intertwined within the monolith.

Example of Refactoring Monolithic Code:

```python
# Original monolithic structure for user operations
class UserManager:
    def create_user(self, user_data):
        # Implementation for creating a user
        pass
    def modify_user(self, user_id, user_data):
        # Implementation for modifying user details
        pass
    def remove_user(self, user_id):
        # Implementation for removing a user
        pass
# Refactored into distinct microservices
# UserService handles user creation
class UserService:
    def create_user(self, user_data):
        # Implementation for creating a user
        pass
# UserManagementService handles modifications and deletions
class UserManagementService:
    def modify_user(self, user_id, user_data):
        # Implementation for modifying user details
        pass
    def remove_user(self, user_id):
        # Implementation for removing a user
        pass
```

In this refactoring, responsibilities are clearly divided among different services, aligning with microservices best practices.

Data Consistency and Communication: Maintaining data consistency across distributed services becomes challenging. Implementing strategies like event-driven communication or command query responsibility segregation (CQRS) can help manage these issues effectively.

Building Resilient Interactions: Ensuring robust and secure interactions between microservices is crucial. Implement reliability patterns such as circuit breakers and fallback mechanisms to maintain system integrity.

Cultural and Organizational Adjustments

Adopting microservices also demands cultural changes within the organization:

- Team Realignment: Transition to cross-functional teams that manage specific microservices from development through deployment, enhancing accountability and speed in delivery.

- DevOps Practices: Integrate DevOps methodologies to foster continuous integration and continuous deployment (CI/CD), which are essential in a microservices setup to streamline updates and minimize downtime.

System Monitoring and Management

Effectively managing a distributed system composed of numerous microservices requires robust monitoring and orchestration tools. Utilizing platforms like Kubernetes for orchestration, Docker for containerization, and Istio for managing service interactions can simplify these tasks. Monitoring solutions like Prometheus and Grafana are vital for real-time health and performance assessments.

Conclusion

Transitioning to a microservices architecture, while complex, provides significant benefits in terms of scalability, agility, and system maintainability. This process demands a strategic approach to redesigning the application architecture, adopting new technical solutions, and fostering an adaptive organizational culture. By methodically addressing these aspects, organizations can significantly enhance their software development practices and infrastructure resilience.

Overview of RESTful API development with Spring Boot

Developing RESTful APIs with Spring Boot is a preferred method for many software developers due to its robustness, straightforwardness, and the extensive functionality offered by the Spring ecosystem. Spring Boot enhances the capabilities of the Spring framework, facilitating the quick development and deployment of production-grade web services with minimal initial setup.

Key Concepts of RESTful APIs

REST (Representational State Transfer) is an architectural style that prescribes using standard HTTP methods to interact with resources, typically represented in JSON or XML, and accessed via straightforward URIs (Uniform Resource Identifiers). This architecture is built for scalable, stateless interactions, key for modern web environments.

Introduction to Spring Boot

Spring Boot extends the Spring framework by streamlining the configuration process through its convention-over-configuration approach. It provides predefined setups for project configurations, reducing manual setup efforts. Spring Boot comes equipped with embedded server options like

Tomcat or Jetty, pre-configured to start automatically with the application, simplifying the deployment process.

Crafting a RESTful API with Spring Boot

The creation of a RESTful API in Spring Boot is streamlined by tools like Spring Initializr. Here's a typical development workflow:

1. Starting the Project: Spring Initializr facilitates the setup of a Spring Boot project by selecting dependencies such as 'Spring Web', 'Spring Data JPA', and optional components like 'H2 Database' for temporary, in-memory database functionality, depending on the project's specifications.

2. Defining Data Models: Resources in RESTful services are defined as DTOs (Data Transfer Objects), for instance:

```java
public class User {
    private Long id;
    private String name;
    private String email;

    // Getters and setters omitted for clarity
}
```

3. Configuring Repositories: Spring Data JPA is used to create repository interfaces that Spring automatically configures to manage data operations:

```java
import org.springframework.data.jpa.repository.JpaRepository;

public interface UserRepository extends JpaRepository<User, Long> {
}
```

4. Service Layer Development: The service layer is responsible for business logic, employing repositories for database interactions:

```java
import org.springframework.stereotype.Service;
import java.util.List;

@Service
public class UserService {
    private final UserRepository userRepository;

    public UserService(UserRepository userRepository) {
        this.userRepository = userRepository;
    }

    public List<User> findAllUsers() {
        return userRepository.findAll();
    }
}
```

5. Setting Up Controllers: Controllers handle HTTP requests and responses. Annotated with `@RestController`, they simplify the creation of web endpoints:

```java
import org.springframework.web.bind.annotation.GetMapping;
import org.springframework.web.bind.annotation.RequestMapping;
import org.springframework.web.bind.annotation.RestController;
import java.util.List;

@RestController
@RequestMapping("/api/users")
public class UserController {
    private final UserService userService;

    public UserController(UserService userService) {
        this.userService = userService;
    }

    @GetMapping
    public List<User> getAllUsers() {
        return userService.findAllUsers();
    }
}
```

This endpoint provides a way to retrieve all users, with Spring Boot handling the JSON conversion automatically.

Benefits of Spring Boot for API Development

Spring Boot is especially beneficial for RESTful API development due to several key features:

- Simplified Configuration: Spring Boot automatically configures based on chosen dependencies, easing initial application setup.

- Productivity Boost: The platform reduces the need for extensive coding by providing ready-to-use features and libraries.

- Operational Efficiency: Embedded servers and comprehensive monitoring tools make deploying and managing Spring Boot applications straightforward.

Conclusion

Spring Boot serves as an excellent framework for developing RESTful APIs by reducing the complexity associated with traditional Spring applications. Its design principle of convention over configuration, combined with the rich set of Spring ecosystem capabilities, makes it an ideal choice for developers seeking to build effective, scalable, and maintainable web services.

Objectives and scope of the book

The primary intent and breadth of this book are tailored for both budding and seasoned professionals in the software development realm who are eager to enhance their grasp of modern programming methodologies, particularly through the application of Spring Boot for crafting robust web applications. This text is designed to furnish readers with an extensive understanding that seamlessly bridges theoretical concepts with hands-on, practical application development.

Objectives of the Book

1. Core Understanding: The book begins by laying a solid groundwork in the fundamental principles underlying modern software development. This includes discussions on software design patterns, programming paradigms, and principles of clean code, aiming to

provide readers with the essential knowledge needed to comprehend the rationale behind recommended practices and their practical applications.

2. Comprehensive Exploration of Spring Boot: Recognizing the widespread adoption and functionalities of Spring Boot, the book dedicates substantial content to delve deep into this framework. It covers everything from initial setup to sophisticated configurations, providing a thorough guide for building scalable and efficient applications.

3. Hands-On Development Guidance: Beyond theoretical explanations, the book guides readers through the construction of a demonstrative application using Spring Boot. This practical approach helps cement the concepts discussed by showing their application in a real-world context.

4. Coding Best Practices and Patterns: The text teaches readers about the best practices in coding, application design, and performance optimization, drawing upon theoretical knowledge and extensive empirical experience from seasoned developers.

5. Advanced Topics: For those already familiar with basic concepts, the book addresses more complex subjects such as microservices architecture, the integration of container technologies like Docker, and interactions with databases and caching solutions.

Scope of the Book

The book is meticulously scoped to provide a detailed yet focused guide on application development using Spring Boot, covering several critical areas:

1. Spring Framework and Spring Boot Introduction: It starts with a look back at the evolution of the Spring framework, setting the context for introducing Spring Boot and its benefits over traditional Spring-based development.

2. Configuration and Setup: Detailed instructions on setting up a Spring Boot project, including configuring the development environment and understanding project structure and annotations, are provided.

3. Building an Initial Application: Step-by-step guidance on creating a Spring Boot application includes:

   - Using Spring Initializr to set up the project.

   - Developing RESTful controllers.

   - Managing data with Spring Data JPA.

   - Securing applications with Spring Security.

4. Advanced Development Concepts: The book introduces more sophisticated development concepts such as:

   - Asynchronous programming.

   - API construction and consumption.

- Implementing microservices with Spring Boot.

- Containerization with Docker.

5. Case Study: A comprehensive project that brings together all the discussed concepts allows readers to see how to integrate various elements of Spring Boot into a cohesive application.

6. Additional Resources: Appendices provide extra resources, troubleshooting tips, and references for further reading and online materials.

Example Code Snippet

Here is an illustrative code snippet from the book demonstrating how to set up a basic RESTful controller in Spring Boot:

```java
import org.springframework.web.bind.annotation.GetMapping;
import org.springframework.web.bind.annotation.RestController;

@RestController
public class SimpleGreetingController {

    @GetMapping("/greet")
    public String greet() {
        return "Hello, World!";
    }
}
```

This example shows the simplicity of setting up a RESTful endpoint in Spring Boot, accessible at `/**greet**`, and is typical of the practical examples provided throughout the book to demonstrate application setup and endpoint creation.

Conclusion

This book aims to not only introduce Spring Boot to novices but also deepen experienced developers' understanding of this potent framework. Covering a spectrum from basic setups to complex implementations, the book is an essential resource for anyone looking to master Spring Boot and advance their capabilities in software development. Through detailed explanations, practical examples, and comprehensive coverage of advanced topics, the book serves as an indispensable guide for mastering contemporary software development techniques.

Chapter One

Deep Dive into Spring Boot

Advanced Spring Boot features and configuration

Spring Boot is renowned for its streamlined approach to setting up and developing new Spring applications, providing out-of-the-box configurations that help get microservices and web applications off the ground quickly. However, Spring Boot also encompasses a plethora of advanced features and configurations that enable developers to meticulously adjust their applications to meet specific requirements for performance, security, and scalability. This exploration delves into some of the sophisticated capabilities of Spring Boot, highlighting how developers can leverage these tools to manage complex application requirements adeptly.

Externalized Configuration

A standout feature of Spring Boot is its robust support for externalized configuration, which permits developers to manage application settings outside the actual codebase. This functionality allows for adjustments in the application's behavior without the need to recompile, supporting configurations through various channels like properties files, YAML files, environment variables, and command-line arguments, with a defined hierarchy for overriding values to adapt across different environments.

For instance, developers can manage database configurations externally and choose configurations specific to profiles at runtime through `application.properties`:

```
# Default database configuration
spring.datasource.url=jdbc:mysql://localhost/test
spring.datasource.username=dbuser
spring.datasource.password=dbpass

# Production profile override
spring.profiles.active=prod
spring.datasource.url=jdbc:mysql://prod-db-server/prod
```

Advanced Networking Configuration

Spring Boot also simplifies the management of networking configurations such as server ports and addresses through settings in `application.properties` or `application.yml`. This feature proves invaluable when deploying across diverse environments that require specific network setups.

For example, configuring the server port and context-path is straightforward:

```
server.port=8080
server.servlet.context-path=/api
```

These settings instruct Spring Boot to serve the application on port 8080, with all controller mappings accessible under the `/api` base URI.

Customizing Spring Boot Actuators

Spring Boot Actuators provide essential out-of-the-box, production-ready features like health checks, metrics, and insights into application operations. Customizing actuators allows developers to enhance the monitoring and management of their applications, critical for maintaining robust production environments. Developers can secure sensitive endpoints and determine which actuators to expose for comprehensive monitoring.

Customization of actuators in `**application.properties**` may include:

```
management.endpoints.web.exposure.include=health,info,metrics
management.endpoint.health.show-details=always
management.endpoints.web.base-path=/manage
```

This setup exposes specified endpoints and changes the base path to `/manage", enhancing security and control over application management.

Asynchronous Execution

Supporting asynchronous execution, Spring Boot allows the handling of long-running tasks without blocking the main application flow. By using `**@Async**` annotations and enabling asynchronous operations through `**@EnableAsync**`, tasks can run in parallel, managed by Spring's task executor.

Here's how to set it up:

```java
import org.springframework.scheduling.annotation.Async;
import org.springframework.scheduling.annotation.EnableAsync;
import org.springframework.stereotype.Service;

@EnableAsync
@Service
public class AsyncService {

    @Async
    public void executeLongRunningTask() {
        // Task implementation details
    }
}
```

This configuration enables `**executeLongRunningTask()**` to operate asynchronously, thus enhancing the application's responsiveness and efficiency.

Advanced Security Configurations

Spring Boot's seamless integration with Spring Security facilitates robust security mechanisms for authentication and authorization. Advanced configurations may include enhancements to method-level security, CORS (Cross-Origin Resource Sharing) settings, and CSRF (Cross-Site Request Forgery) protection customization.

A typical configuration for enabling method-level security could look like this:

```java
import org.springframework.security.config.annotation.method.configuration
    .EnableGlobalMethodSecurity;

@EnableGlobalMethodSecurity(prePostEnabled = true)
public class SecurityConfig extends WebSecurityConfigurerAdapter {
    // Security configuration specifics
}
```

This allows for granular access control using annotations like `@PreAuthorize` at the controller method level.

Conclusion

Spring Boot's advanced features and configurations offer developers comprehensive tools to build highly customized, secure, and efficiently managed applications. From externalized configurations and sophisticated network settings to enhanced actuator customizations and asynchronous processing capabilities, Spring Boot equips developers with an extensive toolkit to tackle complex development challenges, ensuring applications not only launch efficiently but continue to perform and scale effectively in production environments.

Customizing auto-configuration

Spring Boot is celebrated for its auto-configuration capabilities, which facilitate the rapid setup and deployment of new Spring applications by automatically arranging Spring beans and settings. This automation is based on the project's dependencies and the environment's characteristics, enabling developers to quickly get their applications operational. However, particular scenarios might call for specific configurations to address unique operational needs or to enhance performance.

Fundamentals of Auto-Configuration

Auto-configuration in Spring Boot is designed to eliminate much of the manual configuration process. It smartly configures settings and beans based on the libraries detected in the classpath and the properties specified by the developer. For example, if the H2 database libraries are found within the classpath, Spring Boot configures an in-memory database by default.

While auto-configuration offers a highly efficient means of setting up applications, it may not always be perfectly aligned with the specific requirements of every project, often necessitating tailored adjustments or customizations.

Methods for Customizing Auto-Configuration

Customizing auto-configuration in Spring Boot can be approached through various methods, from overriding properties to creating bespoke configuration classes.

1. **Property Overrides**: The simplest customization method involves overriding default properties within the `application.properties` or `application.yml` files. For instance, database connection settings can be customized as follows:

```
spring.datasource.url=jdbc:mysql://localhost:3306/mydb
spring.datasource.username=myuser
spring.datasource.password=mypass
```

This alteration explicitly sets the database URL and access credentials, superseding the default auto-configured settings.

2. **Excluding Auto-Configurations**: Spring Boot permits the exclusion of unwanted auto-configurations using the `exclude` attribute of the `@SpringBootApplication` annotation.

```
import org.springframework.boot.autoconfigure.SpringBootApplication;
import org.springframework.boot.autoconfigure.jdbc.DataSourceAutoConfiguration;

@SpringBootApplication(exclude = {DataSourceAutoConfiguration.class})
public class MyApplication {
    public static void main(String[] args) {
        SpringApplication.run(MyApplication.class, args);
    }
}
```

Here, `DataSourceAutoConfiguration` is excluded, allowing for a custom data source configuration without Spring Boot's interference.

3. **Implementing Custom Configuration Classes**: More intricate customizations can be achieved by defining custom `@Configuration` classes. These classes can specify beans that modify or replace the default configured beans.

```
import org.springframework.context.annotation.Bean;
import org.springframework.context.annotation.Configuration;
import org.springframework.security.crypto.bcrypt.BCryptPasswordEncoder;

@Configuration
public class SecurityConfig {
    @Bean
    public BCryptPasswordEncoder passwordEncoder() {
        return new BCryptPasswordEncoder();
    }
}
```

This configuration introduces a custom `BCryptPasswordEncoder` bean, used by Spring Boot in place of the default security configuration.

4. **Using Conditional Annotations**: Conditional annotations such as `@ConditionalOnClass` and

208

`@ConditionalOnMissingBean` offer a sophisticated method to conditionally load beans based on the presence or absence of certain classes or beans.

```java
import org.springframework.boot.autoconfigure.condition.ConditionalOnMissingBean;
import org.springframework.context.annotation.Bean;
import org.springframework.context.annotation.Configuration;

@Configuration
public class MyFallbackConfig {
    @Bean
    @ConditionalOnMissingBean
    public MyService myService() {
        return new DefaultMyService();
    }
}
```

In this setup, `DefaultMyService` is only instantiated if there is no other `MyService` bean configured, ensuring a default is available without overriding any custom configuration.

Conclusion

Tailoring auto-configuration in Spring Boot enables developers to refine how the framework configures itself to better align with specific business needs and optimize performance. By utilizing property overrides, excluding specific auto-configurations, crafting custom configuration classes, and employing conditional annotations, developers gain precise control over their Spring Boot applications. This customization capability ensures that Spring Boot can adapt to support a diverse range of applications and enterprise demands, thereby maintaining its efficiency and effectiveness in application setups.

Externalizing configuration properties for different environments

In modern software development, it's critical to handle configuration properties adeptly across different environments to ensure applications remain scalable and adaptable. Spring Boot excels in providing robust mechanisms for externalizing configuration settings, allowing these settings to be adjusted outside the application's packaged artifact. This capability is key for differentiating settings across development, testing, and production environments, facilitating seamless environment transitions without the need for code changes or application rebuilds.

The Rationale for Externalized Configuration

As applications transition from development through to production, they often require different settings to accommodate the varying conditions of each environment. For example, configurations for database connections, API keys, and service credentials generally need to vary between environments. Embedding these settings directly in the code not only hampers flexibility but also poses security risks if sensitive data is exposed within source control.

By externalizing configurations, developers can streamline the deployment process and enhance security, as configuration changes do not necessitate direct modifications to the codebase.

Techniques for Externalizing Configurations in Spring Boot

Spring Boot supports a variety of methods for externalizing configuration, prioritizing flexibility and security across different deployment environments.

1. Profile-Specific Configuration Files

Spring Boot can manage environment-specific settings using dedicated configuration files such as `application-dev.properties`, `application-test.properties`, and `application-prod.properties`, which reside in the `/src/main/resources` directory.

```
# application-dev.properties
spring.datasource.url=jdbc:mysql://dev-db.example.com/myapp
spring.datasource.username=dev_user
spring.datasource.password=dev_pass
```

```
# application-prod.properties
spring.datasource.url=jdbc:mysql://prod-db.example.com/myapp
spring.datasource.username=prod_user
spring.datasource.password=prod_pass
```

Developers can activate specific configurations using the **spring.profiles.active** property, either within these files or as a command-line option, such as --`spring.profiles.active=prod`.

2. Using Environment Variables

Environment variables provide a secure way to manage settings, shielding sensitive information from being hardcoded in the application. Spring Boot facilitates this by allowing environment variables to directly map to configuration properties, following a convention where property names are uppercased and dots are replaced with underscores.

```
export SPRING_DATASOURCE_URL=jdbc:mysql://prod-db.example.com/myapp
export SPRING_DATASOURCE_USERNAME=prod_user
export SPRING_DATASOURCE_PASSWORD=prod_pass
```

3. Command-Line Arguments

Command-line arguments are ideal for overriding configuration settings temporarily or during development, providing a high level of flexibility.

```
java -jar myapp.jar --spring.datasource.username=admin --spring.datasource.password=secret
```

4. Centralized Configuration via Spring Cloud Config

For applications that operate within a distributed or microservices architecture, Spring Cloud Config offers a centralized approach to manage configurations. Configurations are stored in a version-controlled repository, enabling changes to be propagated across all client applications without redeployment.

```
# application.yml in Spring Cloud Config Server
spring:
  cloud:
    config:
      server:
        git:
          uri: https://github.com/myorg/config-repo
          clone-on-start: true
```

Recommended Practices for Configuration Management

- Security Practices: Avoid storing sensitive information in version-controlled configuration files. Instead, use environment variables or secure secrets management services.

- Clear Organization: Maintain distinct, well-organized configuration files for different environments to prevent configuration errors.

- Documentation: Ensure all properties are thoroughly documented, highlighting their purposes and permissible values, especially for those that can be overridden during deployments.

Conclusion

Effectively managing configuration properties across various environments is crucial for deploying flexible and secure applications. Spring Boot's externalization capabilities facilitate easy adjustments to configuration settings for different environments, supporting efficient CI/CD processes. This approach not only enhances the operational management of applications but also adheres to best practices for maintaining secure, robust, and flexible software systems in diverse IT landscapes.

Chapter Two

Architecting Microservices with Spring Boot

Principles of microservices architecture

Microservices architecture revolutionizes the traditional approach to software development by advocating for the segmentation of applications into smaller, discrete units. This modern methodology stands in stark contrast to the conventional monolithic architecture by endorsing independent components, each dedicated to a specific function. Such a structure boosts an application's ability to scale, adapt swiftly, and maintain operational resilience, which is critical for enterprises needing to keep pace with rapid technological advances and market demands.

Decentralization

Central to the philosophy of microservices is the concept of decentralization. Rather than maintaining a cohesive, singular application structure, microservices distribute functionalities across multiple, autonomous units. Each microservice is self-sufficient, managing its unique dataset and dependencies, thus enhancing data segregation and integrity. For example, in an e-commerce platform, separate microservices might independently handle user profiles, inventory management, and transaction processing, connecting through defined APIs.

Autonomy

Microservices are characterized by their operational independence, which facilitates separate development, deployment, and scaling activities. This independence aligns well with agile development practices, particularly the methodologies of continuous integration and deployment, allowing for more frequent updates and robust service offerings. Autonomy also ensures that individual service modifications or scalability can occur without disrupting the broader service network.

```java
// Example of a Spring Boot application class for a microservice
@SpringBootApplication
public class PaymentServiceApplication {

    public static void main(String[] args) {
        SpringApplication.run(PaymentServiceApplication.class, args);
    }
}
```

Fault Isolation and Resilience

Microservices architecture enhances system resilience by localizing faults within specific services, thereby preventing widespread system disruptions. Resilience strategies such as the Circuit Breaker pattern mitigate the risk of failure propagation. In the Spring Boot framework, tools like Resilience4j provide mechanisms to fortify service reliability effectively.

```java
// Example of configuring a Circuit Breaker with Resilience4j in Spring Boot
@Bean
public CircuitBreakerConfig customCircuitBreakerConfig() {
    return CircuitBreakerConfig.custom()
        .failureRateThreshold(50)
        .waitDurationInOpenState(Duration.ofMillis(1000))
        .ringBufferSizeInHalfOpenState(5)
        .ringBufferSizeInClosedState(10)
        .build();
}

@Bean
public CircuitBreakerRegistry circuitBreakerRegistry() {
    return CircuitBreakerRegistry.of(customCircuitBreakerConfig());
}
```

Scalability

Microservices excel in scalability due to their independent nature. This feature allows each service to be scaled according to its specific demand, in contrast to monolithic applications which require scaling of the entire system. For example, during peak periods, a service handling user transactions may be scaled up independently from other services.

Modularity

The intrinsic modularity of microservices facilitates easier updates and better system maintainability. Each microservice is developed around a specific business requirement, making it simpler to manage and update without extensive knowledge of the entire system's workings.

Technology Diversity

Microservices permit the use of different technology stacks across various services, enabling developers to choose the most suitable technologies for each service's needs. This flexibility often results in optimized performance and easier maintenance.

Continuous Delivery

The structure of microservices supports continuous delivery practices by allowing individual services to be updated independently of one another. This capability facilitates more frequent releases, vital for adapting quickly to user feedback or changes in business strategy.

Challenges and Considerations

Adopting microservices brings about its set of challenges, including increased complexity in managing multiple services and ensuring data consistency across the system. These issues often lead to higher operational overhead and necessitate sophisticated transaction management strategies, such as the implementation of the Saga pattern for distributed transactions.

In conclusion, the shift towards microservices architecture involves meticulous planning and a deep understanding of its principles. Successfully implemented, it provides a robust framework capable of supporting scalable, flexible, and resilient applications. Organizations must embrace comprehensive strategies that include not only deployment and management but also continuous enhancement of service capabilities to fully leverage the benefits of microservices.

Designing and structuring microservices in a Spring Boot ecosystem

Transitioning to a microservices architecture marks a significant evolution in application development, enabling companies to scale more dynamically, maintain high availability, and rapidly adapt to new business challenges. Spring Boot, renowned for its simplicity and efficiency in building Java applications, serves as an excellent platform for deploying microservices. This exploration covers essential strategies for effectively organizing and managing microservices within the Spring Boot framework.

Identifying Service Boundaries

Key to microservices architecture is the clear demarcation of service boundaries, ensuring that functionalities are appropriately isolated and managed. Spring Boot facilitates this by supporting the creation of bounded contexts, where each service operates as a standalone application, independent of others in the ecosystem.

Domain-Driven Design (DDD) is instrumental in this process, focusing on dividing the system based on business relevance, which aids in maintaining a clean separation and minimal overlap between services. This approach ensures services are highly cohesive yet loosely coupled, enhancing maintainability and resilience.

Architectural Blueprint

Each microservice in Spring Boot is typically architected as an independent application. This structure allows for modular development and deployment, crucial for the microservices approach where services must operate independently.

Here is a simple example demonstrating the setup of a microservice in Spring Boot:

```java
@SpringBootApplication
public class InventoryServiceApplication {

    public static void main(String[] args) {
        SpringApplication.run(InventoryServiceApplication.class, args);
    }

    @Bean
    public InventoryService inventoryService() {
        return new BasicInventoryService();
    }
}
```

In this setup, `**InventoryServiceApplication**` serves as the entry point, encapsulating service operations, configurations, and dependencies, thereby ensuring service isolation.

Managing Configurations

In a distributed environment, managing service configurations without hard-coding them into the service itself is crucial. Spring Boot enables external configuration, allowing services to be configured externally via properties or YAML files, which can be dynamically loaded at runtime.

Spring Cloud Config extends these capabilities by offering a centralized server for managing all configurations across environments, simplifying configuration handling and improving security by separating configuration from the code.

Communication Strategies

Communication between services is a critical component of any microservices architecture. Spring Boot supports various communication methods, from RESTful APIs facilitated by Spring MVC for synchronous communication to asynchronous messaging supported by integrations with platforms like RabbitMQ or Apache Kafka.

For example, here's how a REST controller might look in Spring Boot:

```java
@RestController
@RequestMapping("/api/inventory")
public class InventoryController {

    private final InventoryService inventoryService;

    public InventoryController(InventoryService inventoryService) {
        this.inventoryService = inventoryService;
    }

    @GetMapping("/{itemId}")
    public ResponseEntity<Item> getItemById(@PathVariable Long itemId) {
        Item item = inventoryService.getItemById(itemId);
        return ResponseEntity.ok(item);
    }
}
```

For asynchronous interactions, frameworks like Spring Cloud Stream offer abstractions over messaging systems, enabling event-driven communication that is scalable and manageable.

Independent Data Management

To ensure that microservices are decoupled, each service should control its own database. Spring Data JPA can be leveraged within each microservice to facilitate interaction with its respective database, providing straightforward ways to implement data access layers without extensive boilerplate.

Deployment Considerations

Deployment strategies for microservices often include using Docker for containerization, which encapsulates a microservice and its environment into a container, simplifying deployments and scaling. Orchestration platforms like Kubernetes can manage these containers, providing robust solutions for automatic scaling, load balancing, and service discovery.

In sum, the design and structure of microservices in a Spring Boot environment require thoughtful planning and a strategic approach to both development and deployment. By following established design principles, utilizing Spring Boot's comprehensive toolset, and considering operational dynamics, developers can create effective, scalable, and resilient microservice architectures.

Inter-service communication strategies

In the domain of microservices architectures, crafting the communication protocols between services is pivotal to the system's performance and resilience. This involves selecting the correct methods of interaction, establishing effective communication frameworks, and choosing technologies that enhance connectivity. This exploration focuses on various methods to facilitate communication between services within a Spring Boot setup, with a goal to bolster application scalability, enhance system reliability, and streamline management.

Synchronous vs. Asynchronous Communication

The communication between microservices can be organized into two fundamental types: synchronous and asynchronous. Each type caters to distinct operational requirements and affects the architecture in unique ways.

Synchronous Communication typically employs REST or gRPC for real-time interactions, where a service awaits an immediate response upon request. Although this method is straightforward and effective for direct service interactions, it can lead to high coupling and increased latency, potentially impacting the system's overall fault tolerance.

For example, here is how a synchronous REST controller could be structured in Spring Boot:

```java
@RestController
@RequestMapping("/api/payments")
public class PaymentController {

    private final PaymentService paymentService;

    @Autowired
    public PaymentController(PaymentService paymentService) {
        this.paymentService = paymentService;
    }

    @PostMapping
    public ResponseEntity<Payment> processPayment(@RequestBody Payment payment) {
        Payment processedPayment = paymentService.processPayment(payment);
        return new ResponseEntity<>(processedPayment, HttpStatus.CREATED);
    }
}
```

Asynchronous Communication is preferred when it is crucial to minimize service dependencies. Technologies like RabbitMQ or Apache Kafka facilitate this type of communication, allowing messages to be sent and received without immediate responses, which can significantly enhance performance and system resilience.

An implementation using Kafka in a Spring Boot service could look like this:

```java
@Service
public class AlertService {

    private final KafkaTemplate<String, Alert> kafkaTemplate;

    @Autowired
    public AlertService(KafkaTemplate<String, Alert> kafkaTemplate) {
        this.kafkaTemplate = kafkaTemplate;
    }

    public void sendAlert(Alert alert) {
        kafkaTemplate.send("alertTopic", alert);
    }
}
```

Choosing Communication Patterns

The efficiency of microservices interaction also depends on the selected communication patterns:

- Request/Response: This synchronous pattern is typically used for direct, immediate exchanges where responses are required instantly.

- Publish/Subscribe: This asynchronous mode benefits scenarios where one service broadcasts messages that many other services might be interested in, supporting scalability and flexibility.

- Event-Driven: This pattern involves services responding to events rather than direct calls, promoting a high degree of decoupling by ensuring services only interact through shared events.

Managing Failures and Enhancing Reliability

Robust communication necessitates mechanisms for handling failures and maintaining reliability. Implementing fail-safe strategies such as Circuit Breakers can substantially mitigate the risks associated with single points of failure.

Here's how a circuit breaker might be configured in Spring Cloud:

```
@Bean
public Customizer<Resilience4JCircuitBreakerFactory> resilienceCustomizer() {
    return factory -> factory.configureDefault(id -> new Resilience4jConfigBuilder(id)
        .circuitBreakerConfig(CircuitBreakerConfig.ofDefaults())
        .timeLimiterConfig(TimeLimiterConfig.custom().timeoutDuration(Duration.ofSeconds(3
            )).build())
        .build());
}
```

Securing Service Interactions

Security is paramount, especially when sensitive data is transferred between services. Utilizing security frameworks like OAuth2, JWT, and TLS ensures that communications are both secure and authenticated, safeguarding data integrity and confidentiality.

Conclusion

Developing a sophisticated inter-service communication strategy is integral to the success of a microservices architecture. By adeptly navigating the choices between synchronous and asynchronous communications, employing robust communication patterns, and focusing on securing and maintaining the reliability of these interactions, developers can create systems that are not only functionally effective but also secure and resilient. This approach ensures that the architectural benefits of Spring Boot are fully leveraged, leading to a more stable and efficient network of services.

Chapter Three

Advanced RESTful API Development

Designing RESTful APIs for scalability and maintainability

The creation of RESTful APIs forms the foundation for communication in modern web and mobile platforms, necessitating designs that support extensive growth and easy management. This involves a calculated approach, utilizing best practices and adopting specific design principles to ensure that these APIs can effectively scale and remain manageable as complexities increase.

Core Design Principles for RESTful APIs

1. Adherence to HTTP Methods: It's imperative for RESTful APIs to utilize HTTP methods according to their defined purposes to maintain clarity and consistency. Methods like GET, POST, PUT, DELETE, and PATCH should be used judiciously—GET for retrieving data, POST for creating resources, PUT and PATCH for updates, and DELETE for removing resources.

2. Resource-Centric URLs: Effective REST APIs structure their endpoints around resources, employing nouns to describe resource entities rather than actions. An endpoint might look like `/users` for accessing users or `/users/{id}` for operations concerning a specific user.

3. Embracing Statelessness: Each API request should be self-contained, carrying all necessary information the server needs to understand and respond to the request. This principle aids in load balancing and fault tolerance, essential for scaling as it allows each request to be independently processed by any available server.

4. Sub-Resource Utilization: Hierarchical data relationships should be navigated through sub-resources, for example, `/users/{userId}/orders` to access a user's orders. This design maintains an intuitive and logical structure.

Scalability Techniques

Efficient scalability can be achieved by:

1. Implementing Caching: Temporary data storage, or caching, reduces server load by avoiding repeated data processing and fetching. Effective caching can involve several layers including database-level, application-level, or distributed HTTP caches.

2. Rate Limiting and Throttling: Protecting APIs from being overwhelmed by too many requests from a single source is crucial. Throttling restricts the number of requests a user can make within a specified period, ensuring fair usage and preventing service abuse.

3. Employing Load Balancers: Distributing incoming API traffic across multiple server instances via load balancers can significantly enhance performance and availability.

4. Asynchronous Processes: Offloading tasks that do not require immediate processing to asynchronous workflows helps maintain API responsiveness. This might involve

queuing systems like Kafka or RabbitMQ for background processing.

Practices for Enhanced Maintainability

To ensure APIs remain easy to update and manage:

1. Versioning: Changes to APIs should be version-controlled through methods such as URL paths, query parameters, or headers. This prevents older API versions from breaking when updates are made.

2. Comprehensive Documentation: Utilizing tools like Swagger or OpenAPI for documenting APIs helps maintain clarity and usability, providing a live interface for real-time testing and interaction.

3. Consistent Conventions: Standardizing endpoint naming and structuring conventions across the API improves predictability and ease of use, streamlining developer interactions.

4. Systematic Error Handling: Providing consistent and informative error responses enhances the user experience and debugging process. Responses should include HTTP status codes and error messages that guide users on what went wrong and potential fixes.

5. Prioritizing Security: Security measures, including HTTPS, authentication via tokens like JWT, and rigorous input validation, safeguard against vulnerabilities and unauthorized access

Example of a Well-Designed API Endpoint

Here is an example demonstrating effective RESTful API design practices:

```java
@RestController
@RequestMapping("/api/v1/users")
public class UserController {

    private final UserService userService;

    @Autowired
    public UserController(UserService userService) {
        this.userService = userService;
    }

    @GetMapping("/{id}")
    public ResponseEntity<User> getUserById(@PathVariable String id) {
        User user = userService.findById(id);
        if (user == null) {
            return new ResponseEntity<>(HttpStatus.NOT_FOUND);
        }
        return new ResponseEntity<>(user, HttpStatus.OK);
    }
}
```

This example illustrates the use of HTTP methods, resource-oriented URL design, and appropriate response handling to create a clear, intuitive API.

In summary, crafting RESTful APIs that are scalable and maintainable demands adherence to proven design principles, strategic use of technology, and consistent application of best practices throughout the API's lifecycle. These strategies ensure APIs are robust enough to handle growth and flexible enough to be efficiently managed and adapted over time.

Advanced use of HTTP verbs and status codes

Effective communication within RESTful API design hinges on the precise utilization of HTTP verbs and the strategic implementation of status codes. These components are pivotal for ensuring adherence to REST principles, optimizing API performance, and facilitating error management. This discussion will delve into refined techniques for employing HTTP verbs and status codes, illustrating their potential to craft more robust, intuitive, and efficient APIs.

Refined HTTP Verb Implementation

While the fundamental HTTP methods—GET, POST, PUT, DELETE, and PATCH—are commonly employed, optimizing their use can greatly enhance API functionality:

1. PUT vs PATCH: These methods are integral for updates but serve different functions. PUT is used to replace a resource entirely, whereas PATCH applies partial modifications, which can be more efficient by only transmitting changes.

Example of using PATCH for updating only specific parts of a resource:

```
@PatchMapping("/users/{id}")
public ResponseEntity<User> modifyUser(@PathVariable String id, @RequestBody Map<String,
    Object> partialUpdate) {
    try {
        User updatedUser = userService.updateUserDetails(id, partialUpdate);
        return new ResponseEntity<>(updatedUser, HttpStatus.OK);
    } catch (UserNotFoundException e) {
        return new ResponseEntity<>(HttpStatus.NOT_FOUND);
    }
}
```

2. OPTIONS: The OPTIONS method is often underutilized but is vital for describing the capabilities of an endpoint,

230

particularly useful in dynamic environments where available operations might change.

An implementation example of OPTIONS:

```
@RequestMapping(value = "/users/{id}", method = RequestMethod.OPTIONS)
public ResponseEntity<?> describeOptions() {
    return ResponseEntity
        .ok()
        .allow(HttpMethod.GET, HttpMethod.POST, HttpMethod.PATCH, HttpMethod.DELETE)
        .build();
}
```

Sophisticated Status Code Usage

The careful selection of HTTP status codes can significantly enhance how an API communicates the results of its operations:

1. 201 Created: Essential for indicating successful resource creation via POST, typically accompanied by a **Location** header that points to the new resource's URL.

2. 204 No Content: Useful for DELETE and for PUT or PATCH methods when no response body is necessary, indicating that the request was successful but there is nothing to show.

3. 422 Unprocessable Entity: This status is beneficial for cases where a request is well-formed but cannot be processed due to semantic errors, such as validation failures.

Example usage of 422 in creating a user:

```java
@PostMapping("/users")
public ResponseEntity<?> addUser(@RequestBody User user) {
    if (!user.isValid()) {
        return new ResponseEntity<>(HttpStatus.UNPROCESSABLE_ENTITY);
    }
    User newUser = userService.addUser(user);
    URI location = ServletUriComponentsBuilder
        .fromCurrentRequest()
        .path("/{id}")
        .buildAndExpand(newUser.getId())
        .toUri();

    return ResponseEntity.created(location).body(newUser);
}
```

4. 207 Multi-Status: Useful in batch operations where different parts of the request may have varying outcomes, enabling detailed responses for each segment.

5. 429 Too Many Requests: Critical for APIs with rate limits, this status alerts the client that they have exceeded the number of allowable requests in a given time frame.

Advanced Status Code Scenarios

1. Optimizing Network Usage: Employing `304 Not Modified` in conjunction with ETags or last-modified dates reduces data transmission by informing clients when cached data remains up-to-date.

2. Effective Redirects: Using 301 (Moved Permanently) and 302 (Found) assists in managing client interactions smoothly when API resources are relocated or endpoints are restructured.

3. Handling Service Downtime: The `503 Service Unavailable` status can manage expectations during server downtimes, possibly indicating when to retry with a `**Retry-After**` header.

In conclusion, the advanced application of HTTP verbs and status codes plays a critical role in elevating RESTful API functionality and improving client experiences. By incorporating these refined approaches, developers can ensure their APIs are not only more effective but also provide clearer, more efficient communication and interaction. This enhances API integration, reliability, and overall performance, contributing to better scalability and maintainability.

Implementing HATEOAS for discoverable APIs

Hypermedia as the Engine of Application State (HATEOAS) is a foundational component of RESTful design that elevates the functionality of APIs from static to dynamic. By incorporating HATEOAS, APIs enable clients to interact with their services through hyperlinks included in the responses, much like navigating through a web browser. This implementation not only improves the discoverability of APIs but also facilitates easier maintenance and upgrades by guiding clients through the application's possibilities without prior knowledge of its architecture.

Conceptual Overview of HATEOAS

HATEOAS mandates that API responses should provide not only data but also hyperlinks to the next potential actions based on the application's current state. This design principle helps simulate a self-discovering user interface for APIs, where clients can navigate and interact with resources dynamically, using the links provided in API responses, rather than relying on out-of-band information.

Benefits of Implementing HATEOAS

1. Client-Server Decoupling: Clients interact with the API based on the hypermedia provided dynamically in responses, reducing the need for hardcoded URLs and allowing the API's structure to evolve independently of client implementations.

2. Discoverability: HATEOAS increases the discoverability of API functionalities, allowing clients to explore other actions and resources available from their current state without needing pre-configured routes.

3. API Evolution: With HATEOAS, APIs can undergo changes without significantly impacting existing clients. Clients adapt to API modifications by following new links and actions dynamically presented in the hypermedia responses.

Steps to Implement HATEOAS

The implementation of HATEOAS involves embedding actionable hyperlinks within the API responses, guiding the client through its operations:

1. Hypermedia Format Selection

Choosing a format for embedding hypermedia in API responses is crucial. Formats such as HAL (Hypertext Application Language), JSON-LD, or Siren define how links are structured, making it easier for client applications to interpret and navigate the API dynamically.

An example of a HAL response might look like:

```json
{
    "id": 1,
    "content": "Hello, World!",
    "links": [
        {
            "rel": "self",
            "href": "http://api.example.com/messages/1"
        },
        {
            "rel": "edit",
            "href": "http://api.example.com/messages/1/edit"
        }
    ]
}
```

2. Generating Links on the Server

Using frameworks like Spring HATEOAS in a Spring Boot application can simplify the addition of links to API responses. Here's how you might code it:

```java
@RestController
@RequestMapping("/api/messages")
public class MessageController {

    @GetMapping("/{id}")
    public EntityModel<Message> fetchMessage(@PathVariable Long id) {
        Message message = messageRepository.findById(id).orElseThrow(() -> new
            ResourceNotFoundException("Message not found"));
        EntityModel<Message> resource = EntityModel.of(message);

        // Append hypermedia links to the resource
        resource.add(linkTo(methodOn(MessageController.class).fetchMessage(id
            )).withSelfRel());
        resource.add(linkTo(methodOn(MessageController.class).modifyMessage(id, null
            )).withRel("edit"));

        return resource;
    }

    @PutMapping("/{id}")
    public ResponseEntity<?> modifyMessage(@PathVariable Long id, @RequestBody Message
        messageDetails) {
        // Message modification logic
        return ResponseEntity.ok().build();
    }
}
```

3. Dynamic Client Adaptation

Clients should be designed to understand and utilize the hypermedia links in the responses. By processing these dynamically, clients can adjust to changes in the API without manual updates.

Navigating Challenges

The adoption of HATEOAS can introduce complexities in API and client design, requiring a detailed approach to ensure hypermedia controls are presented consistently and interpreted correctly by the client. Robust testing and clear documentation are essential to aid clients in navigating and utilizing the API effectively.

In conclusion, integrating HATEOAS into your REST APIs transforms the way clients interact with your services, promoting a self-guiding, scalable, and adaptable API environment. By using standardized hypermedia formats and tools like Spring HATEOAS, developers can create APIs that are resilient to changes and provide a rich, dynamic experience for clients.

Chapter Four

Enhanced Data Management in Microservices

Complex data handling with Spring Data JPA

Spring Data JPA enhances the management of data access layers within Java applications by simplifying the integration of complex data operations. This tool is crucial for addressing advanced business requirements and efficiently managing intricate queries and relationships. In this exploration, we will delve into sophisticated approaches and established practices for managing complex data structures utilizing Spring Data JPA, aiming to achieve streamlined, effective, and scalable solutions.

Introduction to Spring Data JPA

As a subset of the broader Spring Data family, Spring Data JPA mitigates the common complexities associated with data persistence in applications. It provides comprehensive repository support and facilitates dynamic query execution, allowing developers to concentrate on business logic rather than database intricacies.

Managing Complex Relationships

Handling intricate data relationships, such as one-to-many, many-to-one, and many-to-many, is a standard requirement in enterprise applications. Spring Data JPA employs annotations like `@OneToMany`, `@ManyToOne`, and `@ManyToMany` to map these relationships efficiently, ensuring both data integrity and optimized query performance.

Example of Many-to-Many Relationship Mapping:

Consider a scenario involving `Student` and `Course` entities where each has a many-to-many relationship. Below is how you might configure these using Spring Data JPA:

```java
@Entity
public class Student {
    @Id
    @GeneratedValue(strategy = GenerationType.IDENTITY)
    private Long id;
    private String name;

    @ManyToMany
    @JoinTable(
        name = "enrollment",
        joinColumns = @JoinColumn(name = "student_id"),
        inverseJoinColumns = @JoinColumn(name = "course_id")
    )
    private Set<Course> courses = new HashSet<>();
}

@Entity
public class Course {
    @Id
    @GeneratedValue(strategy = GenerationType.IDENTITY)
    private Long id;
    private String title;

    @ManyToMany(mappedBy = "courses")
    private Set<Student> students = new HashSet<>();
}
```

This example utilizes a join table `enrollment` to handle the association, effectively managing the many-to-many linkage between `Students` and `Courses`.

Advanced Query Capabilities

Spring Data JPA supports custom queries through JPQL (Java Persistence Query Language) or native SQL, accommodating more sophisticated querying needs beyond basic CRUD operations.

Example of Custom JPQL Usage:

```
public interface StudentRepository extends JpaRepository<Student, Long> {
    @Query("SELECT s FROM Student s JOIN s.courses c WHERE c.title = :title")
    List<Student> findStudentsByCourseTitle(@Param("title") String title);
}
```

This method in the repository demonstrates defining a custom query to retrieve students by course title, showcasing the flexibility of JPQL for complex querying requirements.

Specifications and Criteria API

For dynamically constructing queries based on variable criteria at runtime, Spring Data JPA's Criteria API and Specifications are invaluable. They enable the programmatic building of type-safe queries, particularly useful in scenarios with highly dynamic query parameters.

Example of Specifications Implementation:

```java
public class StudentSpecifications {
    public static Specification<Student> hasName(String name) {
        return (root, query, criteriaBuilder) ->
            criteriaBuilder.equal(root.get("name"), name);
    }

    public static Specification<Student> isEnrolledIn(String courseTitle) {
        return (root, query, criteriaBuilder) -> {
            Join<Student, Course> courses = root.join("courses");
            return criteriaBuilder.equal(courses.get("title"), courseTitle);
        };
    }
}

public interface StudentRepository extends JpaRepository<Student, Long>,
    JpaSpecificationExecutor<Student> {
    List<Student> findAll(Specification<Student> spec);
}
```

This code illustrates how to dynamically combine different `Specification` instances to handle complex filtering in queries.

Performance Optimization

Effective data handling with Spring Data JPA also involves considering potential performance impacts, particularly when dealing with large data volumes or complex entity relationships. Strategies such as choosing between eager and lazy loading, optimizing query structures, and utilizing projections are critical for enhancing performance.

Eager vs. Lazy Loading Considerations:

- Eager Loading can potentially lead to performance bottlenecks if not managed carefully by loading entire sets of related data simultaneously.

- Lazy Loading conserves resources by loading related data only when it is explicitly accessed, though it must be managed to avoid excessive database calls.

Annotations like `@Fetch(FetchMode.JOIN)` or `@BatchSize(size = 10)` help manage data fetching strategies to optimize performance effectively.

Conclusion

Efficient handling of complex data with Spring Data JPA necessitates a deep understanding of its capabilities and thoughtful application of its features. By adeptly managing entity relationships, leveraging advanced querying techniques, and optimizing performance, developers can create robust, efficient, and scalable data access layers tailored to complex application demands.

Implementing transaction management

In the realm of software development, managing transactions is crucial for ensuring reliable and consistent data operations. Transaction management is integral to applications where multiple related changes to data must be executed as a single unit. This article provides a comprehensive overview of transaction management, detailing its importance and offering strategies for its effective deployment.

Key Concepts in Transaction Management

Transaction management controls a sequence of actions so that they either all complete successfully or none at all, preserving the integrity of data across processes. Transactions are governed by the ACID properties:

- Atomicity: This property ensures that all steps in a transaction are treated as a single operation that either succeeds entirely or fails completely.

- Consistency: Transactions must transition the database from one valid state to another, enforcing all data rules.

- Isolation: This ensures that operations within a transaction are concealed from other concurrent transactions until the transaction completes.

- Durability: Guarantees that the results of a transaction are permanent, even in the event of a system failure.

Transaction Management in the Spring Framework

The Spring Framework offers sophisticated transaction management capabilities that can be implemented through declarative or programmatic means, suitable for various application environments.

Declarative Transaction Management

Most developers prefer this approach due to its simplicity and separation from business logic. It utilizes annotations or XML configuration to manage transactions. The `@Transactional` annotation is commonly used to define transaction boundaries.

Example of Declarative Transaction Management:

```java
import org.springframework.transaction.annotation.Transactional;

@Service
public class FinancialService {

    @Autowired
    private BankingRepository bankingRepository;

    @Transactional
    public void processTransaction(Long fromAccountId, Long toAccountId, BigDecimal
        amount) {
        Account from = bankingRepository.findById(fromAccountId).orElseThrow(() -> new
            RuntimeException("Source account not found"));
        Account to = bankingRepository.findById(toAccountId).orElseThrow(() -> new
            RuntimeException("Destination account not found"));

        from.setBalance(from.getBalance().subtract(amount));
        to.setBalance(to.getBalance().add(amount));

        bankingRepository.save(from);
        bankingRepository.save(to);
    }
}
```

In this method marked with `@Transactional`, all operations are part of a single transaction. If any operation fails, the entire transaction is automatically rolled back by Spring, maintaining data consistency.

Programmatic Transaction Management

For scenarios where more control is needed over transactions, Spring supports programmatic transaction management. This approach involves manually managing transaction states using `TransactionTemplate` or `PlatformTransactionManager`.

Example of Programmatic Transaction Management:

```
public void completeTransaction() {
    transactionTemplate.execute(new TransactionCallbackWithoutResult() {
        protected void doInTransactionWithoutResult(TransactionStatus status) {
            try {
                financialService.processTransaction(1L, 2L, new BigDecimal(100.00));
            } catch (RuntimeException e) {
                status.setRollbackOnly();
            }
        }
    });
}
```

This example demonstrates manual control over the transaction. The transaction can be programmatically set to roll back based on specific conditions, providing flexibility in handling transaction outcomes.

Best Practices for Transaction Management

- Define Explicit Transaction Boundaries: It is critical to define where transactions start and end within your application logic.

- Shorten Transaction Lengths: Minimizing the duration of transactions can reduce the likelihood of database locks and improve application responsiveness.

- Choose Correct Isolation Levels: Different isolation levels offer trade-offs between concurrency and data accuracy. Selecting the appropriate level is key to optimizing performance.

- Manage Exceptions Effectively: Proper handling of exceptions in transactions is essential to avoid leaving data in an indeterminate state.

Conclusion

Effective transaction management is vital for applications that depend on accurate and reliable operations involving data. The Spring Framework provides robust tools for managing transactions, ensuring that applications can maintain high levels of data integrity and stability. By implementing sound transaction management practices, developers can safeguard their applications against data anomalies and ensure smooth operation under various conditions.

Strategies for distributed databases and data consistency

Managing distributed databases effectively and ensuring data consistency across various nodes is a central concern in modern, data-intensive applications. Distributed databases enhance scalability, enable better fault tolerance, and facilitate faster data retrieval, but they also introduce challenges in achieving uniform data consistency due to their decentralized nature. This article explores robust strategies for handling distributed databases and maintaining consistent data across different geographic and system boundaries.

Essentials of Distributed Databases

A distributed database system disperses data across several physical locations, which are interconnected through a network. Each site in this configuration functions independently, capable of both reading and writing data. While this setup provides significant advantages in terms of resilience and data accessibility, it complicates the synchronization process across the network, presenting challenges in maintaining consistent data states.

Navigating the CAP Theorem

The CAP theorem provides a framework for understanding the trade-offs between three critical attributes in distributed systems: Consistency, Availability, and Partition Tolerance. It states that a distributed system can only guarantee two of the following three properties at any one time:

- Consistency: All nodes reflect the same data simultaneously.

- Availability: The system remains operational and responsive, even if some components fail.

- Partition Tolerance: The system continues to operate despite any number of message losses or failures within the network.

Deciding which properties to prioritize depends on the application's specific needs; financial systems may need to favor consistency, whereas content delivery networks might prioritize availability.

Strategies to Uphold Data Consistency

1. Replication Methods:

    - Synchronous Replication maintains data uniformity by ensuring that all nodes update simultaneously. Although it guarantees strong consistency, it can slow down the system due to latency issues.

- Asynchronous Replication increases system performance by allowing time lags in data synchronization, which may result in temporary inconsistencies.

2. Conflict Resolution Techniques:

   - Advanced methods like Last Write Wins (LWW), Vector Clocks, and custom Merge Functions are used to resolve data conflicts that arise from simultaneous updates.

   - Example of Vector Clocks Usage:

```java
Map<String, Integer> vectorClock = new HashMap<>();
vectorClock.put("Node1", 1);
vectorClock.put("Node2", 2);

// If Node2 updates
vectorClock.computeIfPresent("Node2", (key, val) -> val + 1);
```

3. Consensus Algorithms:

   - Protocols such as Raft or Paxos are implemented to ensure that all changes to the database are agreed upon by a majority of nodes before they are applied, enhancing consistency across the system.

4. Effective Data Partitioning:

   - Sharding strategies distribute data across nodes based on certain keys, minimizing transaction conflicts and simplifying overall data management.

5. Implementing Caching:

- Caching can significantly reduce read latency, though it requires mechanisms to ensure that cached data remains current as the underlying data changes.

Real-World Applications

In practice, achieving data consistency in distributed databases often involves a combination of these strategies. Systems may employ synchronous replication for critical operations that demand high consistency and asynchronous replication for processes where eventual consistency is permissible. Effective monitoring and proactive anomaly detection are also critical to ensure that the system operates reliably.

Conclusion

Mastering the management of distributed databases and maintaining data consistency demands a strategic approach tailored to the specific needs of the deployment environment. By judiciously selecting the right replication techniques, conflict resolution methods, and additional strategies such as sharding and caching, organizations can ensure that their distributed systems are both effective and reliable. As databases become increasingly distributed across diverse environments, these strategies are vital for ensuring robust data integrity and operational performance.

Chapter Five

Building Resilient Microservices

Error handling and consistency in a microservices architecture

In the dynamic realm of microservices, managing errors effectively and ensuring consistent data across distributed systems are pivotal challenges. These elements are crucial for system reliability and user experience. This article explores sophisticated methods for robust error management and strategies to maintain data consistency across microservices architectures.

Principles of Error Management in Microservices

Error handling within a microservices architecture involves identifying and rectifying issues that arise during service interactions. Errors can be categorized as either internal, occurring within a single service, or external, affecting communication between services. Effective error management not only stabilizes the system but also facilitates rapid recovery and resolution.

Common Error Types in Microservices:

1. Transient Errors: These temporary issues can occur due to network delays or short-term unavailability of services. Strategies such as implementing retries with exponential backoff, along with circuit breakers, are effective for managing these errors.

2. Permanent Errors: These are reproducible errors caused by underlying system faults, such as bugs or incorrect data handling, and typically require significant corrective actions.

Strategies for Effective Error Handling

1. Graceful Degradation: Designing services to fail gracefully can help maintain partial functionality when errors occur. For instance, a fallback to a less personalized experience when a specific microservice fails.

2. Implementing Timeouts and Retries: For transient errors, defining strict timeouts and controlled retries can mitigate the impact of temporary service failures. This requires careful adjustment to prevent overloading services with repeated requests.

```
@Retryable(value = {ServiceUnavailableException.class}, maxAttempts = 3, backoff = @Backoff
    (delay = 1000))
public String resilientServiceCall() {
    return restTemplate.getForObject("http://dependent-service/path", String.class);
}
```

3. Circuit Breaker Pattern: This pattern helps prevent a service from attempting an operation that is likely to fail, based on recent failures. When failures reach a certain threshold, the circuit breaker trips, and the operation is halted temporarily.

```
@CircuitBreaker(name = "targetService", fallbackMethod = "fallbackOperation")
public String processOperation() {
    // operational logic here
}

public String fallbackOperation(Exception ex) {
    return "Fallback response";
}
```

4. Detailed Error Feedback: Providing detailed error logs and incorporating correlation IDs can significantly aid in diagnosing problems across services, improving error resolution times.

Ensuring Data Consistency in Distributed Systems

Maintaining data consistency in a microservices architecture, where each service potentially manages its own database, is inherently complex. Effective strategies to achieve consistency include:

1. Database Transactions: Within the confines of a single service, traditional database transactions can ensure atomicity and consistency.

2. SAGA Pattern: This approach divides a transaction into multiple local transactions, each managed by different services. Each service performs its part of the transaction and communicates with others via events or messages, thus ensuring overall data integrity.

3. Eventual Consistency: This model allows the system to achieve consistency over time rather than immediately. It is particularly useful in environments where absolute consistency is not immediately critical.

4. Two-Phase Commit (2PC): For scenarios that require strict consistency, 2PC ensures that all parts involved in the transaction either commit or rollback together, although this can reduce performance.

5. Compensating Transactions: These are essentially undo operations that revert changes if a part of the

transaction fails after some operations have already been committed.

Example Scenario: Implementing a SAGA

Here's how a SAGA might be implemented in an e-commerce system where placing an order triggers multiple subsequent actions:

```
public class SalesService {
    @Transactional
    public void createSale(Order order) {
        salesRepository.save(order);
        eventPublisher.publish(new OrderInitiatedEvent(order.getId()));
    }

    @TransactionalEventListener
    public void onPaymentSuccess(PaymentSuccessEvent event) {
        Order order = salesRepository.findById(event.getOrderId());
        order.updateStatus(OrderStatus.COMPLETE);
        salesRepository.save(order);
    }
}
```

In this scenario, the `**SalesService**` handles the creation of an order and listens for a successful payment event to finalize the order status, demonstrating the coordination between different services using local transactions.

Conclusion

Effective error handling and data consistency are crucial for the success of a microservices architecture. By employing advanced error handling techniques such as retries, circuit breakers, and detailed logging, along with consistency patterns like SAGA or eventual consistency, microservices can achieve the necessary reliability and integrity. These strategies are fundamental for constructing resilient systems that provide robust service operations and maintain consistent, reliable data management across distributed platforms.

Implementing Circuit Breaker patterns with Resilience4J

In the landscape of modern software architectures, particularly those utilizing microservices, the capability to effectively manage failures is critical for ensuring system resilience and availability. The circuit breaker pattern provides a strategic approach to controlling how failures in one part of the system prevent the entire system from failing. Resilience4J, a Java-based library tailored for building fault-tolerant systems, offers extensive support for implementing this pattern. This article will delve into how to apply the circuit breaker pattern using Resilience4J to bolster system robustness.

Fundamentals of the Circuit Breaker Pattern

The circuit breaker pattern is designed to prevent the continuous return of errors, which could potentially lead to larger failures in parts of the system. It works by monitoring the number of failures over time and "tripping" the circuit if errors reach a predetermined threshold, thereby preventing further failures. After a set cooldown period, the circuit attempts to close again by allowing a limited number of test requests to pass through. If these requests succeed, normal operation resumes. If not, the circuit remains open for another cooldown period.

Key Components of Resilience4J's Circuit Breaker

Resilience4J provides a lightweight, flexible approach to building resilient applications, with modules specifically for circuit breaking. Key configurable parameters in Resilience4J's circuit breaker include:

- Failure Rate Threshold: The percentage of failures that must occur before the circuit breaker trips.

- Wait Duration in Open State: The time the circuit breaker remains in the open state before switching to half-open.

- Ring Buffer Sizes: These define the number of calls considered when calculating the failure rate in closed and half-open states.

Steps to Implement a Circuit Breaker with Resilience4J

To utilize a circuit breaker in your Java application with Resilience4J, begin by integrating the necessary dependencies in your project management tool, like Maven:

```
<dependency>
    <groupId>io.github.resilience4j</groupId>
    <artifactId>resilience4j-circuitbreaker</artifactId>
    <version>1.7.0</version>
</dependency>
```

Next, configure and instantiate a circuit breaker:

```
import io.github.resilience4j.circuitbreaker.CircuitBreaker;
import io.github.resilience4j.circuitbreaker.CircuitBreakerConfig;

CircuitBreakerConfig config = CircuitBreakerConfig.custom()
    .failureRateThreshold(50)
    .waitDurationInOpenState(Duration.ofMillis(1000))
    .ringBufferSizeInHalfOpenState(2)
    .ringBufferSizeInClosedState(10)
    .build();

CircuitBreaker circuitBreaker = CircuitBreaker.of("myService", config);
```

To apply the circuit breaker to specific methods, use Resilience4J's functional style decorators:

```
import io.vavr.control.Try;

public String protectedCall() {
    return Try.ofSupplier(CircuitBreaker.decorateSupplier(circuitBreaker, this
        ::unstableCall))
            .recover(throwable -> "Default Recovery").get();
}

private String unstableCall() {
    // Potentially unstable code
}
```

Here, `unstableCall` is wrapped in a circuit breaker, so all calls are monitored. If the `unstableCall` method fails too often, the circuit breaker trips, and the recovery logic returns a default value.

Monitoring and Managing State

Resilience4J allows you to monitor and manage circuit breaker states effectively through event publishers:

```
circuitBreaker.getEventPublisher()
    .onStateTransition(event -> System.out.println("Circuit Breaker State Changed: " +
        event.getStateTransition()));
```

Best Practices

- Monitoring Integration: Combine Resilience4J with a monitoring system like Prometheus to track the behavior of your circuit breakers.

- Comprehensive Testing: Ensure your system is thoroughly tested to understand how it behaves under different failure scenarios.

- Incremental Implementation: Gradually introduce circuit breakers to critical points in your system to understand their impacts without disrupting existing functionalities.

Conclusion

Implementing the circuit breaker pattern with Resilience4J in a microservices architecture can significantly enhance the system's fault tolerance. By configuring circuit breakers correctly and employing strategic monitoring and testing, developers can ensure that their systems are resilient against a range of failures, thus maintaining stability and service reliability.

Service registry and discovery with Eureka

In modern software architectures, especially those utilizing a microservices approach, effective service discovery is essential. This ensures services can dynamically discover and interact with each other without prior knowledge of their network locations. Netflix's Eureka provides a dependable solution for service registry and discovery, which is integral to handling such dynamic interactions. This article delves into how Eureka operates, its configuration process, and the benefits it brings to microservices architectures.

Fundamentals of Eureka

Eureka serves a dual purpose within a microservices ecosystem—acting as both a service registry and a discovery agent. As a service registry, Eureka allows each service within the system to announce its presence and maintain a heartbeat to ensure availability. As a discovery mechanism, it allows services to query the registry to find and communicate with other services efficiently.

- Eureka Server: This component acts as the heart of the service registry. It keeps a record of all service instances and their statuses. Services must register with this server and periodically send heartbeats to signal their operational status.

- Eureka Client: Each service includes a Eureka client, which handles the registration, deregistration, and discovery duties. It sends periodic heartbeats to the server to affirm the service's availability.

Configuring the Eureka Server

The first step in utilizing Eureka is to set up and configure a Eureka server. This involves several steps detailed below:

1. Dependency Management: Include Eureka Server in your project using Maven or Gradle. Here's how you would set it up using Maven:

```xml
<dependency>
    <groupId>org.springframework.cloud</groupId>
    <artifactId>spring-cloud-starter-netflix-eureka-server</artifactId>
    <version>RELEASE</version>
</dependency>
```

2. Server Initialization: Use Spring Boot to set up and run the Eureka server. Decorate your main application class with `@EnableEurekaServer` to activate Eureka's server features.

```java
@SpringBootApplication
@EnableEurekaServer
public class EurekaRegistrationServerApplication {
    public static void main(String[] args) {
        SpringApplication.run(EurekaRegistrationServerApplication.class, args);
    }
}
```

Configure the server's operational parameters like port and registration settings in the `application.properties` or `application.yml`:

```yaml
server:
  port: 8761
eureka:
  client:
    registerWithEureka: false
    fetchRegistry: false
```

Eureka Client Integration

Integrating Eureka Client into your microservices allows them to register with the Eureka server and discover other services. Here's how to integrate it:

1. Add Client Dependency: Equip each microservice with the Eureka Client by adding the necessary Maven dependency.

```xml
<dependency>
    <groupId>org.springframework.cloud</groupId>
    <artifactId>spring-cloud-starter-netflix-eureka-client</artifactId>
    <version>RELEASE</version>
</dependency>
```

2. Enable Discovery: Annotate the main application class of your service with `@EnableEurekaClient` to activate the discovery capabilities.

```java
@SpringBootApplication
@EnableEurekaClient
public class ProductServiceApplication {
    public static void main(String[] args) {
        SpringApplication.run(ProductServiceApplication.class, args);
    }
}
```

Provide the Eureka server's URL in your service's configuration file to ensure it can locate and register with the server:

```yaml
eureka:
  client:
    serviceUrl:
      defaultZone: http://localhost:8761/eureka/
```

Advantages of Eureka

Using Eureka for service discovery in a microservices architecture offers several benefits:

- Reliability: Eureka's built-in resilience mechanisms ensure that service registry and discovery are consistently available, enhancing overall system reliability.

- Load Balancing: With Eureka, services can perform client-side load balancing based on the information about active service instances available in the registry.

- Simplicity: Eureka's straightforward setup and integration with Spring Cloud applications make it an accessible choice for developers seeking robust service discovery solutions.

Conclusion

Eureka provides a solid foundation for managing service registry and discovery in distributed systems, particularly those based on microservices. Its ability to keep track of service instances and health statuses ensures that services can operate and interact seamlessly, adapting to changes and failures within the environment. By implementing Eureka, developers can significantly boost the efficiency and resilience of their applications.

Chapter Six

API Security and OAuth2

Securing microservices with Spring Security and JWT

In the distributed framework of microservices, implementing robust security is crucial. Using Spring Security alongside JSON Web Tokens (JWT) provides an effective framework for authenticating and authorizing service requests. This combination supports a secure, stateless communication protocol essential for microservices architectures. This article investigates how to deploy Spring Security with JWT to enhance the security of microservices.

The Importance of JWT in Microservices

JWTs are concise, web-safe tokens that facilitate the secure transfer of claims, such as authentication and authorization details, between services. They encapsulate user identities and privileges in a compact format. Each JWT contains encoded JSON claims, including the token issuer, the subject, and expiration time, secured with a cryptographic signature to prevent tampering.

Integrating Spring Security and JWT

Configuring JWT with Spring Security involves a sequence of well-defined steps, starting from dependency management to setting up authentication filters. Here's how you can implement these configurations effectively:

1. Incorporating Necessary Dependencies

Begin by integrating Spring Security and JWT into your project's dependency management tool. For Maven users, the dependencies would look something like this:

```xml
<!-- Spring Security dependency -->
<dependency>
    <groupId>org.springframework.boot</groupId>
    <artifactId>spring-boot-starter-security</artifactId>
</dependency>
<!-- JWT support dependency -->
<dependency>
    <groupId>io.jsonwebtoken</groupId>
    <artifactId>jjwt</artifactId>
    <version>0.9.1</version>
</dependency>
```

2. Configuring Spring Security

Adapt your application's security configurations to integrate JWT by extending `**WebSecurityConfigurerAdapter**`:

```java
@Configuration
@EnableWebSecurity
public class SecurityConfig extends WebSecurityConfigurerAdapter {

    @Override
    protected void configure(HttpSecurity http) throws Exception {
        http
            .csrf().disable()
            .sessionManagement().sessionCreationPolicy(SessionCreationPolicy.STATELESS)
            .and()
            .authorizeRequests()
            .antMatchers("/api/public").permitAll()
            .anyRequest().authenticated()
            .and()
            .addFilter(new JWTAuthenticationFilter(authenticationManager()));
    }
}
```

This configuration ensures that CSRF protection is disabled for API endpoints, sessions are stateless, and all non-public requests require authentication.

3. Implementing a JWT Authentication Filter

Create a custom filter to handle the authentication logic using JWTs:

```
public class JWTAuthenticationFilter extends UsernamePasswordAuthenticationFilter {

    @Override
    public Authentication attemptAuthentication(HttpServletRequest request,
        HttpServletResponse response) {
        String token = request.getHeader("Authorization");
        // Token validation logic here
    }
}
```

4. Token Management Utilities

Manage the lifecycle of JWTs—creation and validation—through a dedicated utility class:

```
public class TokenManager {

    public String generateToken(Authentication authentication) {
        // Generate JWT after successful authentication
    }

    public boolean validateToken(String token) {
        // Validate JWT and extract authentication details
    }
}
```

Recommended Security Practices

- Secure Transmission: Ensure that JWTs are transmitted over HTTPS to prevent interception.

- Token Expiration Management: Use short-lived JWTs to reduce the risk of token misuse, with mechanisms for token renewal where necessary.

- Key Security: Securely manage the keys used for signing JWTs, ideally using automated key rotation and storage solutions.

Conclusion

Leveraging Spring Security with JWT offers a comprehensive approach to securing microservices. This method supports authenticating and authorizing user requests in a manner that is both scalable and manageable across distributed systems. By adhering to best practices in token management and system configuration, organizations can effectively shield their microservices from unauthorized access and ensure a secure operational environment.

Implementing OAuth2 for secure API access

In the evolving landscape of application development, securing API access is critical, particularly within environments that leverage user data across external applications. OAuth2 stands out as a robust authorization framework that enables secure and controlled access to server resources on a user's behalf, without exposing their credentials. This detailed exploration delves into utilizing OAuth2, particularly with Spring Security, to safeguard API interactions in microservices and other distributed systems.

The Mechanics of OAuth2

OAuth2 orchestrates secure interactions among four key players in the authorization process:

- Resource Owner: Typically the user who controls their account data.

- Client: The application seeking access to the user's account.

- Authorization Server: Validates user identity and issues tokens to the client.

- Resource Server: Hosts protected user data and accepts tokens from clients to grant access.

Components of OAuth2

The framework uses several vital components to ensure secure resource access:

1. Access Token: A credential used by the client to access server resources. It is limited by scope and duration.

2. Refresh Token: Used to renew an access token without requiring the user to authenticate again, ideal for long-duration sessions.

3. Scopes: Defines the extent of access granted to the client, limiting operations on the user's behalf.

Authorization Flows in OAuth2

OAuth2 supports various flows to suit different application needs:

- Authorization Code Grant: Best for clients that can securely store credentials. It is commonly used for server-side applications.

- Implicit Grant: Designed for clients unable to securely store credentials, such as mobile apps.

- Resource Owner Password Credentials Grant: Appropriate for highly trusted applications, such as those developed by the service provider.

- Client Credentials Grant: Used when the access request is for the client's own account rather than on behalf of a user.

Implementing OAuth2 Using Spring Security

Spring Security provides comprehensive support for OAuth2, streamlining its implementation in Java applications. Here's a step-by-step guide:

1. Add Required Dependencies

Include the necessary Spring Boot starters for OAuth2 in your build configuration:

```xml
<!-- Spring Boot OAuth2 Client -->
<dependency>
    <groupId>org.springframework.boot</groupId>
    <artifactId>spring-boot-starter-oauth2-client</artifactId>
</dependency>
<!-- Spring Boot OAuth2 Resource Server -->
<dependency>
    <groupId>org.springframework.boot</groupId>
    <artifactId>spring-boot-starter-oauth2-resource-server</artifactId>
</dependency>
```

2. Setup Authorization Server

Configure the authorization server to authenticate users and issue tokens.

```
@EnableAuthorizationServer
@Configuration
public class OAuth2AuthorizationServerConfig extends AuthorizationServerConfigurerAdapter {
    // Implement configurations for client details, token grants, and token management
}
```

3. Configure Resource Server

Ensure your resource server can accept and validate OAuth2 tokens.

```
@EnableResourceServer
@Configuration
public class OAuth2ResourceServerConfig extends ResourceServerConfigurerAdapter {
    @Override
    public void configure(HttpSecurity http) throws Exception {
        http
            .authorizeRequests()
            .antMatchers("/api/private").authenticated()
            .antMatchers("/api/public").permitAll();
    }
}
```

4. Client Configuration

Manage client-side security to enable OAuth2 logins and ensure appropriate user authentication and authorization.

```
@Configuration
public class OAuth2ClientConfig extends WebSecurityConfigurerAdapter {
    @Override
    protected void configure(HttpSecurity http) throws Exception {
        http
            .oauth2Login()
            .and()
            .authorizeRequests()
            .anyRequest().authenticated();
    }
}
```

Best Practices for OAuth2 Security

- Secure Token Handling: Tokens should be securely stored and transmitted using encryption to protect against interception.

- Regularly Update Secrets: Frequently rotate client secrets and refresh tokens to enhance security.

- Stringent Redirect URI Validation: Ensure all redirect URIs are pre-registered with the authorization server to prevent unauthorized use.

Conclusion

Integrating OAuth2 with Spring Security offers a robust solution for securing API access in distributed applications. By setting up detailed client and server configurations and adhering to best practices, developers can effectively protect user data and ensure that only authorized clients can access sensitive resources. This framework not only enhances security but also provides flexibility and scalability in managing authentication and authorization across diverse applications.

Managing API keys and access tokens

In the landscape of digital application development, securing API access is a fundamental concern. API keys and access tokens are essential instruments for authenticating and authorizing user interactions with services. Proper management of these identifiers is crucial for ensuring application security. This article discusses the key practices for managing API keys and access tokens effectively, offering insights into strategies to safeguard your application from unauthorized access and security vulnerabilities.

Overview of API Keys and Access Tokens

API Keys are unique strings that authenticate a user or application to an API. They are primarily used to monitor and control the way an API is being utilized, ensure the right users have access, and provide or restrict functionalities accordingly.

Access Tokens are used to grant access to specific resources and are often provided following a successful authentication process. These tokens generally contain encoded data that servers can use to confirm permission levels and user identities.

Effective Practices for API Key Management

1. Secure Storage Solutions: Avoid embedding API keys directly in the source code. Instead, store them using environment variables or secure, encrypted configuration files. For instance:

```
API_KEY=secure_api_key_value
```

Access this in your application with:

```
String apiKey = System.getenv("API_KEY");
```

2. Restrictive Usage Controls: Implement restrictions on API key usage to prevent misuse. This can include limiting the key's scope by IP address, setting caps on the number of requests that can be made, or specifying accessible endpoints.

3. Routine Key Rotation: Regularly update API keys to mitigate risks associated with potential leaks. Establish protocols for notifying users of key rotations and automate updates to minimize service interruptions.

4. Usage Monitoring: Continuously monitor how API keys are used to detect abnormal activities. Implement alert systems to flag unusual usage patterns and audit trails to track key access histories.

Best Practices for Access Token Management

1. Adherence to Standard Formats: Employ widely recognized token formats like JWT (JSON Web Tokens), which allow for self-contained information storage and straightforward validation processes. Here's how you might generate a JWT in Java:

```java
import io.jsonwebtoken.Jwts;
import io.jsonwebtoken.SignatureAlgorithm;
import java.util.Date;

String token = Jwts.builder()
    .setSubject("user123")
    .setExpiration(new Date(System.currentTimeMillis() + 3600000)) // expires in 1 hour
    .signWith(SignatureAlgorithm.HS512, "your_secret_key")
    .compact();
```

2. Limited Lifespans: Design access tokens to have brief validity periods to minimize the window of potential exposure in case of unauthorized access.

3. Secure Token Transmission: Ensure that tokens are always transmitted over secured connections (HTTPS) to prevent interception by malicious entities.

4. Rigorous Token Validation: Systematically verify the authenticity and integrity of tokens with each use. Check for valid signatures, expiry times, and the correctness of associated claims.

Conclusion

The meticulous management of API keys and access tokens is critical for maintaining the security of applications. By implementing robust management strategies, developers can protect their APIs from unauthorized use and potential security breaches. Keeping up with best practices in security and regularly refining management processes are key steps towards securing API infrastructures effectively.

Chapter Seven

Testing Strategies for Spring Boot Applications

Advanced testing techniques for Spring Boot

Spring Boot is renowned for its ability to streamline the development of complex applications with its convention-over-configuration philosophy. However, as applications scale and become more intricate, advanced testing becomes essential to guarantee functionality and performance. This article outlines sophisticated testing methods tailored for Spring Boot, including integration testing, performance testing, and contract testing, complete with examples for practical application.

Integration Testing in Spring Boot

Integration testing verifies that various components of an application work cohesively. Spring Boot simplifies this process with specialized tools and annotations.

1. `@SpringBootTest` Annotation

The `@SpringBootTest` annotation facilitates the loading of the complete application context to simulate a real-world testing environment, which is ideal for checking the interaction between components.

Example of an integration test using `@SpringBootTest`:

```
@RunWith(SpringRunner.class)
@SpringBootTest
public class ProductServiceIntegrationTest {

    @Autowired
    private ProductService productService;

    @Test
    public void testProductRetrieval() {
        Product product = productService.getProductById("1");
        assertNotNull(product);
        assertEquals("Expected Product Name", product.getName());
    }
}
```

This test ensures that the `ProductService` functions as expected within the application environment, interacting properly with its dependencies.

2. Test Slices

Spring Boot also offers *test slices* such as `@WebMvcTest`, `@DataJpaTest`, and `@JsonTest`, which load only relevant parts of the application context to focus tests on specific layers.

- `@WebMvcTest`: Focuses on Spring MVC controllers.

- `@DataJpaTest`: Tests JPA repositories.

- `@JsonTest`: Checks JSON serialization and deserialization.

Example using `@WebMvcTest`:

```java
@RunWith(SpringRunner.class)
@WebMvcTest(ProductController.class)
public class ProductControllerTest {

    @Autowired
    private MockMvc mockMvc;

    @MockBean
    private ProductService productService;

    @Test
    public void testGetProduct() throws Exception {
        when(productService.getProductById("1")).thenReturn(new Product("1", "Laptop"));

        mockMvc.perform(get("/products/1"))
            .andExpect(status().isOk())
            .andExpect(jsonPath("$.name", is("Laptop")));
    }
}
```

This example tests the `ProductController` by mocking the `ProductService` and asserting the controller's response.

Performance Testing

Performance testing ensures that your application performs optimally under expected workloads.

1. Load Testing with Gatling

Gatling is an effective tool for simulating high user load to test application performance.

Example Gatling script for a Spring Boot application:

```
class BasicSimulation extends Simulation {

  val httpConf = http.baseUrl("http://localhost:8080")

  val scn = scenario("Basic Test")
    .exec(http("Request_1")
    .get("/products/1"))

  setUp(
    scn.inject(atOnceUsers(100))
  ).protocols(httpConf)
}
```

This script uses Gatling to simulate 100 users accessing a product detail page simultaneously.

Contract Testing

Contract testing verifies that interactions between microservices conform to predefined agreements. Spring Cloud Contract is a popular choice for implementing contract testing in Spring Boot applications.

1. Using Spring Cloud Contract

Spring Cloud Contract allows developers to define API contracts that automatically generate tests.

Example contract definition in Groovy:

```groovy
Contract.make {
  request {
    method 'GET'
    url '/products/1'
  }
  response {
    status 200
    body("""
      {
        "id": "1",
        "name": "Laptop"
      }
      """)
    headers {
      contentType(applicationJson())
    }
  }
}
```

This contract stipulates that a GET request to `/**products/1**` should successfully return a JSON object representing a "Laptop."

Conclusion

Employing advanced testing techniques is crucial for developing reliable and scalable Spring Boot applications. Techniques like integration testing, performance testing, and contract testing ensure that applications not only meet development standards but also are prepared for real-world operations. By integrating these testing strategies, developers can significantly enhance the resilience and quality of their software products.

Writing effective unit, integration, and end-to-end tests

Comprehensive testing is fundamental to ensuring that applications are robust, secure, and performant. A well-rounded testing strategy typically includes unit tests, integration tests, and end-to-end tests, each targeting specific aspects of software functionality and interaction. This article focuses on how these testing methodologies can be effectively implemented in Spring Boot projects, providing a guide to enhancing software quality through structured testing.

Unit Testing

Unit testing involves testing individual components in isolation, which is essential for confirming that each part of the application performs as designed without external dependencies.

Best Practices:

- Isolation: Leverage mocking frameworks such as Mockito to isolate components during tests, ensuring no external systems influence the results.

- Coverage: Focus on achieving meaningful test coverage that targets business-critical paths and complex algorithms.

- Clarity and Simplicity: Ensure that tests are straightforward and easily understandable, which simplifies future maintenance.

Example Unit Test in Java:

```java
import static org.mockito.Mockito.*;
import static org.junit.Assert.*;
import org.junit.Test;
import org.mockito.InjectMocks;
import org.mockito.Mock;
import org.springframework.boot.test.context.SpringBootTest;

@SpringBootTest
public class ProductServiceTest {

    @Mock
    private ProductRepository repository;

    @InjectMocks
    private ProductService service;

    @Test
    public void getProductById_ValidId_ReturnsProduct() {
        when(repository.findById(1L)).thenReturn(new Product(1L, "Laptop"));

        Product product = service.getProductById(1L);

        assertNotNull(product);
        assertEquals("Laptop", product.getName());
    }
}
```

In this example, the `**ProductService**` is tested to confirm it correctly fetches and returns a product. The `**ProductRepository**` is mocked to ensure the test remains isolated from other components.

Integration Testing

Integration testing examines the connections and data exchanges between integrated units to detect faults in their interactions. This form of testing is crucial for validating complex systems where modules must work together seamlessly.

Best Practices:

- Use Realistic Data: Test with data that closely resembles what the application will handle in production.

- Environment Similarity: Ensure the test environment mirrors the production environment to reduce inconsistencies.

- Focus on Communication Points: Concentrate tests on areas where components interact or connect.

Example Integration Test in Spring Boot:

```java
import org.springframework.beans.factory.annotation.Autowired;
import org.springframework.boot.test.context.SpringBootTest;
import org.springframework.boot.test.web.client.TestRestTemplate;
import org.springframework.boot.test.context.SpringBootTest.WebEnvironment;
import org.springframework.http.ResponseEntity;
import org.junit.Test;

@SpringBootTest(webEnvironment = WebEnvironment.RANDOM_PORT)
public class UserControllerTest {

    @Autowired
    private TestRestTemplate restTemplate;

    @Test
    public void getUser_RequestVerified_StatusCodeCorrect() {
        ResponseEntity<String> response = restTemplate.getForEntity("/users/1", String
            .class);
        assertEquals(200, response.getStatusCodeValue());
    }
}
```

This script verifies that the `UserController` properly handles requests by simulating interactions within the server environment provided by Spring Boot.

End-to-End Testing

End-to-end testing checks the system's operation from start to finish, ensuring all integrated components function together correctly, simulating real-world usage.

Best Practices:

- User Interaction Simulation: Use tools like Selenium to automate user interactions within the system.

- Comprehensive Scenario Testing: Test common user workflows as well as potential edge cases.

- Production-like Environment: Conduct tests in an environment that closely replicates the live setting.

Example End-to-End Test Using Selenium:

```java
import org.junit.Test;
import org.openqa.selenium.WebDriver;
import org.openqa.selenium.WebElement;
import org.openqa.selenium.firefox.FirefoxDriver;
import org.openqa.selenium.By;

public class FullApplicationTest {

    @Test
    public void verifyLoginProcess_CompleteInteraction() {
        WebDriver driver = new FirefoxDriver();
        try {
            driver.get("http://example.com/login");
            WebElement username = driver.findElement(By.id("username"));
            WebElement password = driver.findElement(By.id("password"));
            WebElement loginButton = driver.findElement(By.id("login"));

            username.sendKeys("demoUser");
            password.sendKeys("demoPass");
            loginButton.click();

            assertEquals("Welcome, demoUser!", driver.findElement(By.id("welcome"
                )).getText());
        } finally {
            driver.quit();
        }
    }
}
```

This test simulates a user logging into an application to verify the end-to-end functionality and user interface interaction, demonstrating the application's behavior as experienced by real users.

Conclusion

Implementing a diverse range of tests—unit, integration, and end-to-end—is crucial for developing Spring Boot applications that are dependable and ready for real-world deployment. These tests ensure that all facets of an application are scrutinized and validated, leading to higher quality software and improved user experiences.

Testing microservices in isolation and as a whole

Microservices architectures decompose complex applications into smaller, independent units, each handling distinct functionalities. This approach enhances scalability and flexibility but introduces specific testing challenges. Effective testing must address both individual service functionality in isolation and the interaction of these services within the full system. This article outlines strategic methodologies for conducting thorough testing of microservices both individually and collectively, supplemented with illustrative examples.

Testing Microservices Individually

Isolated testing of microservices focuses on verifying the functionality of each service independently from others. This testing strategy concentrates on the service's internal operations and its ability to handle expected tasks under varied conditions.

Best Practices:

- Mocking External Dependencies: Utilize tools like Mockito in Java to simulate external services or databases, ensuring the microservice under test operates in a controlled environment.

- Emphasis on Unit and Integration Tests: Direct testing efforts toward validating the core functionalities and internal integrations of the service without external microservice interactions.

- Automate Regression Testing: Implement automated tests to continuously validate the service against its specifications, particularly after modifications.

Example of a Unit Test in Spring Boot:

```java
@RunWith(SpringRunner.class)
@SpringBootTest(classes = ProductServiceApplication.class)
public class ProductServiceTests {

    @MockBean
    private ProductRepository productRepository;

    @Autowired
    private ProductService productService;

    @Test
    public void whenAskedForProductId_EnsureProductIsReturned() {
        Long id = 1L;
        Mockito.when(productRepository.findById(id))
                .thenReturn(Optional.of(new Product(id, "Laptop", "Electronics")));

        Product result = productService.getProductById(id);

        assertThat(result.getName()).isEqualTo("Laptop");
    }
}
```

This unit test isolates the `**ProductService**`, using Mockito to mock the `**ProductRepository**` interactions and validating that the service correctly processes and responds with the expected product.

Comprehensive System Testing of Microservices

System-wide testing or end-to-end testing of microservices ensures that the assembled services interact as intended and fulfill the system requirements cohesively.

Best Practices:

- Leverage End-to-End Testing Tools: Utilize testing frameworks such as Selenium or Cucumber to simulate comprehensive user interactions across the system, encompassing multiple services.

- Contract Testing: Verify that service interactions adhere to predefined protocols using tools like Pact, which ensures that both consumers and providers of an API maintain agreement on the interface.

- Execute Performance Testing: Assess the system's performance under typical and peak load conditions to gauge its capacity and resilience using tools like JMeter or Gatling.

Example of End-to-End Testing Using Selenium:

```java
public class SystemIntegrationTest {

    private WebDriver driver;
    @Before
    public void initialize() {
        driver = new ChromeDriver();
        driver.manage().timeouts().implicitlyWait(10, TimeUnit.SECONDS);
    }
    @Test
    public void verifyCompleteRegistrationProcess() {
        driver.get("http://myapp.com/register");
        driver.findElement(By.id("name")).sendKeys("Alice");
        driver.findElement(By.id("email")).sendKeys("alice@example.com");
        driver.findElement(By.id("submit")).click();
        assertTrue(driver.findElement(By.id("welcome")).getText().contains("Welcome,
            Alice"));
    }
    @After
    public void cleanUp() {
        if (driver != null) {
            driver.quit();
        }
    }
}
```

This Selenium script demonstrates testing a user registration flow from beginning to end, evaluating how well the services work together to complete a user journey.

Conclusion

Testing each microservice in isolation as well as part of the full system is crucial for developing robust microservices architectures. By effectively employing these testing strategies, developers can assure that each microservice performs its specified functions correctly and that the system as a whole operates seamlessly. Such thorough testing practices lead to higher reliability and user satisfaction in the deployed application.

Chapter Eight

API Documentation with Swagger and Springfox

Auto-generating API documentation with Swagger

In contemporary software development, maintaining precise and up-to-date API documentation is imperative for efficient communication across services. Swagger, integrated as a part of the OpenAPI Specification suite, excels in auto-generating documentation for APIs. This system updates documentation automatically to reflect API modifications, which facilitates better team collaboration and understanding. This article explains the process of implementing Swagger to enhance API documentation automatically.

Overview of Swagger

Swagger is an influential open-source project that aids developers in creating, documenting, and consuming RESTful web services. It includes tools that automate documentation generation, client SDK production, and testing procedures. Swagger's core functionality revolves around its specification file, which describes the API's endpoints, operations, and associated parameters in JSON or YAML formats.

Advantages of Using Swagger

1. Automated Documentation: By generating documentation from the API's specification file, Swagger ensures that the documentation is continuously synchronized with the API's current version.

2. Interactive Documentation: Swagger UI provides a dynamic interface for developers and users to interact with the API's functions directly from the browser.

3. Adherence to Standards: Swagger complies with the OpenAPI Specification, ensuring compatibility with a broad range of other development tools and systems, enhancing interoperability.

Integrating Swagger into Spring Boot

Incorporating Swagger into a Spring Boot application boosts API visibility and user interaction. Below is a guide on how to integrate Swagger effectively:

1. Inclusion of Swagger Dependencies

Incorporate Swagger into your Spring Boot project by adding the necessary dependencies. For Maven projects, the required dependencies in the `**pom.xml**` are:

```xml
<dependency>
    <groupId>io.springfox</groupId>
    <artifactId>springfox-swagger2</artifactId>
    <version>2.9.2</version>
</dependency>
<dependency>
    <groupId>io.springfox</groupId>
    <artifactId>springfox-swagger-ui</artifactId>
    <version>2.9.2</version>
</dependency>
```

2. Swagger Configuration

Set up a configuration class to activate and configure Swagger within your application:

```java
import springfox.documentation.builders.PathSelectors;
import springfox.documentation.builders.RequestHandlerSelectors;
import springfox.documentation.spi.DocumentationType;
import springfox.documentation.spring.web.plugins.Docket;
import springfox.documentation.swagger2.annotations.EnableSwagger2;

@Configuration
@EnableSwagger2
public class SwaggerConfig {
    @Bean
    public Docket api() {
        return new Docket(DocumentationType.SWAGGER_2)
            .select()
            .apis(RequestHandlerSelectors.any())
            .paths(PathSelectors.any())
            .build();
    }
}
```

This setup tells Swagger to document every controller and route in your application.

287

3. Accessing Swagger Documentation

After setting up, access the auto-generated documentation by navigating to `**http://localhost:8080/swagger-ui.html**` in your browser. This URL serves the interactive Swagger UI, where all the API's endpoints can be reviewed and tested directly.

Conclusion

Swagger streamlines the documentation process for developers, ensuring API documentation is consistent with the actual API implementation. For developers using Spring Boot, integrating Swagger simplifies generating and updating documentation, improves standard compliance, and enhances interactivity. This makes Swagger an essential tool for developers focusing on creating clear and interactive API documentation.

Customizing API documentation with annotations

In today's tech-driven environment, effective API documentation is crucial for the proper utilization and integration of software services. Annotations are instrumental in customizing this documentation, allowing for the embedding of detailed metadata directly within the codebase. This approach significantly enhances documentation clarity and utility, aiding developers in navigating and integrating APIs efficiently. This article discusses the use of annotations to enrich API documentation, emphasizing practical applications with Swagger (OpenAPI) tools.

288

The Importance of Annotations in API Documentation

Annotations act as metadata that enrich source code by providing additional details that do not alter how code is executed. They are essential in API documentation for offering insights into the functionality of API elements. Tools like Swagger utilize these annotations to automate the generation of rich, comprehensive API documentation.

Core Annotations for Enhanced API Documentation

1. Operation Annotation: This involves using annotations to detail what an API endpoint does, which HTTP methods it supports, and what responses it emits, making the API's functionality explicit and understandable.

2. Parameter Documentation: Annotations help clarify the parameters an API endpoint accepts, including their types, necessary formats, and usage.

3. Request and Response Details: Using annotations to describe expected request formats and potential responses helps set clear expectations for API consumers, showing exactly what data to send and what the outcomes might be.

Deploying Annotations with Swagger in Spring Boot

Swagger is a prominent framework that supports the OpenAPI Specification and facilitates the integration of annotations to automatically generate detailed API documentation. Here's how to implement Swagger annotations in a Spring Boot environment:

1. Initial Swagger Setup

To incorporate Swagger, start by adding its dependencies to your Spring Boot project. For Maven projects, this involves adding the following to your `**pom.xml**`:

```xml
<!-- Maven dependencies for integrating Swagger -->
<dependency>
    <groupId>io.springfox</groupId>
    <artifactId>springfox-swagger2</artifactId>
    <version>2.9.2</version>
</dependency>
<dependency>
    <groupId>io.springfox</groupId>
    <artifactId>springfox-swagger-ui</artifactId>
    <version>2.9.2</version>
</dependency>
```

```java
@Configuration
@EnableSwagger2
public class SwaggerConfiguration {
    @Bean
    public Docket apiDocket() {
        return new Docket(DocumentationType.SWAGGER_2)
            .select()
            .apis(RequestHandlerSelectors.basePackage("com.example.application"))
            .paths(PathSelectors.any())
            .build();
    }
}
```

2. Utilizing Swagger Annotations

Once configured, Swagger annotations can be applied within your controller classes to enrich your API documentation:

```
import org.springframework.web.bind.annotation.RestController;
import org.springframework.web.bind.annotation.GetMapping;
import org.springframework.web.bind.annotation.RequestParam;
import io.swagger.annotations.Api;
import io.swagger.annotations.ApiOperation;
import io.swagger.annotations.ApiParam;


@RestController
@Api(description = "User management operations")
public class UserController {

    @ApiOperation(value = "Fetch a user by their ID", response = User.class)
    @GetMapping("/users/{id}")
    public User fetchUser(@ApiParam(value = "ID of the user to retrieve", required = true)
        @RequestParam Long id) {
        return userService.findById(id);
    }
}
```

This snippet demonstrates the use of `@Api`,
`@ApiOperation`, and `@ApiParam` annotations,
providing detailed descriptions and expected interactions for
the API's endpoints.

Benefits of Annotation-Based API Documentation

Utilizing annotations for API documentation brings several
key advantages:

- Improved Documentation Quality: Annotations ensure
  the documentation is precise, detailed, and directly
  aligned with the API's functionality.

- Efficiency in Development: Accurate documentation
  decreases the time developers spend understanding and
  using an API.

- Consistency Across Teams: Detailed and clear
  annotations help maintain a consistent understanding
  and prevent discrepancies in how API functionalities
  are interpreted.

Conclusion

Annotations are a powerful means of customizing API documentation, seamlessly integrating detailed descriptions directly with the code to enhance both its accuracy and usability. When used in conjunction with tools like Swagger, annotations provide a dynamic method to generate and maintain API documentation. This strategy not only optimizes the documentation process but also improves the overall developer experience by ensuring APIs are easily understood and correctly utilized.

Integrating Springfox for seamless Spring Boot integration

In contemporary software development, having detailed and current API documentation is vital for maximizing the efficiency and interoperability of web services. Springfox is a tool designed to integrate seamlessly with Spring Boot, enabling automated Swagger-compliant API documentation. This automation ensures that developers have access to real-time, interactive documentation, which aligns perfectly with the API's operations. This article details how to implement Springfox within a Spring Boot environment to streamline API documentation effectively.

Understanding Springfox

Springfox facilitates the automatic generation of API documentation for Spring Boot applications using the Swagger 2 specification. It reads annotations from your Spring controllers and models to generate a JSON or YAML document. This document is then used by Swagger UI to render a comprehensive and interactive documentation interface, which simplifies both the creation and maintenance of API documentation.

Benefits of Springfox with Spring Boot

The integration of Springfox with Spring Boot offers significant advantages:

- Automatic Documentation: Springfox generates up-to-date documentation directly from the application's codebase, reflecting the latest changes to the API.

- Documentation Enhancement: Developers can enrich the auto-generated documentation using annotations to provide additional details, examples, and descriptions.

- Effortless Integration: Designed specifically for Spring Boot, Springfox integrates directly into the application with minimal setup, enhancing developer productivity.

How to Integrate Springfox into Spring Boot

Integrating Springfox into a Spring Boot application involves several straightforward steps:

1. Incorporate Springfox Dependencies

Add the required Springfox dependencies to your project to enable Swagger documentation. For Maven users, include these in your project's pom.xml:

```xml
<!-- Dependencies for Springfox and Swagger UI -->
<dependency>
    <groupId>io.springfox</groupId>
    <artifactId>springfox-swagger2</artifactId>
    <version>2.9.2</version>
</dependency>
<dependency>
    <groupId>io.springfox</groupId>
    <artifactId>springfox-swagger-ui</artifactId>
    <version>2.9.2</version>
</dependency>
```

2. Create a Swagger Configuration

Set up Springfox by configuring it within your Spring Boot application. This involves creating a new configuration class that specifies how Swagger documentation should be generated:

```java
import springfox.documentation.builders.RequestHandlerSelectors;
import springfox.documentation.spi.DocumentationType;
import springfox.documentation.spring.web.plugins.Docket;
import springfox.documentation.swagger2.annotations.EnableSwagger2;
import org.springframework.context.annotation.Bean;
import org.springframework.context.annotation.Configuration;

@Configuration
@EnableSwagger2
public class SwaggerConfiguration {
    @Bean
    public Docket apiConfig() {
        return new Docket(DocumentationType.SWAGGER_2)
            .select()
            .apis(RequestHandlerSelectors.basePackage("com.yourorganization.yourproject"))
            .build();
    }
}
```

This configuration tells Springfox to document APIs found within a specified package, making it simple to control what gets documented.

294

3. Access Swagger UI

After the application is configured and running, access the Swagger UI by navigating to `http://localhost:8080/swagger-ui.html` on your browser. This URL serves the Swagger UI, where you can interact with your documented API endpoints.

Using Swagger Annotations for Detailed Documentation

To further improve the documentation, Swagger annotations can be applied extensively throughout your API code:

- @ApiOperation and @ApiResponses to describe methods and their possible HTTP responses.

- @ApiParam to detail method parameters.

Example of enhanced API documentation using Swagger annotations:

```java
import io.swagger.annotations.ApiOperation;
import io.swagger.annotations.ApiParam;
import io.swagger.annotations.ApiResponse;
import io.swagger.annotations.ApiResponses;
import org.springframework.web.bind.annotation.GetMapping;
import org.springframework.web.bind.annotation.RequestParam;
import org.springframework.web.bind.annotation.RestController;

@RestController
public class ExampleController {

    @ApiOperation(value = "Get details for a user", notes = "Fetches details of a user by
        their unique identifier.")
    @ApiResponses({
        @ApiResponse(code = 200, message = "User details retrieved successfully"),
        @ApiResponse(code = 404, message = "User not found")
    })
    @GetMapping("/user")
    public String getUserDetails(@ApiParam(value = "User ID to retrieve details for",
        required = true) @RequestParam String userId) {
        return "Details for user " + userId;
    }
}
```

Conclusion

Integrating Springfox with Spring Boot simplifies API documentation tasks by automating the generation process and providing an interactive documentation interface. This seamless integration ensures that documentation is both accessible and aligned with the current API, greatly enhancing usability and developer experience. Through detailed annotations and minimal setup, Springfox serves as an indispensable tool in modern API development environments.

Chapter Nine

Asynchronous Communication and Messaging

Introduction to asynchronous communication in microservices

Asynchronous communication is a key technique for enhancing the scalability and functionality of microservices architectures. It enables services to exchange messages without waiting for direct responses, facilitating independent and parallel operations across different services. This approach stands in contrast to synchronous communication where each interaction waits for a response before proceeding. This article examines the role of asynchronous communication in microservices, its advantages, potential pitfalls, and prevalent implementation methods.

Fundamentals of Asynchronous Communication

Asynchronous communication allows microservices to send messages without necessitating an immediate response from the receiver. This method reduces dependencies among services, allowing each to function autonomously and continue operations without being held up by others, which is especially beneficial in distributed systems where service responsiveness can vary.

Advantages of Asynchronous Communication

Implementing asynchronous communication within microservices offers multiple benefits:

- Scalability: It facilitates easier scaling of services as they are not tightly coupled to the response times of other services.

- Resilience: Systems are more robust and can better handle individual service failures, as the overall system doesn't rely on synchronous responses.

- Operational Efficiency: Services are not idly waiting for responses and can perform other tasks, thereby improving resource utilization.

Challenges of Asynchronous Communication

However, asynchronous communication also introduces specific challenges that need careful handling:

- Maintaining Data Consistency: As services operate independently, ensuring consistent data across the system becomes more complex.

- Complexity in Monitoring: The asynchronous nature makes it harder to trace the complete path of requests and responses, complicating debugging and monitoring.

- Infrastructure Demands: Establishing a reliable messaging infrastructure to support asynchronous communication can increase system complexity and overhead.

Key Patterns in Asynchronous Communication

Effective asynchronous communication can be achieved through several design patterns that cater to different needs within microservices architectures:

1. Event-Driven Architecture: Services operate based on events rather than direct calls, which decreases direct dependencies and enhances decoupling.

2. Message Queues: Technologies such as RabbitMQ and Apache Kafka manage messages between services, ensuring that communications are maintained even during high loads or failures.

3. Command Query Responsibility Segregation (CQRS): This pattern separates the read and write operations into different components, facilitating asynchronous and efficient handling of data.

Implementing Asynchronous Communication with RabbitMQ and Spring Boot

Setting up asynchronous messaging within a Spring Boot application using RabbitMQ can be straightforward. Below is an example of how a message listener might be implemented:

```java
import org.springframework.amqp.rabbit.annotation.RabbitListener;
import org.springframework.messaging.handler.annotation.Payload;
import org.springframework.stereotype.Component;

@Component
public class AlertServiceListener {

    @RabbitListener(queues = "#{alertsQueue.name}")
    public void processAlert(@Payload String alertMessage) {
        System.out.println("Alert received: " + alertMessage);
        // Logic to handle the alert
    }
}
```

This snippet sets up a RabbitMQ listener in Spring Boot, allowing the service to asynchronously receive and process alert messages.

Conclusion

Asynchronous communication offers substantial benefits for microservices by improving scalability, resilience, and efficiency. While it introduces challenges such as data consistency and increased system complexity, these can be effectively managed through appropriate architectural patterns and technologies. Understanding and leveraging asynchronous communication strategies allow developers to build more dynamic and robust microservices architectures.

Implementing message queues with RabbitMQ and Kafka

In the landscape of modern distributed systems, employing message queuing technologies enhances the robustness and responsiveness of services. RabbitMQ and Apache Kafka are two of the predominant platforms in this field, each bringing specialized capabilities to meet diverse requirements. This discussion will highlight how RabbitMQ and Kafka facilitate effective message queuing implementations, focusing on their unique strengths, configuration steps, and applicable use cases.

RabbitMQ in Messaging Systems

RabbitMQ, an open-source message broker, is esteemed for its robustness and versatility in handling complex messaging scenarios.

Core Features:

- Complex Routing Mechanisms: It supports various routing configurations including direct, topic, headers, and fanout, enabling sophisticated message distribution strategies.

- Reliable Message Handling: Guarantees that messages are reliably sent and received with confirmation features.

- Support for Persistent Messaging: Ensures that messages are stored safely across system restarts, preventing data loss.

Spring Boot Integration with RabbitMQ: Here's how to integrate RabbitMQ into a Spring Boot application:

1. Dependency Setup in pom.xml:

```xml
<dependency>
    <groupId>org.springframework.boot</groupId>
    <artifactId>spring-boot-starter-amqp</artifactId>
</dependency>
```

2. RabbitMQ Configuration in application.properties:

```
spring.rabbitmq.host=localhost
spring.rabbitmq.port=5672
spring.rabbitmq.username=guest
spring.rabbitmq.password=guest
```

3. Implementing a Message Publisher:

```java
import org.springframework.amqp.rabbit.core.RabbitTemplate;
import org.springframework.beans.factory.annotation.Autowired;
import org.springframework.stereotype.Component;

@Component
public class MessagePublisher {

    @Autowired
    private RabbitTemplate rabbitTemplate;

    public void publishEvent(String message) {
        rabbitTemplate.convertAndSend("myExchange", "myRoutingKey", message);
    }
}
```

4. Setting Up a Message Consumer:

```java
import org.springframework.amqp.rabbit.annotation.RabbitListener;
import org.springframework.stereotype.Component;

@Component
public class MessageConsumer {

    @RabbitListener(queues = "myQueue")
    public void handleReceivedMessage(String message) {
        System.out.println("Received message: " + message);
    }
}
```

Kafka for Event Streaming

Apache Kafka is renowned for its capacity to handle massive data streams, making it a go-to for high-throughput requirements.

Notable Features:

- Exceptional Throughput: Capable of managing millions of messages per second, Kafka supports extensive data streams.

- Horizontal Scalability: Can be scaled out to accommodate increased traffic without downtime.

- Comprehensive Data Retention: Enables detailed configuration of data retention policies to suit long-term storage needs.

Integrating Kafka with Spring Boot: Configuring Kafka within a Spring Boot setup is facilitated by the Spring Kafka library.

1. Kafka Dependency Addition in `**pom.xml**`:

```xml
<dependency>
    <groupId>org.springframework.kafka</groupId>
    <artifactId>spring-kafka</artifactId>
</dependency>
```

2. Kafka Settings in `**application.properties**`:

```
spring.kafka.bootstrap-servers=localhost:9092
spring.kafka.consumer.group-id=myGroup
spring.kafka.consumer.auto-offset-reset=earliest
```

3. Kafka Producer Configuration:

```java
import org.springframework.beans.factory.annotation.Autowired;
import org.springframework.kafka.core.KafkaTemplate;
import org.springframework.stereotype.Component;

@Component
public class KafkaEventProducer {

    @Autowired
    private KafkaTemplate<String, String> kafkaTemplate;

    public void sendEvent(String topic, String message) {
        kafkaTemplate.send(topic, message);
    }
}
```

4. Kafka Consumer Setup:

```java
import org.springframework.kafka.annotation.KafkaListener;
import org.springframework.stereotype.Component;

@Component
public class KafkaEventConsumer {

    @KafkaListener(topics = "myTopic", groupId = "myGroup")
    public void processMessage(String message) {
        System.out.println("Received Kafka message: " + message);
    }
}
```

Conclusion

RabbitMQ and Kafka offer critical capabilities for building advanced message queuing systems in microservices and distributed environments. RabbitMQ is ideal for applications requiring detailed message routing and delivery assurances, while Kafka excels in scenarios needing high throughput and robust data retention. Proper integration of these platforms into Spring Boot applications can significantly enhance the performance and scalability of services, aligning with the needs of modern enterprise systems.

Using Spring Boot with asynchronous messaging systems

Spring Boot simplifies the development of Spring-based applications, particularly in enhancing microservices architectures with asynchronous messaging capabilities. This method of messaging allows services to communicate without synchronous wait times, boosting system efficiency and scalability. This article provides insights into integrating Spring Boot with well-known messaging systems like RabbitMQ and Apache Kafka, complete with implementation examples.

Asynchronous Messaging Overview in Spring Boot

In asynchronous messaging frameworks, services send messages without waiting for immediate responses, enabling them to continue other processes simultaneously. This model is crucial for improving throughput and reducing latency. Spring Boot facilitates this with seamless integrations for RabbitMQ and Kafka, tailored for various messaging needs.

RabbitMQ Integration with Spring Boot

RabbitMQ is an adaptable open-source message broker, highly regarded for its reliability and diverse messaging functionalities.

Spring Boot Configuration for RabbitMQ: To incorporate RabbitMQ into Spring Boot, specific dependencies are added, and connection properties are configured.

1. Include Spring AMQP Dependency: Spring Boot integrates with RabbitMQ using the Spring AMQP starter package. This can be added to the Maven configuration:

```xml
<dependency>
    <groupId>org.springframework.boot</groupId>
    <artifactId>spring-boot-starter-amqp</artifactId>
</dependency>
```

2. RabbitMQ Configuration Setup: Configure RabbitMQ settings in the application's properties file:

```
spring.rabbitmq.host=localhost
spring.rabbitmq.port=5672
spring.rabbitmq.username=guest
spring.rabbitmq.password=guest
```

3. Creating a Message Publisher: Develop a service to publish messages using RabbitMQ:

```java
import org.springframework.amqp.rabbit.core.RabbitTemplate;
import org.springframework.beans.factory.annotation.Autowired;
import org.springframework.stereotype.Service;

@Service
public class MessageDispatcher {

    @Autowired
    private RabbitTemplate rabbitTemplate;

    public void dispatchMessage(String exchange, String routingKey, String message) {
        rabbitTemplate.convertAndSend(exchange, routingKey, message);
    }
}
```

4. Implementing a Message Receiver: Set up a component to asynchronously receive messages:

```java
import org.springframework.amqp.rabbit.annotation.RabbitListener;
import org.springframework.stereotype.Component;

@Component
public class MessageHandler {

    @RabbitListener(queues = "yourQueue")
    public void onMessageReceived(String message) {
        System.out.println("Message received: " + message);
    }
}
```

Kafka Integration with Spring Boot

Apache Kafka excels in processing high-volume data streams, suitable for real-time data handling.

Spring Boot Setup for Kafka: Spring Boot's Kafka support is managed through the Spring Kafka project, facilitating easy producer and consumer configuration.

1. Spring Kafka Dependency: Include the Spring Kafka dependency in your project:

```xml
<dependency>
    <groupId>org.springframework.kafka</groupId>
    <artifactId>spring-kafka</artifactId>
</dependency>
```

2. Kafka Configuration: Define Kafka connection settings in your configuration file:

```
spring.kafka.bootstrap-servers=localhost:9092
spring.kafka.consumer.group-id=myGroup
spring.kafka.consumer.auto-offset-reset=earliest
```

3. Kafka Producer Service: Establish a service to send data to specified Kafka topics:

```java
import org.springframework.beans.factory.annotation.Autowired;
import org.springframework.kafka.core.KafkaTemplate;
import org.springframework.stereotype.Service;

@Service
public class MessageService {

    @Autowired
    private KafkaTemplate<String, String> kafkaTemplate;

    public void sendMessage(String topic, String message) {
        kafkaTemplate.send(topic, message);
    }
}
```

4. Kafka Consumer Component: Create a listener to process messages from Kafka:

```java
import org.springframework.kafka.annotation.KafkaListener;
import org.springframework.stereotype.Component;

@Component
public class MessageProcessor {

    @KafkaListener(topics = "yourTopic", groupId = "myConsumerGroup")
    public void processMessage(String message) {
        System.out.println("Message from Kafka: " + message);
    }
}
```

Conclusion

Leveraging Spring Boot with asynchronous messaging systems such as RabbitMQ and Kafka enhances the capability of microservices to perform efficiently and scale dynamically. These systems facilitate non-blocking communications that are essential for applications dealing with high volumes of data or requiring high responsiveness. Spring Boot's streamlined configuration and management tools make it simpler to integrate these powerful messaging solutions, enabling developers to focus more on creating value-driving features while maintaining high performance and reliability in their applications.

Chapter Ten

Containerization with Docker

Basics of Docker and containerization

Docker has significantly reshaped how software deployment is approached by harnessing the power of containerization. This method involves encapsulating an application along with all its dependencies into a unified, portable container that ensures consistent behavior across various computing environments. This discussion delves into Docker's fundamental principles, explores its advantages, and examines its application in modern software development cycles.

Docker and Containerization Explained

Docker is a groundbreaking open-source platform that enhances application deployment, operation, and scaling through the use of containers. Containers package an application with all its prerequisites, which standardizes its operational environment across any machine, regardless of underlying differences.

Containerization contrasts with traditional virtualization by isolating at the operating system level rather than emulating a complete hardware stack. This allows containers to share the host's OS kernel, promoting efficiency and reducing resource overhead compared to full virtual machines that virtualize hardware resources.

Core Docker Components

Docker comprises several vital elements that facilitate the streamlined management of containers:

- Docker Engine: At the heart of Docker, this runtime component manages the creation and running of containers.

- Docker Images: These are the static templates from which Docker containers are launched, containing all the necessary executable application content and libraries.

- Docker Containers: These are active environments that run applications encapsulated within Docker images, ensuring consistent operation across different systems.

Advantages of Docker

1. Uniformity Across Environments: Docker standardizes the application environment across development, testing, and production, addressing the "works on my machine" problem effectively.

2. Speed of Deployment: Containers are lightweight and initiate faster than traditional methods, enabling rapid deployment and scaling.

3. Scalable and Modular: Docker supports effective scaling strategies by managing containers as separate entities, simplifying updates and modularization of applications.

4. Resource Efficiency: Since containers share the host OS, they are more resource-efficient than virtual machines, which require individual OS instances.

Fundamental Docker Commands

Handling Docker typically involves several command-line instructions. Essential commands include:

- Pull an Image:

```
docker pull redis
```

This retrieves the Redis image from Docker Hub.

- Run a Container:

```
docker run -d redis
```

Starts a Redis container in detached mode.

- List Containers:

```
docker ps -a
```

Lists all containers, showing both running and stopped.

- Stop a Container:

```
docker stop [CONTAINER_ID]
```

Halts the specified container.

- Remove a Container:

```
docker rm [CONTAINER_ID]
```

Removes a non-running container from the system.

- Build a Docker Image:

```
docker build -t your-app-name .
```

Builds a Docker image named 'your-app-name' from a Dockerfile in the current directory.

Docker in Development Processes

Docker is integral to contemporary development operations, particularly in Continuous Integration/Continuous Deployment (CI/CD) environments. It is also effectively paired with orchestration platforms like Kubernetes for managing large-scale containerized applications. Docker's reliability ensures developers can focus on creating software, free from environmental discrepancies that can lead to unexpected issues.

Conclusion

Docker and containerization have transformed the paradigms of software deployment and management, fostering efficiency and consistency across operational landscapes. As Docker continues to evolve, its deeper integration with cloud services and microservices architectures will likely enhance its pivotal role in modern IT infrastructures.

Containerizing Spring Boot applications

Containerization has significantly changed how applications are developed and deployed, ensuring consistent functionality across diverse environments. Docker is particularly effective for Spring Boot applications, allowing them to be packaged with all necessary components into one deployable unit. This article outlines how to containerize a Spring Boot application using Docker, detailing each step from Dockerfile creation to application execution within a container.

Fundamentals of Containerization with Spring Boot

Spring Boot facilitates the rapid development of Spring applications by simplifying configuration and deployment processes. Integrating Docker with Spring Boot further enhances this by providing a uniform environment that can seamlessly transition from development to production, thereby solving the common dilemma of discrepancies between environments.

Pre-requisites for Containerizing a Spring Boot Application

To begin the process of containerization, you need:

- An existing Spring Boot application: A functional Spring Boot application is necessary.

- Docker installation: Docker must be correctly installed on your system. Installation instructions can be found on Docker's official website.

- Familiarity with Dockerfile: Understanding Dockerfile syntax is crucial as these files instruct Docker on how to build application images.

Developing a Dockerfile for Spring Boot

A Dockerfile contains commands a user could call on the command line to assemble an image. Here's an example Dockerfile for a Spring Boot application:

```
# Starting with a base image with Java installed
FROM openjdk:8-jdk-alpine

# Setting the working directory in the container
WORKDIR /app

# Copying the application's jar file into our working directory
COPY target/my-spring-app-1.0.jar app.jar

# Exposing port 8080 for application access
EXPOSE 8080

# Environment variable for Java options
ENV JAVA_OPTS=""

# Command to run the application
ENTRYPOINT ["sh", "-c", "java $JAVA_OPTS -Djava.security.egd=file:/dev/./urandom-jar /app/app.jar"]
```

This Dockerfile performs the following actions:

- FROM: Establishes the base image for subsequent instructions.

- WORKDIR: Sets the directory where CMD or ENTRYPOINT commands are executed.

- COPY: Places files from the local file system into the container.

- EXPOSE: Marks the port on which the container will listen for connections.

- ENV: Sets an environment variable.

- ENTRYPOINT: Specifies the executable command when the container starts.

315

Building and Running the Docker Container

With the Dockerfile ready, proceed to build and run the container:

1. Build the Docker Image: Execute the following in your project directory where the Dockerfile resides:

```
docker build -t my-springboot-app .
```

This command creates a Docker image named `my-springboot-app`.

2. Start the Docker Container: Launch your container using:

```
docker run -p 8080:8080 my-springboot-app
```

This maps port 8080 of the container to port 8080 on the host, making the application accessible via `localhost:8080`.

Best Practices for Containerization

-   Streamline the Build Context: Position the Dockerfile at the project's root and utilize `.dockerignore` to exclude unnecessary files.

-   Implement Multi-Stage Builds: These allow for a leaner final image by separating build stages.

-   Regular Updates: Keep your images secure by updating to the latest base images to incorporate security patches.

Conclusion

Containerizing Spring Boot applications with Docker not only simplifies the deployment process but also ensures that applications perform consistently across all stages of development. By following the outlined steps, developers can effectively leverage Docker's capabilities to enhance the portability and reliability of their Spring Boot applications.

Best practices for Dockerfiles and docker-compose

Docker is an essential tool for the deployment and management of applications in containers, providing a framework that simplifies the process from development to production. Central to effective Docker utilization are Dockerfiles and Docker Compose files, which help automate and streamline container configuration. This article will outline key best practices for crafting Dockerfiles and Docker Compose files to ensure your containers are efficiently built and easy to maintain.

Optimizing Dockerfiles

A Dockerfile is essentially a batch script composed of commands and arguments that define the steps to create a Docker container image. Here are some critical guidelines for optimizing Dockerfile effectiveness:

1. Specify Base Image Precisely: Always use a specific tag or digest when referencing base images to prevent the

ambiguity of the `latest` tag, ensuring consistency across builds.

```
# Less Ideal
FROM python

# Preferred
FROM python:3.8-slim
```

2. Reduce Image Layers: Combine related commands into single `RUN` statements to decrease the number of layers in the image, improving build performance and reducing the image size.

```
# Less Ideal
RUN apt-get update
RUN apt-get install -y curl

# Preferred
RUN apt-get update && apt-get install -y curl
```

3. Utilize .dockerignore: Exclude unnecessary files from being included in the Docker context with a `.dockerignore` file, akin to `.gitignore`, which enhances build speed and efficiency.

```
# Example .dockerignore content
.git
.vscode
tmp/
logs/
```

4. Minimize Installed Packages: Keep your images lean by only installing essential packages, reducing exposure to vulnerabilities and minimizing resource use.

5. Smart Use of Build Cache: Docker reuses intermediate layers from previous builds for unchanged steps. Structure your Dockerfile to exploit this by adding frequently changed steps last.

6. Use ARG and ENV for Flexibility: Parameterize build-time variables using `**ARG**` and runtime configurations with `**ENV**` to increase Dockerfile flexibility and reusability.

```
ARG PORT=8080
ENV LISTEN_PORT=$PORT
```

Best Practices for Docker Compose

Docker Compose is instrumental for managing multi-container Docker applications. A YAML file configures all application services, making it crucial for streamlined operations.

1. Specify Compose File Version: Always declare the Compose file version to avoid compatibility issues with Docker engines.

```
version: '3.9'
```

2. Separate Configuration for Environments: Maintain distinct Docker Compose files for different environments (development, staging, production) to customize configurations and manage extensions effectively.

```
docker-compose -f docker-compose.yml -f docker-compose.override.yml up
```

319

3. Manage Volumes and Logs: Configure volumes for data persistence where necessary and set up appropriate logging drivers to suit operational needs.

```yaml
services:
  db:
    image: postgres
    volumes:
      - db_data:/var/lib/postgresql/data
    logging:
      driver: json-file
      options:
        max-size: "10m"
        max-file: "3"
```

4. Deployment Strategies: Implement strategies in your Compose file to manage how updates and rollbacks affect running services, ensuring minimal downtime.

```yaml
services:
  web:
    image: webapp:latest
    deploy:
      replicas: 4
      update_config:
        order: start-first
```

5. Non-Root User: Run services as non-root whenever possible to enhance security.

```yaml
services:
  app:
    image: myapp
    user: nonrootuser
```

Conclusion

Adhering to these best practices for Dockerfiles and Docker Compose can greatly enhance the development, deployment, and maintenance of Docker applications. Efficient Dockerfile and Docker Compose setups not only streamline the container management process but also bolster security and performance across your deployments. By implementing these strategies, developers can foster more robust and manageable containerized environments.

Chapter Eleven

Deploying Microservices to the Cloud

Overview of cloud deployment options (AWS, Azure, GCP)

As the digital era continues to expand, cloud computing has become essential for organizations seeking enhanced scalability, agility, and technological advancement. The cloud services marketplace is dominated by three major platforms: Amazon Web Services (AWS), Microsoft Azure, and Google Cloud Platform (GCP). Each offers unique features tailored to different business needs. This article provides an in-depth look at these platforms, highlighting their key services, advantages, and points to consider for optimal application deployment.

Amazon Web Services (AWS)

Overview and Services AWS, initiated in 2006 by Amazon, is a comprehensive and widely adopted cloud platform that offers a broad spectrum of services across computing, storage, networking, database, and more, spread across numerous global regions. It's designed to cater to all scales of businesses from startups to large enterprises.

Principal Services:

- EC2 (Elastic Compute Cloud): Scalable virtual servers.

- S3 (Simple Storage Service): Object storage with high durability.

- RDS (Relational Database Service): Managed relational database service.

- Lambda: Serverless computing service.

Strengths:

- Extensive assortment of services.

- Vast global presence and high availability.

- Robust security features.

- Comprehensive ecosystem of partners and third-party tools.

Considerations:

- The sheer volume of services can be overwhelming.

- Managing costs effectively requires diligence and understanding of pricing models.

Microsoft Azure

Overview and Services Introduced in 2010, Microsoft Azure is Microsoft's cloud computing solution providing a wide range of cloud services, including those for computing, analytics, storage, and networking. Its integration capabilities make it especially favorable for businesses embedded in Microsoft environments.

Core Services:

- Azure Virtual Machines: Deploy virtual machines.

- Azure SQL Database: Managed database service.

- App Services: Develop and host web applications.

- Azure Kubernetes Service (AKS): Manage Kubernetes environments.

Strengths:

- Seamless integration with Microsoft products.

- Comprehensive solutions for hybrid cloud deployments.

- Extensive tools for developers.

Considerations:

- Complex service configuration.

- Hybrid cloud solutions can be costly.

Google Cloud Platform (GCP)

Overview and Services Launched by Google in 2008, GCP provides a range of services based on the same infrastructure that fuels Google's end-user products like YouTube and Gmail. It offers services primarily in computing, data storage, and machine learning.

Notable Services:

- Google Compute Engine: Customizable virtual machines.

- Google App Engine: Platform for building scalable applications.

- Google Cloud Storage: Reliable data storage solution.

- Google Kubernetes Engine (GKE): Managed Kubernetes service.

Strengths:

- Strong offerings in big data and machine learning.

- Commitment to openness and portability.

- High-performing global infrastructure.

Considerations:

- Less extensive marketplace compared to its competitors.

- The interface and tools might have a steeper learning curve for those not familiar with Google's platforms.

Example Deployment on AWS

Here is a simple example to deploy a web application on AWS using EC2:

```
# Launch an EC2 instance
aws ec2 run-instances --image-id ami-0abcdef1234567890 --count 1 --instance-type t2.micro --key-name MyKe

# Connect to the instance
ssh -i /path/to/my-key-pair.pem ec2-user@ec2-198-51-100-1.compute-1.amazonaws.com

# Deploy your application
git clone https://github.com/exampleuser/exampleapp.git
cd exampleapp
npm install
npm start
```

Conclusion

Choosing a cloud platform involves careful consideration of the organization's specific needs, existing infrastructure, and future goals. AWS provides an extensive range of services with global reach, Azure offers strong integration with Microsoft technologies and hybrid capabilities, and GCP excels in data-intensive and machine learning applications. Each platform has its strengths and challenges, making the selection crucial for long-term success in cloud deployments.

Deploying containerized applications to Kubernetes

Kubernetes, or K8s, is recognized as the gold standard for orchestrating containerized applications, allowing for efficient management of deployment, scaling, and operational control over clusters. This guide delves into the fundamental procedures and strategies for deploying applications effectively within a Kubernetes ecosystem.

Introduction to Kubernetes

Kubernetes orchestrates the management of containerized applications by automating deployment, scaling, and operations across a cluster of machines. It is designed to help maintain high availability, facilitate load balancing, and manage application deployments dynamically.

Essential Kubernetes Components

To effectively utilize Kubernetes for deployment, it is important to understand its core components:

- Pods: The basic operational unit of Kubernetes, pods encapsulate one or more containers, their storage resources, and their unique network IP.

- Services: A service defines a logical set of pods and a policy by which to access them. Services enable the external exposure of application URLs to the internet or other services within the cluster.

- Deployments: Manages the deployment and scaling of a set of pods, and maintains the desired state of the application.

Preparing for Deployment with Kubernetes

Deployment on Kubernetes starts with proper containerization, usually via Docker. Below is the process for setting up your application for Kubernetes:

1. Construct a Dockerfile: This file provides the instructions for building your application's Docker image.

```
FROM golang:1.15
WORKDIR /go/src/app
COPY . .
RUN go get -d -v ./...
RUN go install -v ./...
CMD ["app"]
```

2. Build and Distribute the Docker Image: Compile your Docker image from the Dockerfile and upload it to a container registry accessible to Kubernetes.

```
docker build -t mygolangapp:latest .
docker push mygolangapp:latest
```

Kubernetes Deployment Process

With your Docker image prepared and stored in a registry, you can proceed with deploying it on Kubernetes:

1. **Develop a Deployment YAML File:** Define your application deployment using a YAML configuration file.

```yaml
apiVersion: apps/v1
kind: Deployment
metadata:
  name: mygolangapp
spec:
  replicas: 2
  selector:
    matchLabels:
      app: mygolangapp
  template:
    metadata:
      labels:
        app: mygolangapp
    spec:
      containers:
      - name: mygolangapp
        image: mygolangapp:latest
        ports:
        - containerPort: 8080
```

2. **Implement the Deployment Using kubectl:** Apply the deployment configuration to your Kubernetes cluster.

```
kubectl apply -f deployment.yaml
```

3. **Monitor Deployment Status:** Ensure that the deployment is successfully executed and that the pods are running.

4. Expose the Deployment Through a Service: Create a Kubernetes service to expose your application to external traffic.

```
apiVersion: v1
kind: Service
metadata:
  name: mygolangapp-service
spec:
  type: LoadBalancer
  ports:
  - port: 80
    targetPort: 8080
  selector:
    app: mygolangapp
```

Deploy this service configuration:

```
kubectl apply -f service.yaml
```

5. Access the Application: Once the service is operational, Kubernetes will provide an external IP to access your application.

Kubernetes Deployment Best Practices

- Resource Allocation: Define resource requests and limits for your pods to optimize the utilization of resources.

- Health Monitoring: Set up readiness and liveness probes to maintain the health and availability of applications.

- Consistent Image Tagging: Use specific version tags for your Docker images to ensure deployment consistency and reliability.

Conclusion

Deploying applications on Kubernetes provides a scalable and efficient framework for managing complex applications. By adhering to these outlined steps and best practices, organizations can ensure successful deployments, achieving operational excellence and robust application management in Kubernetes environments.

Managing configurations and secrets in cloud environments

In the realm of cloud computing, the management of configurations and secrets holds paramount importance for safeguarding applications and their data. Effective handling ensures the security of sensitive information while supporting consistent application performance across various deployment environments. This article discusses strategic approaches to manage configurations and secrets in cloud environments effectively, highlighting best practices and practical methodologies.

Definitions of Configurations and Secrets

Configurations encompass the adjustable external parameters that an application might use to vary its behavior without being sensitive in nature. These can include URLs for service endpoints, database connections (sans credentials), or operational parameters like timeout settings.

Secrets entail highly sensitive data that should never be exposed or included directly in the source code. Such data typically includes passwords, token credentials, private encryption keys, and other access credentials that must be strictly controlled to avoid unauthorized access and breaches.

Best Practices for Configuration Management

1. Use of Environment Variables: Storing configuration settings in environment variables is a standard practice that isolates them from the application's codebase, enhancing both security and flexibility.

```
import os
database_url = os.getenv('DATABASE_URL')
```

2. Configuration Files: It's advisable to maintain distinct configuration files for different deployment stages (development, production, etc.), which helps prevent the mixing of settings across environments.

```
// config.production.json
{
    "database_url": "http://prod.example.com/db"
}
```

3. Automated Configuration Tools: Tools such as Terraform or Ansible can automate the deployment and management of configurations, ensuring consistency and reducing manual errors across environments.

Best Practices for Secret Management

1. **Dedicated Secret Management Tools:** Employ tools designed for secret management like Azure Key Vault, AWS Secrets Manager, or HashiCorp Vault to handle sensitive information securely. These tools provide encrypted storage, access controls, and audit logs.

Example using Azure Key Vault:

```
az keyvault secret show --name mySecret --vault-name myKeyVault
```

2. **Encryption Practices:** Always encrypt secrets both at rest and in transit. Leverage built-in encryption solutions provided by the cloud provider or use key management services like Google Cloud KMS for managing your encryption keys.

3. **Strict Access Controls:** Limit access to secrets by enforcing strict permissions and using role-based access control. Ensure that only the necessary parts of the application or authorized personnel can retrieve secrets.

4. **Routine Rotation of Secrets:** Set up automated processes to regularly rotate secrets, reducing the risk of secret exposure or misuse over time.

```
# Command to rotate a secret in Vault
vault write -f sys/rotate-secrets/mysecret
```

5. **Auditing and Monitoring:** Continuously monitor the access and use of secrets. Implement logging to track

access patterns and review them periodically to detect potential unauthorized access attempts.

Integrating Secrets and Configuration Management into CI/CD Workflows

Embedding configuration and secret management into Continuous Integration/Continuous Deployment (CI/CD) pipelines ensures that security considerations are inherent throughout the development and deployment process:

- Dynamic Secrets and Configuration Injection: Utilize plugins that integrate with secrets management systems to dynamically inject secrets directly into the deployment workflows without hard coding them.

- Environment-Specific Secrets: Maintain different sets of secrets and configurations for each deployment stage, ensuring that they are appropriately isolated.

- Secure Parameter Passing in CI/CD Pipelines: Pass environment-specific configurations and secrets as parameters in CI/CD jobs to avoid exposing them in the pipeline configuration files.

Conclusion

Effective management of configurations and secrets is crucial in cloud environments to safeguard sensitive information and ensure consistent application operations. By implementing robust management practices, utilizing appropriate tools, and integrating these processes into CI/CD workflows, organizations can enhance their security posture while maintaining flexibility and scalability in their cloud deployments. This holistic approach not only secures data but also facilitates a resilient and adaptable cloud infrastructure.

Chapter Twelve

Monitoring and Logging for Microservices

Implementing centralized logging with ELK Stack

Centralized logging is a key component in effectively managing logs within microservices architectures, and the ELK Stack—comprising Elasticsearch, Logstash, and Kibana—provides an excellent set of tools for consolidating, analyzing, and visualizing data across multiple sources in real-time.

Introduction to the ELK Stack

The ELK Stack represents a combination of three powerful open-source tools: Elasticsearch, Logstash, and Kibana. Elasticsearch is a high-performance search and analytics engine. Logstash serves as the data processor that ingests and transforms data before sending it to Elasticsearch. Kibana is the visual interface on top of Elasticsearch, offering tools for sophisticated querying and data visualization.

Configuration of the ELK Stack

Elasticsearch: This is the storage hub for all log data, optimized for rapid retrieval and capable of handling vast amounts of data efficiently. You can start by downloading and running Elasticsearch locally, generally on port 9200. Ensure that your setup is secure and accessible only within your secured network environment.

Logstash: This tool is crucial for collecting, enhancing, and transporting data to Elasticsearch. After installing Logstash, configure it to parse and modify logs before they're forwarded to Elasticsearch. For example, to handle JSON logs, your configuration might look like this:

```
input {
  file {
    path => "/path/to/your/logs/*.log"
    start_position => "beginning"
  }
}

filter {
  json {
    source => "message"
  }
}

output {
  elasticsearch {
    hosts => ["localhost:9200"]
    index => "logstash-logs-%{+YYYY.MM.dd}"
  }
}
```

This setup instructs Logstash to read log files from a specific path, parse them as JSON, and then send them to Elasticsearch, where logs are indexed daily.

Kibana: This tool provides the front-end visualization of data stored in Elasticsearch. By setting up Kibana on a web server and linking it to Elasticsearch, users can create and customize dashboards that suit their monitoring preferences.

Centralization of Logs

With each microservice generating its logs, managing these logs can be complex when they are dispersed across numerous servers or containers. Centralizing logs in one place simplifies the task of diagnosing and analyzing data across all services.

Centralizing logs with the ELK Stack involves configuring each microservice to send its logs to Logstash, which can be facilitated using specific logging drivers or agents that are compatible with Logstash, or even directly into Elasticsearch. For Docker users, setting up the GELF driver to route logs directly to Logstash might look like this:

```
services:
  web:
    image: my-web-app:latest
    logging:
      driver: gelf
      options:
        gelf-address: "udp://localhost:12201"
```

Data Analysis and Visualization

With logs centralized in Elasticsearch, data can be visually analyzed through Kibana. Kibana supports real-time dashboard updates and allows for comprehensive visual representations using charts, graphs, and maps, enabling detailed monitoring of metrics such as response times and error rates.

Security and Maintenance

It is crucial to secure your centralized logging system by encrypting data transmissions and safeguarding access with strong authentication and authorization protocols. Regularly maintaining and monitoring the ELK Stack is also essential to avert data loss and maintain system performance and availability.

Conclusion

Implementing centralized logging with the ELK Stack in microservices infrastructures enables significant insights and operational efficiencies. It enhances the capacity to identify and address issues promptly, thereby reducing system downtime and improving reliability.

Monitoring microservices with Prometheus and Grafana

For robust and efficient operation of microservices architectures, deploying effective monitoring systems is indispensable. Prometheus and Grafana are quintessential in this regard, providing comprehensive tools for metric collection and data visualization. These capabilities are vital for both real-time operational oversight and historical performance analysis.

Foundations of Prometheus and Grafana

Prometheus is a sophisticated open-source monitoring framework engineered to manage the intricacies of modern distributed architectures such as microservices. It functions by collecting data in a time-series format, ideal for observing temporal variations and trends within microservice operations. Prometheus consistently fetches metrics from defined HTTP endpoints on the microservices it is tasked to monitor.

Grafana serves to augment the data processing abilities of Prometheus. As an open-source analytics platform, Grafana enables the creation of intricate and interactive dashboards that display the data collected by Prometheus, facilitating an intuitive understanding of detailed metrics.

Implementing Prometheus for Microservices Monitoring

Effective data collection with Prometheus necessitates that each microservice exposes a `/metrics` endpoint for Prometheus to scrape. This is typically achieved by incorporating client libraries that are compatible with the microservice's development framework.

For example, in microservices crafted in Java, leveraging the Prometheus Java client library allows for the exposure of JVM metrics along with tailored metrics specific to the application:

```java
import io.prometheus.client.spring.web.EnablePrometheusTiming;
import org.springframework.context.annotation.Configuration;

@Configuration
@EnablePrometheusTiming
public class MonitoringConfig {
    // This section allows for the configuration of custom metrics collection
}
```

This setup facilitates Prometheus in accessing metrics through a Spring Boot application's `/metrics` endpoint.

Prometheus must be properly configured to recognize where it should collect metrics from, as specified in the `prometheus.yml` configuration file:

339

```
scrape_configs:
  - job_name: 'java-application'
    scrape_interval: 5s
    static_configs:
      - targets: ['localhost:8080']
```

This configuration compels Prometheus to periodically scrape metrics from the `/**metrics**` endpoint of a Java application hosted locally.

Utilizing Grafana for Metric Visualization

Following the setup of Prometheus, Grafana is employed to visualize the collected metrics. Grafana can be linked to Prometheus as a data source, which then allows for the development of rich dashboards that provide insights into various metrics.

Configuring Grafana to work with Prometheus involves:

1. Going to "Configuration > Data Sources" in Grafana.

2. Selecting "Add data source."

3. Choosing "Prometheus" as the type.

4. Inputting the URL of the Prometheus server (e.g., `**http://localhost:9090**`).

5. Saving and testing the configuration to ensure functionality.

Once configured, Grafana enables the creation of visual tools like diagrams and graphs to display essential metrics such as resource consumption, traffic data, and unique business metrics.

Advanced Monitoring Techniques

To elevate the functionality of monitoring with Prometheus and Grafana, several enhancements can be considered:

- Alerting: Setting up alerting rules in Prometheus to trigger notifications via multiple channels, including email or Slack, based on specific metric thresholds.

- High Availability: Configuring Prometheus in a high-availability arrangement ensures that monitoring is continuously operational.

- Enhanced Data Retention: Since Prometheus may fall short in long-term data retention, integrating with systems like Thanos or Cortex can extend its capabilities, allowing for more detailed data storage and complex queries.

Conclusion

Utilizing Prometheus and Grafana for the monitoring of microservices not only sharpens visibility into system functions but also assists in proactive infrastructure management. These tools are instrumental in maintaining operational health and optimizing response measures, thereby ensuring that services run smoothly and efficiently.

Tracing requests with Zipkin

In environments where applications are distributed across multiple services, tracing requests is vital for pinpointing performance issues and optimizing system operations. Zipkin, a renowned open-source distributed tracing tool, stands out by enabling comprehensive monitoring and analysis of how requests move through an application, thereby identifying any performance bottlenecks.

Zipkin at a Glance

Zipkin is designed to capture and analyze timing information, which helps in identifying latency issues across a system's architecture. It is modeled after Google's Dapper and consists of several components that streamline the tracing process:

1. Instrumentation: Libraries that collect timing data from the application.

2. Collector: A component that compiles data from various services.

3. Storage: Facilities for storing trace data, compatible with several systems including In-Memory, MySQL, Cassandra, and Elasticsearch.

4. Web UI: An interface for visualizing and investigating traces to understand service latencies.

How Zipkin Operates

Zipkin uses a trace ID to monitor each request that travels through the system, recording detailed information about every segment of the request's path as "spans". These spans document the operations performed, their duration, and other relevant metadata.

Integrating Zipkin within microservices is typically achieved through libraries like Brave or Spring Cloud Sleuth for Java-based applications. To illustrate, setting up Zipkin in a Spring Boot application involves adding specific dependencies to manage tracing:

```xml
<dependency>
    <groupId>org.springframework.cloud</groupId>
    <artifactId>spring-cloud-starter-sleuth</artifactId>
</dependency>
<dependency>
    <groupId>org.springframework.cloud</groupId>
    <artifactId>spring-cloud-sleuth-zipkin</artifactId>
</dependency>
```

These libraries facilitate automatic configuration of trace collection and interaction with Zipkin. The application configuration might look something like this:

```yaml
spring:
  zipkin:
    baseUrl: http://localhost:9411
  sleuth:
    sampler:
      probability: 1.0
```

Here, the application is configured to send trace data to a Zipkin server hosted locally and to trace a specified fraction of requests.

Analyzing Traces Using Zipkin

Zipkin's Web UI allows for efficient trace analysis by enabling queries based on trace IDs, service names, or annotations. It provides a timeline view for each trace, showing the sequence and duration of spans. This visualization is crucial for quickly locating where delays occur in the service chain, facilitating faster troubleshooting and optimization.

Advantages of Using Zipkin

1. Visibility: Provides a transparent view into the request flow across services, making it easier to diagnose issues.

2. Performance Optimization: Identifies slow points within the system, allowing for targeted performance improvements.

3. Error Detection: Facilitates quick determination of errors' root causes, enhancing system reliability.

4. Scalability: Handles increasing system complexity effectively with various storage backend options.

Conclusion

Using Zipkin for request tracing in distributed systems provides a detailed and actionable view into the performance and operational dynamics of microservices. It is an indispensable tool for developers and system administrators seeking to enhance their application performance and reliability. As systems scale and grow in complexity, Zipkin's capabilities become even more crucial, ensuring that performance issues are quickly detected and resolved.

Chapter Thirteen

Scaling Microservices

Strategies for scaling microservices horizontally and vertically

In the field of microservices, ensuring robust performance and continuous availability as user demands evolve is essential. This necessitates the implementation of scaling strategies, predominantly categorized into horizontal and vertical scaling. Each method serves specific purposes and introduces different complexities.

Horizontal Scaling

Also referred to as scaling out, horizontal scaling involves augmenting the number of service instances to distribute workload more efficiently across a broader array. This strategy is particularly advantageous in microservices architectures due to its inherent flexibility and adherence to distributed system principles.

Key Advantages:

- Fault Tolerance: By operating multiple instances, the impact of a single instance failure is mitigated, ensuring service continuity.

- Load Distribution: Distributing the workload across various instances prevents overload on any single service, enhancing overall system performance.

345

Technical Implementation: Employing a load balancer is crucial for horizontal scaling, as it directs incoming traffic across all service instances equitably. Technologies such as NGINX or HAProxy, or cloud services like AWS Elastic Load Balancing, are commonly utilized. Below is an example configuration for NGINX that facilitates load balancing across three instances:

```
http {
    upstream myapp {
        server srv1.example.com;
        server srv2.example.com;
        server srv3.example.com;
    }

    server {
        listen 80;

        location / {
            proxy_pass http://myapp;
            proxy_set_header Host $host;
            proxy_set_header X-Real-IP $remote_addr;
            proxy_set_header X-Forwarded-For $proxy_add_x_forwarded_for;
            proxy_set_header X-Forwarded-Proto $scheme;
        }
    }
}
```

Challenges:

- State Management: Managing state across multiple instances can introduce complexity, especially in maintaining consistency. Ideally, services should operate statelessly, but stateful configurations may necessitate session affinity or the use of distributed caches like Redis.

- Service Discovery: Effective scaling requires dynamic service discovery to manage the registration and deregistration of instances as they come online or go offline. Service discovery mechanisms such as Eureka or Kubernetes provide essential capabilities to manage these dynamics.

Vertical Scaling

Known as scaling up, vertical scaling involves increasing the computational resources (CPU, RAM) of an existing instance. This approach is simpler but less flexible compared to horizontal scaling.

Key Advantages:

- Simplicity: Fewer instances to monitor and manage reduces operational complexity.

- Immediate Impact: Upgrading resources can quickly address performance bottlenecks, providing a swift enhancement in service performance.

Technical Considerations: Vertical scaling adjustments are typically managed through direct modifications in service settings, particularly in cloud environments. For example, adjusting an AWS EC2 instance to a more robust configuration can be accomplished with the following command:

```
aws ec2 modify-instance-attributes --instance-id i-1234567890abcdef0 --instance-type newInstanceType.t2.large
```

Challenges:

- Hardware Limitations: Physical constraints cap the scalability of a single instance.

- Potential Downtime: Resource upgrades can necessitate service restarts, though some modern cloud services support resource adjustments without downtime.

Choosing Between Horizontal and Vertical Scaling

The decision to employ horizontal or vertical scaling depends on the application's specific requirements, desired fault tolerance levels, and the management complexity the organization is prepared to undertake. Horizontal scaling is typically more suitable for long-term growth and scalability, while vertical scaling can provide quick, albeit temporary, relief from resource constraints.

In many cases, a combination approach is effective, beginning with vertical scaling to optimize individual instance performance before implementing horizontal scaling by adding more instances. This strategy utilizes the ease of vertical scaling along with the expansive benefits of horizontal scaling.

Conclusion:

Implementing appropriate scaling strategies is vital for microservices to efficiently handle increased demands and ensure robust performance. Both horizontal and vertical scaling are integral to a well-rounded scalability strategy, influenced by the application's specific needs and the operational strategies of the organization. It is crucial for system architects and developers to thoughtfully evaluate their scalability requirements to deploy the most effective solutions.

Load balancing techniques

Load balancing is a fundamental technique in managing distributed systems, especially within microservices architectures, where it crucially redistributes network traffic or client requests across multiple servers. This distribution ensures no single server is overwhelmed, which enhances the responsiveness and boosts the availability of applications, offering a more reliable user experience.

Crucial Role of Load Balancing in Microservices

In the architecture of microservices, services often have multiple instances running to increase reliability and performance. Here, load balancing becomes indispensable as it spreads out traffic evenly across all available instances. This not only optimizes the use of resources but also heightens the system's overall dependability through added redundancy.

Categories of Load Balancers

Load balancers are typically divided into two main types: hardware-based and software-based. Hardware load balancers are physical devices that manage network traffic and are recognized for their robust performance and reliability. However, they tend to be more expensive and less flexible than software load balancers. Software load balancers, on the other hand, offer greater flexibility and cost-effectiveness, integrating seamlessly into the application's environment and allowing for extensive customization.

Effective Load Balancing Algorithms

The effectiveness of a load balancer is significantly influenced by the algorithms it employs. These include:

- Round Robin: This basic algorithm allocates requests evenly across all servers, without considering the current load on each server, which might lead to inefficiencies if server capacities vary widely.

- Least Connections: This algorithm is more dynamic, directing traffic to the server with the fewest active connections, thus better adapting to variations in server load.

- IP Hash: This method uses the client's IP address to consistently direct them to the same server, which helps maintain session continuity.

Here is a Python snippet illustrating a simple Round Robin algorithm:

```python
class RoundRobinBalancer:
    def __init__(self, servers):
        self.servers = servers
        self.count = 0

    def get_server(self):
        server = self.servers[self.count]
        self.count = (self.count + 1) % len(self.servers)
        return server

# Setting up servers and demonstrating usage:
servers = ["Server1", "Server2", "Server3"]
balancer = RoundRobinBalancer(servers)

for _ in range(10):
    print(balancer.get_server())
```

Software-Based Load Balancing Options

Software solutions like NGINX and HAProxy are prominent for their versatility and comprehensive feature sets.

NGINX: Commonly used as a web server, NGINX also functions effectively as a load balancer. It is lauded for its performance efficiency and stability. Below is a sample NGINX configuration for load balancing:

```
http {
    upstream myapp {
        server server1.example.com;
        server server2.example.com;
        server server3.example.com weight=3;
    }

    server {
        listen 80;

        location / {
            proxy_pass http://myapp;
        }
    }
}
```

This configuration demonstrates how NGINX can manage traffic across multiple servers, with the `weight` parameter allowing for adjustments based on server capacity.

HAProxy: Known for its robustness, HAProxy serves as a reliable open-source option for balancing and proxying TCP and HTTP traffic, especially suitable in environments with substantial traffic.

Load Balancing Challenges

While load balancing offers numerous benefits, it also presents challenges such as configuration complexity, especially in large or dynamic environments. Effective health checks are essential to prevent routing to dysfunctional servers, thus complicating administrative efforts. Moreover, as services are scaled or modified, keeping load balancer configurations current requires ongoing vigilance.

Conclusion

Load balancing is vital for the effective management of distributed systems like microservices, significantly enhancing operational efficiency and system reliability. Choosing the appropriate load balancing solution and keeping abreast of new developments can greatly improve an organization's application performance and stability. As the field evolves, it is imperative for system managers to continuously update their practices and embrace new technologies.

Autoscaling in a cloud environment

Autoscaling within cloud environments is an essential feature that dynamically adjusts the allocation of computing resources in response to fluctuating workloads. This capability significantly enhances application responsiveness, optimizes the utilization of resources, and reduces operational costs by automatically scaling resources up or down based on real-time demand.

The Role of Autoscaling

Applications hosted on cloud platforms often experience variable levels of demand that can be unpredictable, stemming from user interactions, planned events, or sudden traffic spikes. Traditional resource provisioning, aimed at accommodating peak demand, typically results in overcapacity and underutilization or, conversely, might fail during unexpected surges. Autoscaling smartly circumvents these issues by offering a dynamic resource management solution that scales automatically with the needs of the application.

Operation of Autoscaling

Autoscaling continuously monitors designated performance metrics such as CPU usage, memory demands, or network traffic. It operates under rules set or through intelligent algorithms that determine when to scale up or down. For instance, an increase in CPU utilization above 70% might trigger the system to launch additional instances to balance the load, whereas a decrease below 20% could lead to reducing the number of active instances to decrease costs.

Fundamental Elements of Autoscaling

The autoscaling architecture generally comprises several components:

- Launch Configurations: These define the configurations for each instance that is initiated by the autoscaler, including settings like instance type, image used, security group configurations, and associated storage.

- Autoscaling Groups: These are clusters of instances managed as a unit, which specifies the minimum and maximum number of instances, desired operational capacity, and the preferred deployment zones.

- Scaling Policies: These rules or guidelines dictate the scaling actions, based on specific triggers or metrics. These can be predictive, based on historical data, reactive to current metrics, or scheduled according to known traffic patterns.

In the context of AWS, for example, setting up autoscaling involves creating a launch configuration and an autoscaling group through the AWS Management Console, AWS CLI, or SDKs. Below is an illustration using AWS CLI commands to establish these components:

```
# Command to create a launch configuration
aws autoscaling create-launch-configuration --launch-configuration-name my-config
    --image-id ami-abc123 --instance-type t2.medium --security-groups my-sec-group

# Command to create an autoscaling group
aws autoscaling create-auto-scaling-group --auto-scaling-group-name my-group
    --launch-configuration-name my-config --min-size 1 --max-size 10 --desired
    -capacity 2 --availability-zones us-east-2a us-east-2b
```

Benefits of Autoscaling

Autoscaling provides several key advantages:

- Cost Reduction: It ensures cost efficiency by adjusting resource levels to match actual usage, avoiding overspending on unneeded capacity.

- Maintained Performance: It safeguards optimal application performance by allocating resources in accordance with current demands.

- Improved Availability and Fault Tolerance: By distributing instances across multiple zones and adjusting resource counts, autoscaling enhances the robustness of the application infrastructure.

- Responsiveness to Traffic Fluctuations: Autoscaling swiftly adapts to changes in application load, crucial for handling peak usage periods effectively.

Challenges Associated with Autoscaling

Despite its benefits, autoscaling introduces certain challenges:

- Complex Setup: Determining effective scaling thresholds and parameters can be complex and typically necessitates a deep understanding of application behavior under various loads.

- Operational Costs: While it generally reduces overall costs, autoscaling can incur expenses related to the scaling processes themselves, such as API calls and the costs associated with ramping up new instances.

- Response Times: There may be delays in the system's response to scaling needs, affecting how quickly new resources become fully functional and integrated.

Conclusion

Autoscaling in cloud environments plays a vital role in modern IT strategies by aligning resource provisioning directly with application demand, ensuring operational efficiency, cost-effectiveness, and high performance. As cloud technologies advance, the importance of effectively managing autoscaling strategies grows, prompting organizations to continually optimize their resource management approaches to stay aligned with evolving application and business needs. This adaptive resource management tool requires meticulous planning and ongoing adjustment to meet the dynamic requirements of cloud-hosted applications effectively.

Chapter Fourteen

Maintaining and Evolving Microservices

Strategies for maintaining a growing microservices ecosystem

Navigating the complexities of an expanding microservices ecosystem requires strategic approaches to ensure stability, efficiency, and scalability. As the ecosystem grows, the challenges related to managing interdependencies, administration overhead, and potential failures increase. Implementing effective strategies becomes crucial to maintaining a resilient and adaptive system.

Focusing on Design Fundamentals

Robust design principles are vital in an expanding microservices architecture. Ensuring that services are loosely coupled allows each service to function and evolve independently, minimizing the risk of widespread system disruptions and simplifying updates and maintenance. Additionally, each service should demonstrate high cohesion by having a clearly defined role and responsibility, reducing unnecessary inter-service dependencies.

Adopting Domain-Driven Design (DDD) can facilitate the organization of services around the business domain, aligning the architecture with business goals and processes more effectively. This approach not only leads to better-designed

356

services but also enhances team communication by employing a consistent language that mirrors the business domain.

Advancing Automation

In the realm of a growing microservices ecosystem, automation is key. Automating Continuous Integration (CI) and Continuous Deployment (CD) processes helps minimize human error and accelerates the ability to update or fix services rapidly.

Tools like Jenkins or GitLab CI are instrumental for implementing these automated processes. Here's an example of how a CI pipeline can be configured in GitLab CI to automatically manage testing and deployment upon code updates:

```
stages:
  - test
  - deploy

run_tests:
  stage: test
  script:
    - echo "Running tests"
    - ./run-tests.sh
  only:
    - main

deploy_service:
  stage: deploy
  script:
    - echo "Deploying service"
    - ./deploy.sh
  only:
    - main
  when: manual
```

This setup allows for automated testing with the `run_tests` job on changes to the `main` branch, while the `deploy_service` job can be triggered manually, providing control over deployment activities.

Enhancing Monitoring and Observability

As microservices multiply, effective monitoring and observability are crucial for detecting and addressing potential issues early. Advanced monitoring tools and techniques can offer deep insights into microservices' performance and their interactions.

Incorporating extensive logging, distributed tracing, and performance metrics is essential. Using tools like Prometheus for monitoring, Grafana for visualizations, and Jaeger or Zipkin for tracing helps create a comprehensive view of system health and functionality. Here's an example of setting up Prometheus to monitor multiple microservices:

```
scrape_configs:
  - job_name: 'microservices'
    static_configs:
      - targets: ['service1:9090', 'service2:9090']
```

Promoting a DevOps Culture

Establishing a DevOps culture is essential for fostering collaboration between development and operations teams, which is crucial in a microservices environment. This cultural shift towards shared responsibility for the full lifecycle of services, from design through to maintenance, enhances decision-making and problem-solving capabilities.

Empowering teams with the necessary tools and authority to oversee the services they develop from start to finish helps streamline processes and reduce bottlenecks.

Reinforcing Security Measures

Security considerations become more critical as the number of microservices—and consequently, potential vulnerabilities—increases. Developing a comprehensive security framework that includes secure communications between services, regular security audits, and adherence to best practices is crucial.

Utilizing technologies such as mutual TLS for encrypted communications, service meshes like Istio for managing security policies, and incorporating security gates in CI/CD pipelines can effectively bolster security. Deploying API gateways for handling authentication and authorization also centralizes and simplifies security management.

Conclusion

Effectively managing a growing microservices ecosystem involves adopting solid design principles, leveraging automation, implementing sophisticated monitoring, fostering a DevOps culture, and ensuring robust security practices. These strategies are fundamental to handling the complexities of scalability, maintaining system reliability, and ensuring agility as the architecture evolves. Continuously refining these strategies and integrating new technologies are imperative for sustaining a robust and dynamic system.

Implementing continuous integration/continuous deployment (CI/CD)

Adopting Continuous Integration and Continuous Deployment (CI/CD) is crucial in the modern landscape of software development, enabling teams to improve speed and adaptability in delivering product enhancements. CI/CD effectively automates essential steps in the software delivery process, significantly boosting software quality by freeing developers to focus more on feature development instead of manual processes.

Fundamentals of CI/CD

Continuous Integration (CI) involves developers consistently integrating their code changes into a central repository, typically several times per day. Each integration triggers automated builds and tests, ensuring quick identification of integration issues. This approach facilitates the early detection of defects, simplifying resolution, and reducing the cost of corrections.

Continuous Deployment (CD) expands on CI by automatically deploying every change to the codebase, after successful tests, into a testing or production environment. This automation includes not only testing but also the deployment processes, ensuring that new functionalities are quickly operational and available to users, while also reducing the errors associated with manual deployment processes.

Benefits of CI/CD

The transition to CI/CD offers multiple significant benefits:

- Increased Deployment Frequency: Automation facilitates faster integration and deployment, leading to higher release rates.

- Enhanced Developer Productivity: Eliminating manual tasks allows developers to concentrate on adding value through new features.

- Superior Software Quality: Frequent testing and integration help catch issues early, improving the quality of the final product.

- Lower Deployment Risks: Regular, incremental updates mean each deployment is smaller and more controlled, making the process more reliable.

- Rapid Feedback Incorporation: Continuous deployment enables immediate real-world feedback from users, which can be quickly integrated into the development cycle.

Implementing CI/CD

Implementing CI/CD necessitates the setup of a CI/CD pipeline, a defined series of stages a piece of software undergoes to reach production readiness. Tools commonly used to facilitate these pipelines include Jenkins, GitLab CI, and CircleCI.

Here's a straightforward example using Jenkins:

1. Code: Developers push their code changes to a shared repository.

2. Build: Jenkins detects these changes, pulls the latest version, and begins the build process.

3. Test: If the build is successful, Jenkins proceeds to run a set of predefined tests to validate the code.

4. Deploy: Successful tests lead to automatic deployment to a staging environment, and upon successful validation there, to production.

A Jenkins pipeline is typically defined in a `**Jenkinsfile**`, which clearly outlines the necessary steps:

```
pipeline {
    agent any
    stages {
        stage('Build') {
            steps {
                sh 'make'
            }
        }
        stage('Test') {
            steps {
                sh 'make test'
            }
        }
        stage('Deploy') {
            steps {
                sh 'make deploy'
            }
        }
    }
}
```

This file specifies the Build, Test, and Deploy stages, including the commands that Jenkins will execute during each stage.

CI/CD Best Practices

To effectively leverage CI/CD, several best practices should be followed:

- Effective Code Repository Management: Employ version control solutions like Git to manage and maintain the codebase in a deployable state.

- Automated Testing: Develop a comprehensive suite of automated tests to ensure software functionality and performance.

- Fast Build Processes: Streamline the build process to maintain quick feedback loops for developers.

- Consistent Deployments: Deploy changes frequently to minimize risk and adapt swiftly to user feedback.

- Proactive Monitoring and Validation: Continuously monitor application performance in production to ensure successful deployment and functionality.

Conclusion

Integrating CI/CD revolutionizes traditional software development and deployment approaches, creating a highly efficient, automated workflow that enhances the quality and speed of software delivery. This methodology allows organizations to swiftly adapt to changes in the market and user preferences. As complexity and team sizes increase, the importance of CI/CD becomes more critical, affirming its essential role in competitive software development.

Managing technical debt and refactoring

Effectively handling technical debt and engaging in systematic refactoring are crucial for maintaining the integrity and scalability of software projects over their lifespans. Technical debt represents the extra work that arises when quick and easy code solutions are chosen over better approaches that are more laborious but would pay off in the long run. This debt, if not managed, can accumulate and make future changes harder and more expensive.

Overview of Technical Debt

Technical debt can stem from several sources, including rushed development cycles, inconsistent coding practices among developers, or continuous changes in project requirements. It usually falls into two categories: intentional and unintentional. Intentional technical debt is taken on knowingly, with a plan for remediation, whereas unintentional debt accumulates without immediate recognition due to less optimal practices or outdated methodologies.

Proper management of technical debt involves identifying its origins and deploying strategies to control and reduce it effectively. Regular code reviews, maintaining thorough documentation, and adhering to coding standards help in mitigating the accrual of unwanted technical debt.

Effective Management Techniques

1. Consistent Refactoring: Refactoring is the modification of existing code without changing its functionality to improve non-functional attributes of the software. Integrating refactoring into the development routine can significantly

enhance code quality. Consider this simple example of code refactoring in Java:

Before Refactoring:

```java
public double calculateTotal(Vector<OrderLine> orderLines) {
    double total = 0.0;
    for (int i = 0; i < orderLines.size(); i++) {
        OrderLine line = orderLines.elementAt(i);
        total += line.getPrice() * line.getQuantity();
    }
    return total;
}
```

After Refactoring:

```java
public double calculateTotal(List<OrderLine> orderLines) {
    return orderLines.stream()
                .mapToDouble(line -> line.getPrice() * line.getQuantity())
                .sum();
}
```

The revised code utilizes Java's Stream API, improving readability and reducing error potential by eliminating manual iteration.

2. Debt Prioritization: It's critical to identify and prioritize technical debt by its impact on the project. Focus on resolving high-impact debts that compromise essential functionalities first.

3. Allocating Time for Reduction: Just as time is set aside for feature development, time should also be allocated for reducing technical debt. This can be built into the development cycles, such as sprints in Agile frameworks.

4. Automation Tools: Automated testing and continuous integration tools can prevent minor issues from becoming significant debts. Tools like SonarQube can help in continuously monitoring code quality and technical debt.

5. Developer Education: Regularly educating developers about best coding practices and the importance of minimizing technical debt is essential. Workshops and ongoing training sessions can equip developers with the necessary skills to maintain high code quality from the outset.

Leadership's Role

Leadership plays a vital role in the management of technical debt. Leaders must ensure their teams understand the importance of addressing technical debt and provide them with the necessary resources and time to tackle it effectively. They must balance the need for immediate feature development against the benefits of debt reduction, making informed decisions that will benefit the software project in the long term.

Conclusion

Addressing technical debt and performing regular refactoring are strategic practices essential for sustaining software project health and agility. By prioritizing these practices, organizations ensure their software remains robust, flexible, and cost-effective to maintain. Ignoring technical debt can result in a fragile codebase, difficult to adapt and expensive to maintain. A proactive approach to technical debt management and refactoring is therefore pivotal for successful software development.

Conclusion

Recap of advanced concepts covered

This recapitulation focuses on sophisticated software development practices, detailing essential concepts that elevate the expertise and effectiveness of development teams. These advanced topics, pivotal for contemporary development frameworks, span various strategies and technologies that streamline development processes and boost efficiency.

Microservices Architecture

Microservices architecture decomposes applications into smaller, self-contained units, each managing a distinct functionality. This approach enhances flexibility and scalability, which is particularly advantageous in cloud environments, allowing for the independent deployment of each service component. Typically, microservices communicate using lightweight protocols like HTTP/REST or asynchronous messaging systems such as AMQP.

Containerization and Docker

Containerization involves isolating an application and its dependencies into a container that provides consistency across any computing environment. Docker, a prominent tool in this field, facilitates the deployment and scaling of applications by containerizing them. For example, the following Docker command runs a containerized application:

```
docker run -d -p 8080:80 myapp
```

This command tells Docker to execute 'myapp' in detached mode, while mapping port 80 inside the container to port 8080 on the host, thus making the application externally accessible.

Continuous Integration and Continuous Deployment (CI/CD)

CI/CD integrates automation into various stages of application development, from integration to deployment, ensuring consistent and efficient delivery through a CI/CD pipeline. Utilizing tools such as Jenkins, CircleCI, and GitLab CI, this practice continuously integrates and monitors the application throughout its lifecycle, promoting rapid and dependable delivery.

Cloud Services Management

Advanced management of cloud services entails orchestrating and managing cloud resources effectively to deploy, scale, and maintain applications. Kubernetes is central to orchestrating containerized applications, automating their deployment and scaling across host clusters, thereby boosting operational efficiency.

DevOps Practices

DevOps merges software development (Dev) and IT operations (Ops), aiming to shorten the development lifecycle and achieve continuous delivery with high-quality software. Stemming from Agile methodologies, DevOps emphasizes enhanced collaboration and integration across teams involved in various stages of the development process.

Advanced Programming Concepts

Adopting sophisticated programming techniques such as asynchronous programming, reactive extensions, and functional programming can significantly enhance the responsiveness and performance of applications. Techniques like asynchronous programming in JavaScript or C# optimize the handling of operations that do not block threads.

Security and Compliance

Security considerations are critical and integrated throughout the development process from design through deployment. Ensuring compliance with standards like GDPR for data protection and PCI DSS for payment security is essential. Security practices such as using OAuth for authentication, implementing role-based access control, and encrypting data both at rest and in transit form the backbone of robust security strategies.

Conclusion

This summary underscores the critical advanced concepts in software development that contribute to a vibrant and effective development environment. From the modular nature of microservices to the comprehensive automation capabilities of Kubernetes and CI/CD pipelines, these practices promote innovation and robustness. As technology continues to evolve, mastering these advanced methodologies equips development teams to address both present and future challenges effectively. Adopting these practices ensures teams are well-prepared to navigate the complexities of the modern software development landscape.

Challenges and solutions in microservices and API development

The implementation of microservices architecture and API development has revolutionized software development, introducing agility and efficient management of complex applications. However, these innovative approaches also present unique challenges that must be carefully managed to fully harness their potential.

Microservices Architecture Challenges

1. Complexity in Management The management of a vast array of microservices, each potentially developed with different technologies and running in varied environments, introduces significant complexity.

Solution: Leveraging orchestration platforms like Kubernetes simplifies the complexities involved by automating deployment, scaling, and operations of microservices across clusters, thus facilitating easier management and better reliability.

2. Data Consistency Issues Ensuring consistent data across independently managed microservice databases is a common challenge, especially in environments that require high transactional integrity.

Solution: Adopting an event-driven approach with technologies like Apache Kafka enables services to communicate changes instantly and maintain data integrity across the ecosystem.

3. Network Latency and Service Resilience The distributed nature of microservices may lead to increased latency and higher risk of service failure.

Solution: Implementing resilience patterns like circuit breakers can help manage failures effectively. Using a circuit breaker framework like Hystrix, services can isolate points of failure and prevent a system-wide cascade of failures.

Example of implementing Hystrix:

```
HystrixCommand.Setter config = HystrixCommand.Setter
    .withGroupKey(HystrixCommandGroupKey.Factory.asKey("ServiceGroup"))
    .andCommandPropertiesDefaults(HystrixCommandProperties.Setter()
        .withExecutionTimeoutInMilliseconds(1000));
HystrixCommand<String> command = new HystrixCommand<String>(config) {
    @Override
    protected String run() {
        // logic to call a service that might fail
        return potentiallyFailingServiceCall();
    }

    @Override
    protected String getFallback() {
        return "Safe Fallback Response";
    }
};

String result = command.execute();
```

4. Complex Service Interactions As the number of microservices increases, so does the complexity of interactions between them, which can impact performance.

Solution: An API Gateway can simplify complex service interactions by handling request routing, composition, and protocol translation, making it easier for services to communicate efficiently.

API Development Challenges

1. Ensuring Security APIs expose critical business logic and data, making them targets for security breaches.

Solution: Implementing comprehensive security measures such as OAuth 2.0 for secure access, and applying rate limiting to prevent abuse, ensures robust API security.

2. Effective Version Control APIs evolve over time, necessitating effective version control to manage changes without disrupting existing clients.

Solution: Applying semantic versioning helps manage changes transparently, and maintaining old versions alongside new ones allows clients to migrate at their own pace.

3. Maintaining Documentation Up-to-date and accurate documentation is crucial for facilitating ease of use and integration by developers.

Solution: Using tools like Swagger or OpenAPI to automatically generate and update API documentation ensures that developers have reliable guides, enhancing usability and developer experience.

Conclusion

Adopting microservices and API development strategies brings significant benefits to software projects, enhancing scalability, flexibility, and performance. However, these advantages come with their own set of challenges which, when effectively managed, allow organizations to leverage these advanced technological frameworks fully. By implementing strategic solutions to address these challenges, companies can innovate and maintain a competitive edge in the rapidly evolving digital landscape.

Pathways for further mastery in Spring Boot and microservices

Delving into advanced Spring Boot and microservices involves a focused approach to boosting agility, scalability, and facilitating the development of cloud-native applications. Developers and organizations eager to deepen their expertise in these areas can follow several paths to enhance their knowledge and skills.

Advanced Expertise in Spring Boot

Spring Boot streamlines the setup and deployment of Spring applications, minimizing much of the manual configuration traditionally required. It offers a plethora of ready-to-use features suitable for backend applications, such as embedded servers, metrics, health checks, and external configuration capabilities.

1. Advanced Configuration and Customization Understanding the intricacies of Spring Boot's auto-configuration is essential. Developers should learn to modify and tailor these configurations to meet specific requirements, grasping how Spring Boot decides on certain configurations and how to override them when necessary.

For instance, crafting custom starters can significantly streamline common patterns:

```
@Configuration
public class MyCustomStarter {

    @Bean
    @ConditionalOnMissingBean
    public MyService myService() {
        return new MyServiceImpl();
    }
}
```

This example demonstrates a custom Spring Boot starter that conditions the creation of a MyService bean to its absence, thus allowing for customization in different applications.

2. Enhancing Monitoring and Profiling Skills Leveraging Spring Boot Actuator can provide developers with powerful monitoring tools that can be customized to gain deep insights into application operations. Linking these tools with external systems like Prometheus or Grafana can greatly improve the observability of the applications.

3. Reactive Programming Mastery Spring WebFlux facilitates reactive programming within Spring Boot, accommodating asynchronous data streams and high numbers of concurrent connections, which are ideal for high-performance applications.

Proficiency in Microservices Architecture

Microservices architecture breaks down applications into smaller, independent services that communicate over well-defined APIs. Mastering this architecture requires both technical acumen and strategic planning.

1. Utilizing Design Patterns Knowing critical microservices patterns such as API Gateways, Circuit Breakers, Service Registries, and Config Servers is essential. These patterns help solve prevalent issues in distributed systems.

For example, implementing the Circuit Breaker pattern with Resilience4j can safeguard services from cascading failures:

```
CircuitBreakerConfig config = CircuitBreakerConfig.custom()
    .failureRateThreshold(50)
    .waitDurationInOpenState(Duration.ofMillis(1000))
    .ringBufferSizeInHalfOpenState(2)
    .ringBufferSizeInClosedState(2)
    .build();

CircuitBreakerRegistry registry = CircuitBreakerRegistry.of(config);
CircuitBreaker circuitBreaker = registry.circuitBreaker("myCircuitBreaker");

Supplier<String> decoratedSupplier = CircuitBreaker
    .decorateSupplier(circuitBreaker, this::serviceCall);

String result = Try.ofSupplier(decoratedSupplier)
    .recover(throwable -> "Hello from Recovery").get();
```

This configuration demonstrates how to manage service dependencies effectively to prevent a single point of failure from affecting the entire system.

2. Effective Scaling Strategies Developers should also understand how to scale microservices efficiently to manage increased loads, which involves mastering load balancing, dynamic scaling, and caching techniques.

3. Ensuring Security Across Services Security in distributed microservices environments is critical. Developers need to implement comprehensive security protocols such as OAuth

and JWTs, secure service communications, and ensure all data transactions are protected.

Ongoing Education and Community Engagement

Keeping pace with the rapidly evolving technologies of Spring Boot and microservices is essential. Active participation in tech communities, contributing to open-source projects, attending industry conferences, and staying informed through current literature are all effective ways to remain updated with the latest trends and practices.

Conclusion

Paths to mastery in Spring Boot and microservices are varied but require a commitment to ongoing learning and practical application. By deepening their understanding of complex configurations, staying engaged with the tech community, and keeping abreast of new advancements, developers can significantly enhance their capabilities and make substantial contributions to the field of modern software development.

Introduction

The critical role of performance in enterprise-grade applications

In the domain of enterprise-grade software, performance stands as a fundamental pillar, not merely an optional feature. The effectiveness of expansive applications is critically dependent on their ability to efficiently manage substantial workloads, process large volumes of data, and accommodate numerous concurrent users without any compromise in service quality. This crucial aspect underlines a key insight: performance is as integral to the software as its functional capabilities.

The Essential Role of Performance in Enterprise Applications

1. User Experience and Satisfaction: At the core of performance importance is its impact on user experience. For enterprise applications that typically support a high volume of users, subpar performance can lead to slower response times and tedious interactions with the system. This directly affects user satisfaction and can significantly hamper productivity across the organization, leading to notable economic implications.

2. Scalability: Enterprise applications are expected to scale efficiently; they must manage increases in data, user activity, and transaction volumes without faltering. Optimal performance is key because it ensures that applications can

expand their capabilities to meet rising demands without necessitating extensive infrastructure redesigns.

3. Competitive Advantage: In competitive markets, businesses can achieve a significant edge by offering faster and more dependable services. Superior performance can differentiate a company's software solutions from those of its competitors, particularly when functionalities are comparable. Enhanced system speed improves customer retention, reduces user turnover, and attracts new users.

4. Cost Efficiency: Performance also affects cost efficiency. Applications that operate efficiently utilize fewer resources (CPU, memory, bandwidth), which can lead to substantial cost reductions, especially in environments where resources are metered and billed based on usage.

5. Compliance and SLAs: Numerous enterprise applications are governed by specific performance metrics outlined in Service Level Agreements (SLAs). Non-compliance can result in financial penalties and loss of business, thus making performance not just a matter of efficiency but also of contractual adherence.

Overcoming Performance Challenges

Achieving optimal performance in enterprise environments involves navigating several challenges, from robust data management to scalable infrastructure solutions. Here's how these challenges can be effectively addressed:

1. Handling Massive Data Volumes: Enterprise applications often deal with extensive datasets, which can decelerate performance if not managed properly.

Solution: Effective data management strategies such as intelligent data partitioning, indexing, and implementing caching mechanisms can dramatically enhance system responsiveness. Data partitioning across multiple servers can expedite data access and retrieval, significantly improving performance.

2. Ensuring High Availability and Fault Tolerance: The high costs associated with downtime or data loss in enterprise applications necessitate robust fault tolerance and high availability.

Solution: Techniques such as load balancing and redundant system configurations ensure that services remain available and operational, even when individual components fail. Server clustering, for instance, allows for seamless failover, minimizing service interruptions.

3. Alleviating Network Issues: Performance of distributed applications can be severely affected by network problems, particularly latency and limited bandwidth.

Solution: Utilizing content delivery networks (CDNs), optimizing data transfer protocols, and implementing data compression are effective ways to mitigate these issues, enhancing data flow and reducing latency.

4. Optimizing Application Performance: Inherent issues in software architecture or code can also lead to performance bottlenecks.

Solution: Application profiling tools can be used to identify slowdowns and optimize code. Employing asynchronous programming methods can also improve the responsiveness of applications. For instance:

```
CompletableFuture.supplyAsync(() -> database.fetchData())
    .thenAccept(data -> process(data));
```

This non-blocking approach allows the application to remain responsive, handling other tasks while awaiting data from the database, thus significantly enhancing user interaction.

Conclusion

Performance in enterprise-grade applications is a critical factor that influences not only operational effectiveness but also user satisfaction, competitive positioning, cost management, and compliance with industry standards. Continuous investment in performance optimization and embracing technological advancements ensures that applications meet and exceed expected performance criteria. Such sustained commitment to performance is essential for maintaining the viability and success of critical enterprise systems well into the future.

Overview of performance tuning and advanced configurations in Spring Boot

In the realm of enterprise-grade software, performance is more than a feature—it's a cornerstone of development. Applications built with Spring Boot, when optimized correctly, not only facilitate development but also excel in operational environments by handling high loads efficiently. Tuning

Spring Boot for optimal performance involves adjusting configurations that enhance the application's effectiveness without compromising functionality.

Key Aspects of Spring Boot Performance Tuning

Performance tuning in Spring Boot is crucial for ensuring that applications run efficiently in production. It primarily focuses on optimizing database connections, memory management, server settings, and implementing effective caching mechanisms.

1. Optimizing Database Connections

The management of database connections significantly impacts application performance. Spring Boot's default settings may not always be optimal for production needs.

Example configuration adjustments include:

```
spring.datasource.hikari.maximum-pool-size=20
spring.datasource.hikari.minimum-idle=5
```

Using HikariCP, Spring Boot's default connection pool, these properties help manage the pool size to match the application's needs, ensuring efficient database connectivity.

2. Memory Management Enhancements

Adjusting JVM settings is critical for managing how an application uses memory, which is vital for maintaining performance under various loads. Key JVM parameters include:

- `-Xmx` for maximum heap size,

- `-Xms` for the initial heap size,

- `-XX:+UseG1GC` for enabling modern garbage collection.

Example JVM launch command:

```
java -Xmx512m -Xms256m -XX:+UseG1GC -jar myapp.jar
```

3. Web Server Tuning

Configuring the embedded server settings directly can lead to significant improvements in how the application handles requests. For example:

```
server.tomcat.max-threads=200
server.tomcat.min-spare-threads=10
```

These settings adjust the Tomcat server's capacity to handle more concurrent requests, enhancing throughput and response time.

4. Effective Caching Strategies

Implementing caching can drastically reduce the load on the database and improve response times by storing frequently accessed data temporarily.

```
@EnableCaching
public class CachingConfig {

    @Bean
    public CacheManager cacheManager() {
        return new ConcurrentMapCacheManager("entities");
    }
}
```

Advanced Configurations for Spring Boot

Going beyond performance tuning, advanced configurations in Spring Boot involve leveraging profiles, conditional settings, and creating custom auto-configurations to enhance flexibility and reusability across applications.

1. Utilizing Profiles

Profiles allow developers to define environment-specific configurations to segregate settings for development, testing, and production.

Example development profile settings:

```
# application-dev.properties
spring.datasource.url=jdbc:h2:mem:testdb
spring.datasource.driverClassName=org.h2.Driver
spring.datasource.username=sa
spring.datasource.password=password
```

2. Conditional Configuration

Spring Boot supports conditional configurations, enabling developers to include or exclude beans based on certain conditions.

```
@Bean
@ConditionalOnProperty(name = "feature.enabled", havingValue = "true")
public MyFeature myFeature() {
    return new MyFeatureImpl();
}
```

This approach ensures that specific configurations are activated based on environment properties.

3. Creating Custom Auto-Configuration

Developers can create their own auto-configurations to encapsulate and reuse common patterns or settings across multiple Spring Boot applications.

```
@Configuration
@ConditionalOnClass(MyService.class)
@EnableConfigurationProperties(MyServiceProperties.class)
public class MyAutoConfiguration {

    @Bean
    @ConditionalOnMissingBean
    public MyService myService(MyServiceProperties properties) {
        return new MyService(properties.getConfig());
    }
}
```

This auto-configuration checks for the presence of `MyService` class and defines a bean accordingly.

Conclusion

Enhancing performance and configuring advanced settings in Spring Boot are essential for deploying robust, efficient applications. Mastery of database tuning, memory management, server configuration, and caching strategies ensures that Spring Boot applications perform optimally. Additionally, utilizing advanced configuration features like profiles and custom auto-configurations promotes flexibility and maintainability, crucial for modern software development.

Setting the stage for high-performance computing with Spring Boot

Spring Boot has transformed how developers build and deploy enterprise applications, providing a streamlined framework that simplifies Java development without sacrificing performance. With the right strategies and configurations, Spring Boot can be tailored for high-performance computing, enabling applications to efficiently manage large datasets, complex transactional systems, and extensive user loads.

Harnessing Spring Boot for High-Performance Computing

1. Tailored Configuration

Spring Boot simplifies setup with its convention-over-configuration paradigm, but high-performance computing demands meticulous tuning of system and application settings. Adjustments may include optimizing garbage collection, JIT compilations, and application-specific parameters like database connections and thread management.

For example, to enhance the server's ability to handle more concurrent connections, you might adjust Tomcat's settings in `**application.properties**`:

```
server.tomat.max-threads=500
server.tomcat.accept-count=100
server.tomcat.max-connections=10000
```

These configurations help the server manage higher loads by allowing more simultaneous connections.

2. Effective Resource Utilization

Efficient resource management is crucial in high-performance environments. Spring Boot's actuator module provides vital insights into application performance, enabling real-time monitoring and optimization. Moreover, leveraging Spring Boot's support for externalized configuration ensures that applications are tuned to the specific needs of their deployment environments.

3. Advanced JVM Optimization

At the heart of Spring Boot applications lies the Java Virtual Machine (JVM). For high-performance scenarios, advanced JVM tuning is essential. Configurations might involve setting heap sizes, selecting appropriate garbage collection algorithms, and optimizing the JIT compiler.

For instance, to optimize for high-load environments using the Garbage First Garbage Collector (G1GC), the JVM settings would be:

```
java -jar -XX:+UseG1GC -Xmx4G -Xms4G myapp.jar
```

This setup specifies the use of G1GC with a heap of 4 GB, aiming to enhance performance under significant load.

4. Embracing Reactive Programming

Spring Boot integrates with Spring WebFlux to support reactive programming, which is ideal for managing I/O-bound operations efficiently in high-performance contexts. Reactive programming enables non-blocking I/O, which conserves resources and allows the application to perform other tasks concurrently.

Here's an example of a non-blocking REST endpoint using Spring WebFlux:

```java
@RestController
public class DataController {

    @GetMapping("/data")
    public Mono<String> getData() {
        return Mono.just("Here is some data");
    }
}
```

This controller utilizes reactive principles to improve throughput and responsiveness.

5. Implementing Asynchronous Processing

Spring Boot's native support for asynchronous processing is vital for high-performance computing, allowing tasks to be executed in parallel or without interrupting the main application flow. This is implemented using Spring's asynchronous methods and scheduling capabilities.

For example, an asynchronous service might look like this:

```java
@Service
public class AsyncService {

    @Async
    public CompletableFuture<String> process() {
        // Simulate a time-consuming task
        try {
            Thread.sleep(5000);
        } catch (InterruptedException e) {
            Thread.currentThread().interrupt();
        }
        return CompletableFuture.completedFuture("Processing complete");
    }
}
```

This method processes tasks asynchronously, enhancing application throughput and scalability.

Conclusion

Spring Boot provides a robust foundation for developing applications that require high performance by allowing detailed configuration adjustments, efficient resource management, and advanced optimizations. Incorporating modern programming techniques such as reactive programming and asynchronous operations further empowers developers to build applications that are not only fast and responsive but also scalable. By fine-tuning these elements, Spring Boot stands as a formidable platform for high-performance computing in the enterprise domain.

Chapter One

Advanced Spring Boot Configuration

Deep dive into external configurations and profiles

Spring Boot's architecture significantly streamlines the process of application development and deployment, by providing robust support for managing diverse environments through external configurations and profiles. Proper utilization of these tools can greatly enhance deployment strategies and ensure consistent behavior across various environments from development to production.

Mastering External Configurations in Spring Boot

External configurations enable Spring Boot applications to adapt seamlessly across different operational environments without needing to recompile the code. This functionality is critical when distinct settings are necessary for development, testing, and production environments, which may differ in database connections, API endpoints, and other operational parameters.

Spring Boot supports several methods for externalizing configurations, including the use of properties files, YAML files, environment variables, and command-line arguments. This allows developers to choose the best method that aligns with their deployment strategy or personal preferences.

Properties Files: Spring Boot automatically recognizes and loads `application.properties` or `application.yml` files from the classpath. Developers can create separate configuration files for different environments, such as `application-dev.properties` for development and `application-prod.properties` for production.

Here's how you might configure database URLs for different environments:

```
# application-dev.properties
spring.datasource.url=jdbc:mysql://localhost/devdb
spring.datasource.username=devuser
spring.datasource.password=devpass

# application-prod.properties
spring.datasource.url=jdbc:mysql://prodserver/proddb
spring.datasource.username=produser
spring.datasource.password=prodpass
```

Environment Variables and Command-Line Arguments: These are especially useful in cloud deployments or other environments where modifying files is impractical. For example:

```
java -jar app.jar --spring.profiles.active=prod --spring.datasource.url=jdbc:mysql://prodserver/proddb
```

Leveraging Profiles in Spring Boot

Profiles are a foundational feature in Spring Boot that enable the specification of environment-specific configurations, facilitating conditional settings and bean registrations based on the environment. This capability is crucial for isolating application configurations to ensure they are only activated in appropriate contexts.

Profiles can be activated by specifying the `**spring.profiles.active**` property in configuration files, as an environment variable, or via command-line arguments.

Example Usage:

```
# application.yml
spring:
  profiles:
    active: dev

---
spring:
  config:
    activate:
      on-profile: dev
    datasource:
      url: jdbc:mysql://localhost/devdb
      username: devuser
      password: devpass

---
spring:
  config:
    activate:
      on-profile: prod
    datasource:
      url: jdbc:mysql://prodserver/proddb
      username: produser
      password: prodpass
```

This YAML configuration enables different datasource settings based on the active profile, allowing the application to adapt its database connections depending on the environment.

Exploring Advanced Configuration Techniques in Spring Boot

Spring Boot also offers sophisticated configuration techniques for developers aiming to further refine their applications.

@ConfigurationProperties: This annotation binds external configurations to a POJO (Plain Old Java Object), providing a type-safe way to configure properties, particularly useful for consolidating related configuration properties:

```
@Component
@ConfigurationProperties(prefix="mail")
public class MailProperties {
    private String hostname;
    private int port;
    private String from;

    // standard getters and setters
}
```

Properties prefixed with `**mail**` in external configurations will be mapped to this object, which can then be utilized across the application.

@Profile with @Configuration: Combining `@**Profile**` with `@**Configuration**` enables the definition of environment-specific configuration classes, encapsulating beans that are only registered when certain profiles are active:

```
@Configuration
@Profile("development")
public class DevDatabaseConfig {
    @Bean
    public DataSource dataSource() {
        return new EmbeddedDatabaseBuilder().build();
    }
}
```

This configuration class will be active only under the "development" profile, using an embedded database.

Conclusion

Effectively utilizing external configurations and profiles in Spring Boot is crucial for developers to effectively manage applications across diverse environments. By externalizing configurations and strategically deploying profiles, developers can ensure that their applications perform optimally in each environment, streamline deployment processes, and maintain cleaner, more organized codebases. Such practices are indispensable for any professional working with Spring Boot in dynamic deployment environments.

Customizing Spring Boot starters and auto-configurations

Spring Boot stands out for streamlining application development through its convention-over-configuration strategy, largely by leveraging starters and auto-configurations. These mechanisms are designed to quickly establish a Spring application with reasonable defaults. Nonetheless, as applications expand in complexity and operational demands, customizing these configurations is crucial. Adapting Spring Boot starters and auto-configurations not only enhances application adaptability but also tailors performance to meet specific business requirements.

Delving into Spring Boot Starters and Auto-Configurations

Spring Boot starters bundle essential dependencies together to add specific functionalities to your application, such as web capabilities or secure authentication, ensuring these dependencies work harmoniously and are maintained regularly. Examples include `**spring-boot-starter-web**` for web apps and `**spring-boot-starter-security**` for securing applications.

Auto-configuration in Spring Boot is designed to automatically tailor your application based on the libraries detected in your classpath. It reduces the need for manual configuration by adjusting automatically based on the detected environment.

Customizing Spring Boot Starters

Customizing or creating new starters involves understanding their structure, which typically includes:

- A `**pom.xml**` file that specifies required dependencies.

- Configuration properties classes that aid in binding properties.

- Auto-configuration classes tagged with `**@Configuration**`, which conditionally configure beans depending on the presence of classes or properties.

To develop a custom starter, follow these steps:

1. Define Starter Dependencies: Start by creating a new Maven project and adding necessary dependencies. For example, a `**spring-boot-starter-payment**` would include libraries pertinent to payment processing.

2. Develop Auto-Configuration: Create configuration classes that define beans under certain conditions, tailored to the needs of your starter. Use annotations

such as `@ConditionalOnClass` and `@ConditionalOnMissingBean` to ensure compatibility and avoid conflicts.

3. Configure Properties: If your starter requires configurable options, use the `@ConfigurationProperties` annotation to set up a properties class.

Consider this example of an auto-configuration class:

```
@Configuration
@ConditionalOnClass(PaymentService.class)
@EnableConfigurationProperties(PaymentProperties.class)
public class PaymentAutoConfiguration {

    @Bean
    @ConditionalOnMissingBean
    public PaymentService paymentService(PaymentProperties properties) {
        return new DefaultPaymentService(properties.getApiKey());
    }
}
```

This configuration ensures that a `PaymentService` bean is only set up if `PaymentService` is available on the classpath and no other `PaymentService` beans have been defined.

Advanced Configuration Strategies

For more detailed customizations, deeper insights into how Spring Boot manages auto-configurations are necessary:

- Override Auto-Configuration: Occasionally, it may be necessary to override the default auto-configurations. This can be done by specifying exclusions in your `application.yml` or `application.properties` through the `spring.autoconfigure.exclude` property, or directly within your `@SpringBootApplication` annotation using the `exclude` attribute.

- Manage Auto-Configuration Order: The sequence in which auto-configurations are applied can significantly influence functionality. Use annotations like `@AutoConfigureOrder`, `@AutoConfigureBefore`, or `@AutoConfigureAfter` to control this order relative to other configurations.

Conclusion

Customizing Spring Boot starters and auto-configurations is vital for developers aiming to align the framework more closely with their specific application needs. Whether by creating new starters, modifying existing ones, or managing the sequence of auto-configurations, these customizations can significantly enhance both the functionality and efficiency of a Spring Boot application. Such flexibility is essential for developing complex, high-performing applications that are finely tuned to meet specific business goals.

Fine-tuning Spring Boot applications with environment-specific parameters

Optimizing Spring Boot applications by adjusting configurations specific to deployment environments is a crucial strategy for enhancing performance, security, and resource management. Distinct environments, such as development, testing, and production, often necessitate different settings due to their unique resource availability, security needs, and other operational parameters. Utilizing Spring Boot's capabilities for externalizing configurations and setting environment-specific parameters can significantly improve an application's efficiency and effectiveness.

The Importance of Environment-Specific Tuning

Optimizing applications for specific environments offers numerous benefits:

- Performance Optimization: Adjusting configurations like JVM settings and database connections according to the available resources in each environment can boost application performance.

- Security Enhancements: Security configurations may vary greatly between environments, with production environments generally requiring stricter security controls than development settings.

- Resource Management: Tailoring resource usage and service integrations based on the environment can lead to cost savings and enhanced system reliability.

Implementing Environment-Specific Configurations in Spring Boot

Spring Boot facilitates environment-specific configuration primarily through the use of profiles, which enable developers to define and activate sets of configurations based on the environment.

Utilizing Profiles

Spring Boot profiles allow configurations to be grouped and activated only in specified environments. This is commonly managed through the `spring.profiles.active` property in configuration files like `application.properties` or `application.yml`, or can be specified programmatically or via command-line options at runtime.

For example, defining different database settings for `dev` and `prod` profiles in `application.yml` might look like this:

```yaml
spring:
  profiles:
    active: dev

---

spring:
  config:
    activate:
      on-profile: dev
  datasource:
    url: jdbc:postgresql://localhost/devdb
    username: devuser
    password: devpass

---

spring:
  config:
    activate:
      on-profile: prod
  datasource:
    url: jdbc:postgresql://production-host/proddb
    username: produser
    password: prodpass
```

This configuration ensures that the application connects to the appropriate database depending on whether it is in development or production mode.

Externalizing Configurations

Configurations in Spring Boot can be externalized through:

- Properties Files: Profiles can have associated `application-{profile}.properties` or `.yml` files containing environment-specific settings.

- Environment Variables: Useful in cloud deployments or with Docker/Kubernetes, allowing settings to be passed without altering code.

- Command-line Arguments: These can override existing configurations and are handy for passing sensitive or critical last-minute adjustments.

For instance, to override the active profile and database URL at launch, one might use:

```
java -jar myapp.jar --spring.profiles.active=prod --spring.datasource.url=jdbc
    :postgresql://alternate-host/proddb
```

Configuration Properties for Fine-Tuning

Spring Boot's `@ConfigurationProperties` annotation helps in defining grouped properties within structured objects, enhancing type safety and centralized management.

```java
@Component
@ConfigurationProperties(prefix = "app.messaging")
public class MessagingProperties {
    private String brokerUrl;
    private String queueName;

    // getters and setters
}
```

Properties like these can be customized in environment-specific files or through other external sources, tailoring behavior across different deployment scenarios.

Conclusion

Tailoring Spring Boot applications with specific parameters for each environment is crucial for ensuring optimal operation, security, and resource utilization. By leveraging profiles and externalized configurations, developers can create versatile applications that adapt seamlessly across different deployment environments. This adaptability not only ensures consistent performance but also simplifies ongoing application maintenance and lifecycle management.

Chapter Two

JVM Performance Optimization

Understanding JVM internals and its impact on Spring Boot

The Java Virtual Machine (JVM) is fundamental to the performance and efficiency of Java applications, including those developed on the Spring Boot platform. Profound comprehension of JVM internals is paramount for enhancing and stabilizing Spring Boot applications. This deep insight allows developers to strategically adjust the application's behaviors to suit varied operational environments effectively.

Critical JVM Elements Impacting Spring Boot Applications

1. Memory Management

The JVM manages system memory across the heap, stack, and method areas. The heap stores runtime data such as objects and Java Runtime Environment (JRE) class representations and is managed by the garbage collector. The stack holds local variables and method calls essential for executing methods, while the method area stores class structure, including constants, field and method data, plus the code for methods and constructors.

For Spring Boot applications, particularly in microservices where multiple service instances may run across various containers, adept memory management is crucial. Configuring the heap size and garbage collection settings appropriately can prevent memory overflows and maintain a responsive application performance.

Example JVM Memory Management Configuration:

```
java -Xms512m -Xmx1024m -XX:+UseG1GC -jar myapplication.jar
```

This command configures the initial (`-Xms`) and maximum (`-Xmx`) heap sizes and employs the G1 Garbage Collector (`-XX:+UseG1GC`), favored for its efficiency in handling large memory spaces with minimal pause times.

2. Just-In-Time (JIT) Compilation

The JIT compiler enhances Java applications' performance by converting bytecode into native machine code at runtime. Understanding and managing JIT compilation is crucial for optimizing compute-intensive sections of a Spring Boot application.

Enabling insights into JIT compilation processes can be facilitated by specific JVM tools and flags that delineate method compilation frequencies and behaviors.

3. Classloading

The JVM's classloader is integral, loading classes into memory upon first access. Given Spring Boot's extensive class and dependency inventory, efficient classloading is essential for reducing startup times and optimizing memory use.

You can monitor classloading activities with JVM diagnostic commands:

```
jcmd <pid> VM.classloader_stats
```

4. Thread Management

The JVM handles threads crucial for executing concurrent tasks in Java applications. Spring Boot uses thread pools to efficiently manage request handling. Proper configuration of these pools is crucial for maintaining performance under various load conditions.

Example Spring Boot Thread Pool Configuration:

```java
@Bean
public TaskExecutor taskExecutor() {
    ThreadPoolTaskExecutor executor = new ThreadPoolTaskExecutor();
    executor.setCorePoolSize(10);
    executor.setMaxPoolSize(50);
    executor.setQueueCapacity(100);
    executor.initialize();
    return executor;
}
```

5. Garbage Collection (GC)

Garbage collection is a vital JVM function impacting application performance. Effective garbage collection is especially crucial in web and microservices environments, where applications frequently create and discard numerous short-lived objects. Choosing and tuning the right garbage collector can significantly minimize disruptive pauses and enhance application fluidity.

Here is how to specify a garbage collector:

```
java -XX:+UseG1GC -jar myapplication.jar
```

In this example, the G1 Garbage Collector is activated, known for its effective management of heap space and predictable garbage collection pauses.

Conclusion

A deep understanding of JVM internals is essential for optimizing Spring Boot applications effectively. Through meticulous memory management, leveraging JIT compilation, optimizing class loading, managing threads effectively, and choosing the appropriate garbage collection strategy, developers can markedly improve the performance and robustness of their Spring Boot applications. This comprehensive knowledge facilitates refined adjustments to the application, ensuring alignment with JVM operations and meeting specific application demands.

JVM options and garbage collection tuning for Spring Boot applications

Optimizing the Java Virtual Machine (JVM) settings is crucial for maximizing the efficiency and performance of Spring Boot applications. Adjustments to JVM options, particularly those governing garbage collection (GC), play a vital role in resource management and can significantly impact the application's throughput and responsiveness.

Key JVM Options Impacting Spring Boot

The JVM offers various options that affect its behavior, many of which involve memory management and garbage collection. Properly configuring these options can enhance application response times, boost throughput, and ensure efficient resource utilization.

Important JVM Parameters

1. Heap Memory Options: Setting the `-Xms` and `-Xmx` parameters appropriately defines the initial and maximum heap size, respectively. These settings are crucial as they dictate how much memory the JVM will allocate, impacting both performance and resource consumption.

```
java -Xms512m -Xmx2048m -jar myapplication.jar
```

This line sets the initial heap size to 512 MB and the maximum size to 2 GB, optimizing memory usage for the application's needs.

2. Thread Stack Size: Configuring the `-Xss` option adjusts the stack size per thread, which is essential for controlling memory allocation and avoiding stack overflow errors in applications with deep recursion or high concurrency.

```
java -Xss256k -jar myapplication.jar
```

This command sets each thread's stack size to 256 KB, which is typically adequate for moderately complex applications.

Garbage Collection Optimization for Spring Boot

Tuning the garbage collection process is key for applications that generate a significant number of short-lived objects, a common scenario in web applications built with Spring Boot.

Selecting an Appropriate Garbage Collector

Choosing the right garbage collector is dependent on the application's specific needs:

1. Throughput Collector (Parallel GC): Suitable for applications where overall throughput is the priority, with longer GC pauses being acceptable. It is enabled with `-XX:+UseParallelGC`.

2. Concurrent Mark Sweep (CMS): Aimed at applications that require lower latency, it uses additional CPU resources to minimize pause times. Enabled using `-XX:+UseConcMarkSweepGC`.

3. G1 Garbage Collector: Best for multi-core systems with large memory, where scalability and predictable pauses are required. Activated with `-XX:+UseG1GC`.

Example of G1 GC usage:

```
java -XX:+UseG1GC -jar myapplication.jar
```

Fine-Tuning Garbage Collection Parameters

Optimizing GC involves adjusting specific parameters to refine the garbage collection behavior:

1. Young Generation Size: Managed by `-Xmn` or `-XX:NewRatio`, adjusting this affects how often minor collections occur.

2. Targeting GC Pause Times: The `-XX:MaxGCPauseMillis` setting helps establish goals for maximum GC pause times, influencing the JVM's attempt to meet these targets.

3. Adaptive Size Policy: Using `-XX:+UseAdaptiveSizePolicy` lets the JVM adjust the sizing of the young and old generations dynamically based on the application's behavior.

Monitoring and Diagnostics

Monitoring the effects of JVM configurations on a Spring Boot application is critical. Tools like VisualVM, JConsole, and command-line utilities such as `jstat` provide insights into memory consumption and garbage collection efficiency.

Example of using `jstat` for GC monitoring:

```
jstat -gc <pid> 1000
```

This tool monitors garbage collection metrics in real time, outputting data every second to help identify potential issues with the current GC settings.

Conclusion

Fine-tuning JVM options and garbage collection settings is integral to enhancing the performance and stability of Spring Boot applications. By thoughtfully selecting and configuring these options, developers can significantly improve application efficiency and responsiveness. Continuous monitoring and adaptive adjustments based on actual performance data are essential to maintain optimal settings as application demands evolve.

Profiling and monitoring JVM for optimal performance

Profiling and monitoring the Java Virtual Machine (JVM) are essential techniques for enhancing the performance of Java applications, particularly those built using Spring Boot. These methods enable developers to identify performance issues, optimize resource allocation, and ensure that applications run smoothly under varying operational conditions.

Importance of Profiling and Monitoring the JVM

Gathering detailed runtime data through JVM profiling and monitoring is crucial. It allows developers to observe CPU utilization, memory consumption, threading behavior, and garbage collection processes in real-time. These insights enable the refinement of application performance, ensuring proactive optimization and maintenance.

Effective Tools for JVM Profiling and Monitoring

A range of tools is available for detailed profiling and monitoring of the JVM, offering capabilities that range from basic to advanced, catering to different needs whether in development or production environments.

1. VisualVM

VisualVM integrates multiple command-line JDK tools into a single graphical interface, providing a comprehensive monitoring tool for the JVM.

- Capabilities: It tracks memory and CPU usage, provides thread dumps, analyzes heap content, monitors garbage collection activities, and profiles application performance.

- How to Use:

```
jvisualvm
```

Launch VisualVM and link it to a JVM instance to initiate detailed monitoring and profiling.

2. JConsole

JConsole is another graphical monitoring tool included in the Java Development Kit (JDK) that leverages Java Management Extensions (JMX) to collect data on Java application performance.

- Capabilities: It monitors memory usage, threading information, class loading statistics, and long-term JVM behavior.

- How to Use:

```
jconsole
```

Start JConsole to connect it to any Java process running locally or remotely.

3. jStat

jStat is a command-line utility focused on JVM performance statistics, ideal for environments where GUI-based tools are impractical.

- Capabilities: It specializes in tracking garbage collection and JVM heap statistics.

- How to Use:

```
jstat -gcutil <pid> 1000
```

Run jStat to monitor garbage collection metrics continuously, updating every second, for a specified JVM process.

Best Practices for Profiling and Monitoring JVM

Implementing best practices in JVM profiling and monitoring can significantly improve the efficiency of Java applications:

- Continuous Monitoring: Regular monitoring should be an integral part of system operations to quickly detect and address performance issues and to evaluate the impact of any modifications.

- Development and Testing Profiling: Conduct frequent profiling during the development and testing stages to identify and fix performance issues before they affect production environments.

- Garbage Collection Fine-Tuning: Adjust garbage collection settings based on profiling outcomes to minimize disruption and enhance application responsiveness.

410

- Resource Configuration Based on Data: Modify JVM configurations such as heap size and thread settings according to real-time data to ensure optimal performance and resource utilization.

- Automated Alerts: Set up alerts for key JVM metrics such as high memory usage or thread spikes to promptly address deviations from expected performance.

Conclusion

Regular profiling and monitoring of the JVM are vital for maintaining optimal performance and stability in Java applications. Utilizing tools like VisualVM, JConsole, and jstat provides developers with the detailed insights needed to manage application resources effectively. Systematic application of these monitoring and profiling techniques ensures that Java applications are robust, efficient, and ready to meet the challenges of diverse operational environments.

Chapter Three

Spring Boot Application Tuning

Optimizing Spring framework core components (IoC, AOP)

Refining the Spring Framework's pivotal components, Inversion of Control (IoC) and Aspect-Oriented Programming (AOP), is essential for enhancing the functionality, performance, and scalability of applications developed using Spring. Proper adjustment and fine-tuning of these components greatly improve development efficiency and application execution.

Fine-Tuning Inversion of Control (IoC)

The IoC container is integral to the Spring Framework, responsible for managing the lifecycle and configurations of application components. This functionality supports loose coupling and simplifies the testing process. Optimizing how the IoC container is utilized can accelerate application startup and improve runtime efficiency.

1. Appropriate Bean Scoping: Spring offers various bean scopes—singleton, prototype, request, session, and global session. Choosing the correct scope is vital for optimizing resource use and reducing overhead. Typically, the singleton scope, which is the default, optimizes performance by limiting the number of bean instances created. However, beans that

need to maintain state per user or request might be better suited to request or session scopes.

```
@Component
@Scope("singleton") // Explicitly setting the scope for clarity
public class SingletonService {
    // Implementation details
}
```

2. Implementing Lazy Initialization: Spring usually instantiates all singleton beans at application startup by default. Enabling lazy initialization for some beans can lessen initial load times by delaying bean creation until they are first required.

```
@Component
@Lazy
public class LazyService {
    // Implementation details
}
```

3. Preferring Constructor Injection: Using constructor injection over field injection improves testability, supports immutability, and ensures that necessary dependencies are present at construction, which simplifies application context management.

```
@Component
public class CustomerService {
    private final AccountService accountService;

    @Autowired
    public CustomerService(AccountService accountService) {
        this.accountService = accountService;
    }
}
```

Optimizing Aspect-Oriented Programming (AOP)

AOP separates concerns like logging, security, and transaction management from business logic, improving code modularity and clarity. However, AOP needs meticulous management to prevent it from becoming a source of performance overhead.

1. Efficient Pointcut Expressions: Crafting precise and minimal pointcut expressions prevents unnecessary advice execution, which can hinder performance.

```
@Aspect
@Component
public class AuditAspect {
    @Before("execution(* com.example.service.*.*(..))") // Targeted pointcut
    public void logMethodEntry(JoinPoint joinPoint) {
        // Logging logic
    }
}
```

2. Selecting Proxy Types: Spring AOP supports JDK dynamic proxies for interfaces and CGLIB proxies for classes. Where possible, interface-based proxies are preferred as they are generally faster and consume fewer resources.

```
@Aspect
@Component
@Scope(proxyMode = ScopedProxyMode.INTERFACES) // Opting for interface-based proxies
public class EncryptionAspect {
    // Aspect implementation
}
```

3. Conditional Advice Application: Applying AOP advice conditionally, especially for operations that are resource-intensive, can optimize performance and prevent slowdowns in production.

```java
@Aspect
@Component
public class MonitoringAspect {

    @Around("@annotation(Monitor) && execution(* com.example..*(..))")
    public Object monitor(ProceedingJoinPoint joinPoint) throws Throwable {
        if (!monitoringEnabled()) {
            return joinPoint.proceed();
        }

        long startTime = System.currentTimeMillis();
        try {
            return joinPoint.proceed();
        } finally {
            logDuration(joinPoint, System.currentTimeMillis() - startTime);
        }
    }

    private void logDuration(JoinPoint joinPoint, long duration) {
        logger.info(joinPoint.getSignature() + " took " + duration + "ms");
    }

    private boolean monitoringEnabled() {
        // Check if monitoring is enabled
        return false; // Example
    }
}
```

Conclusion

Effectively optimizing IoC and AOP within the Spring Framework can dramatically improve the performance and manageability of Spring applications. By adopting strategies such as correctly scoping beans, enabling lazy initialization, and precisely applying AOP, developers can ensure their applications are not only efficient but also robust and scalable. Continuous refinement based on performance feedback is crucial for maintaining optimal application functionality as needs evolve.

415

Efficient database interaction and connection pooling

Streamlining database interactions and managing connection pooling effectively are key for enhancing the performance of database-driven applications. Proper handling of these elements can significantly decrease latency, boost throughput, and scale applications efficiently by minimizing the overhead associated with managing database connections and executing SQL commands.

Importance of Connection Pooling

Connection pooling is a technique used to manage and reuse a fixed set of database connection objects instead of repeatedly opening and closing new connections. This approach is beneficial for several reasons:

Advantages of Connection Pooling:

1. Reduced Latency: Reusing existing connections eliminates the time-consuming process of establishing new connections, which is particularly valuable in high-traffic scenarios.

2. Controlled Resource Usage: Connection pools restrict the number of open connections to the database, preventing excessive use that could lead to database slowdowns or failures.

3. Scalability Improvements: By managing connections efficiently, applications can handle more transactions or users simultaneously without proportionally increasing resource usage.

Best Practices for Database Interaction and Connection Pooling

1. Choosing a Connection Pool Library: Various libraries such as HikariCP, Apache Commons DBCP, and C3P0 offer connection pooling capabilities. HikariCP is often favored for its superior performance and minimal configuration overhead. Select a library that aligns with the specific requirements and performance criteria of your application.

Example configuration for HikariCP in Spring Boot:

```java
@Configuration
public class DataSourceConfiguration {

    @Bean
    public DataSource dataSource() {
        HikariConfig hikariConfig = new HikariConfig();
        hikariConfig.setDriverClassName("com.mysql.jdbc.Driver");
        hikariConfig.setJdbcUrl("jdbc:mysql://localhost:3306/sampledb");
        hikariConfig.setUsername("root");
        hikariConfig.setPassword("password");

        hikariConfig.setMaximumPoolSize(10);
        hikariConfig.setAutoCommit(true);
        hikariConfig.addDataSourceProperty("cachePrepStmts", "true");
        hikariConfig.addDataSourceProperty("prepStmtCacheSize", "250");
        hikariConfig.addDataSourceProperty("prepStmtCacheSqlLimit", "2048");

        return new HikariDataSource(hikariConfig);
    }
}
```

2. Optimizing SQL Execution: Improving SQL command efficiency and employing prepared statements can reduce database server strain and enhance application throughput.

- Prepared Statements: These are essential for both performance and security. They enable SQL statement pre-compilation and efficient reuse.

```
String sql = "UPDATE accounts SET balance = ? WHERE account_id = ?";
PreparedStatement statement = connection.prepareStatement(sql);
statement.setDouble(1, newBalance);
statement.setInt(2, accountId);
statement.executeUpdate();
```

3. Tuning Connection Pool Settings: Regular adjustment of connection pool parameters is crucial to align with application demand and ensure optimal performance:

- Pool Size: Adjust the pool size based on peak load observations and database capability.

- Connection Timeout: Configure suitable timeouts for connection acquisitions to manage demand spikes effectively.

- Management of Idle Connections: Optimize the handling of idle connections to balance resource efficiency against instant availability.

4. Managing Transactions Efficiently: Effective transaction management helps reduce database lock times and resource contention, thus improving overall application responsiveness. Use appropriate isolation levels and manage transaction timeouts strategically to avoid long-held locks that could degrade performance.

Conclusion

Mastering database interactions and connection pooling is fundamental for optimizing the performance of applications that rely heavily on databases. By implementing effective connection pooling strategies, optimizing SQL interactions, and continuously refining these configurations, developers can ensure their applications are robust, responsive, and capable of scaling effectively. Regular updates and tuning in response to application changes and load variations are crucial to sustain optimal performance levels.

Best practices for managing application contexts and beans

In the world of Spring Framework development, proficient management of application contexts and beans is crucial for crafting efficient, scalable, and maintainable applications. Application contexts serve as the backbone of Spring's potent dependency injection capabilities, while beans represent the objects managed within these contexts. Below, we delve into the top practices for overseeing these vital components.

Grasping Application Contexts and Beans

Within Spring, an application context acts as a sophisticated factory that maintains a registry of diverse beans and their dependencies. By employing an application context, Spring can handle bean lifecycles, configure beans, and facilitate dependency injection, among other functions.

Prime Practices for Application Contexts Management

1. Embrace Configuration Classes: In contemporary Spring applications, preference is given to Java-based configuration, offering greater type safety and ease of refactoring compared

to XML configurations. Configuration classes, annotated with `@Configuration`, serve as a logical space to define and compose beans.

```
@Configuration
public class AppConfig {
    @Bean
    public MyService myService() {
        return new MyServiceImpl();
    }
}
```

This approach provides clear and concise management of bean definitions, particularly beneficial for large applications necessitating modular configuration.

2. Leverage Component Scanning: To minimize manual bean registration, Spring can automatically detect and register beans through `@ComponentScan`. This is often coupled with stereotype annotations like `@Component, @Service`, `@Repository`, and `@Controller`, which aid in semantically distinguishing the roles of each bean within the application.

```
@Configuration
@ComponentScan(basePackages = "com.example.app")
public class AppConfig {
}
```

This setup directs Spring to scan the specified package and automatically register all appropriately annotated classes, simplifying configuration.

3. Implement Lazy Initialization: To expedite application startup time, lazy initialization can be employed so that beans

are instantiated only upon their first request, rather than at startup.

```java
@Configuration
@Lazy
public class LazyConfig {
    @Bean
    public ExpensiveToCreateBean expensiveBean() {
        return new ExpensiveToCreateBean();
    }
}
```

Applying `@Lazy` at the configuration level ensures that all beans defined in this configuration are lazy by default, resulting in noticeable performance improvements, particularly in sizable applications.

Prime Practices for Bean Management

1. Scope Appropriately: Spring manages bean scoping to determine how instances of a bean should be shared. While the default scope is singleton, other scopes like prototype, request, session, and application may be more suitable depending on the use case.

```java
@Bean
@Scope(ConfigurableBeanFactory.SCOPE_PROTOTYPE)
public MyPrototypeBean prototypeBean() {
    return new MyPrototypeBean();
}
```

Choosing the appropriate scope ensures the application behaves as intended and optimally utilizes resources.

2. Prioritize Constructor Injection: Preferring constructor injection over field injection enhances code testability and

guarantees that required dependencies are not null. It also promotes immutability and simplifies application debugging.

```
@Service
public class BookService {
    private final BookRepository bookRepository;

    @Autowired
    public BookService(BookRepository bookRepository) {
        this.bookRepository = bookRepository;
    }
}
```

This pattern is highly recommended as it clearly defines mandatory dependencies and adheres to the principle of inversion of control.

3. Employ Profile-Driven Beans: For applications operating in diverse environments, employing profiles to conditionally register beans is a sound practice. This enables developers to define beans that are only accessible in specific environments.

```
@Configuration
@Profile("development")
public class DevConfig {
    @Bean
    public DataSource dataSource() {
        return new EmbeddedDatabaseBuilder().build();
    }
}
```

Profiles aid in maintaining a clean separation between development, testing, and production configurations, mitigating the risk of misconfiguration across environments.

In Conclusion

Effectively managing application contexts and beans is paramount for harnessing the full potential of the Spring Framework. By adhering to best practices such as employing configuration classes, implementing lazy initialization, scoping beans appropriately, prioritizing constructor injection, and utilizing profiles, developers can create Spring applications that are both performant and easily maintainable. These strategies ensure that applications are not only robust but also adaptable to evolving business requirements.

Chapter Four

High-Performance RESTful Services

Techniques for optimizing RESTful service performance

Enhancing the performance of RESTful services is crucial in the development of modern web applications where high efficiency and swift responsiveness are required. RESTful services, which operate on the principles of representational state transfer, are fundamental to seamless web interactions. This article outlines essential strategies for improving their performance, vital for boosting user experience and application scalability.

1. Proper Use of HTTP Methods

RESTful services rely on standard HTTP methods for operations, each serving a specific function. Correctly using these methods not only clarifies API operations but also enhances performance through effective caching and streamlined data processing:

- **GET** for retrieving resources.

- **POST** to create new resources.

- **PUT** for updating existing resources.

- **DELETE** to remove resources.

Employing the correct method facilitates optimal caching and efficient data retrieval, thereby reducing server load.

2. Implementing Caching Mechanisms

Caching is a powerful technique to elevate RESTful service performance. By storing previously fetched data, caching cuts down redundant server requests and speeds up response times.

- **Client-side caching** can be implemented with HTTP cache headers like `Cache-Control`, `ETag`, and `Last-Modified`, which help manage cache freshness and revalidation.

```
Cache-Control: max-age=3600
ETag: "a1b2c3d4"
```

- **Server-side caching** involves temporary storage of data or computed results using in-memory stores such as Redis or Memcached, reducing the need to recompute or fetch data frequently.

3. Database Interaction Optimization

The efficiency of database operations is critical for RESTful APIs, particularly those that manage extensive datasets. Enhancing database performance can be achieved through:

- **Indexing:** Apply indexes to frequently queried fields to reduce lookup times.

- **Query Optimization:** Streamline SQL queries to avoid unnecessary data processing and costly joins.

- **Connection Pooling:** Utilize connection pools to manage database connections, which minimizes the overhead of opening and closing connections repeatedly.

4. Asynchronous Operations

Handling operations asynchronously can significantly improve the throughput of RESTful services, particularly for processes that are not instantaneously completed.

- **Asynchronous Requests:** Frameworks like Spring WebFlux and technologies such as Node.js allow for non-blocking request handling, enabling other processes to execute without waiting for the current one to finish.

- **Message Queues:** For deferred or time-consuming tasks, using message queues such as RabbitMQ or Kafka helps by offloading these tasks from the request-response cycle.

5. Load Balancing Techniques

Utilizing load balancing improves service availability and responsiveness by distributing incoming network traffic across multiple servers.

- Strategies include:

    - **Round-Robin** – evenly distributing requests across all servers.

    - **Least Connections** – sending requests to the server with the fewest active connections.

- **IP Hash** – directing user requests based on IP hash to the same server consistently.

Tools like NGINX or cloud services such as AWS Elastic Load Balancing can facilitate effective load distribution.

6. Reducing Payload Sizes

Minimizing the size of the data transmitted in requests and responses can lead to quicker transmissions, particularly over slower networks.

- **Compression:** Implementing gzip compression reduces the data size, facilitating faster data transfer.

- **Field Selection:** Allowing clients to specify required fields, through techniques like GraphQL or RESTful sparse fieldsets, minimizes the data transferred.

```
Accept-Encoding: gzip
```

7. Continuous Monitoring and Profiling

Regular monitoring and profiling of RESTful services are necessary to identify and resolve performance bottlenecks. Using performance monitoring tools like New Relic or Prometheus can provide valuable metrics on response times, error rates, and server resource utilization, guiding further optimizations.

Conclusion

Optimizing RESTful service performance involves multiple strategies from the effective use of HTTP methods to sophisticated caching and load balancing. By adopting these techniques, developers can ensure their RESTful APIs are not only functional but also performant across varied load conditions. Continuous monitoring and iterative improvements based on usage data are critical for maintaining superior performance.

Advanced content negotiation and versioning strategies

In modern web development, proficiently handling content negotiation and API versioning is crucial to ensure that applications stay adaptable, maintainable, and backward-compatible. These advanced techniques allow services to cater to varied client requirements and evolve seamlessly without disrupting existing functionalities.

Advanced Content Negotiation

Content negotiation allows a web server to select the most suitable content format to send in response to a client's request, based on the client's expressed preferences in HTTP headers. Employing advanced techniques in content negotiation enhances the adaptability and user experience of web services.

1. Utilizing the Accept Header:

The `Accept` header in an HTTP request lets clients indicate the media types they are prepared to accept from the server. The server uses this information to determine the optimal format for the response. For instance, the server might choose to return data in HTML or JSON format depending on the client's preferences expressed through the Accept header.

```
GET /api/resource HTTP/1.1
Host: example.com
Accept: application/json
```

2. Defining Custom Media Types:

A sophisticated approach involves using custom media types. This not only specifies the media type but also embeds version information, enabling precise control over the content format.

```
Accept: application/vnd.myapp.v1+json
```

This tells the server that the client expects JSON formatted according to version 1 of "myapp's" specific format.

3. URL or Parameter-based Negotiation:

Some APIs provide format options directly in the URL path or through query parameters. This method is straightforward for clients but can complicate server logic.

URL suffix example:

```
GET /api/resource.json
```

Query parameter example:

```
GET /api/resource?format=json
```

API Versioning Strategies

Proper versioning is essential for the evolutionary growth of APIs without breaking existing client integrations. Several strategies effectively manage different API versions:

1. URI Versioning:

Including the version number in the URI is a common method that clearly communicates the API version, simplifying routing and maintenance.

```
GET /api/v1/resource
```

2. Header Versioning:

Versioning can also be managed through custom headers. This approach keeps URLs clean and unchanging but may make version management less visible and potentially more complex for some clients.

```
GET /api/resource HTTP/1.1
API-Version: v1
```

3. Query Parameter Versioning:

Using a query parameter for versioning is an intuitive method but mixes resource identification with meta-attributes of the request.

```
GET /api/resource?version=1
```

Key Considerations for Effective Versioning and Negotiation

Implementing sophisticated content negotiation and versioning strategies involves several important considerations:

- Clear Documentation: Ensure that the mechanisms for content negotiation and versioning are well-documented, including all available media types and version identifiers.

430

- Structured Deprecation Strategy: Develop a structured policy for phasing out older versions of your API and media types, giving clients sufficient notice and guidance for migration.

- Comprehensive Testing: Implement comprehensive testing for all API versions to confirm that updates do not impact existing client integrations adversely.

Conclusion

Mastering advanced content negotiation and versioning is fundamental in modern API architecture, enabling APIs to efficiently meet diverse client needs and smoothly transition through updates. By carefully implementing and documenting these capabilities, developers can craft APIs that are both powerful and straightforward to use, ensuring compatibility as new functionalities are introduced. The choice of strategy should align with the application's specific requirements and its users' needs, balancing between flexibility, simplicity, and robustness.

Implementing caching and compression for API responses

Optimizing API responses through caching and compression significantly boosts web service performance and scalability. These methods decrease both server and network strain, leading to quicker response times and more efficient data transmission, ultimately enhancing user experience.

Overview of Caching Mechanisms

Caching is a technique where data is temporarily stored to facilitate quick retrieval without the need for repeated processing or fetching from the backend, effectively reducing server load and latency.

1. Server-Side Caching:

This involves storing commonly requested data on the server or an intermediate caching server. This arrangement allows data to be served quickly, avoiding the need for frequent database hits or complex computations. Implementing such a caching layer often involves using technologies like Redis or Memcached.

```
// Implementing Redis caching in Spring Boot
@Bean
public CacheManager cacheManager(RedisConnectionFactory connectionFactory) {
    RedisCacheConfiguration config = RedisCacheConfiguration.defaultCacheConfig
        ()
        .entryTtl(Duration.ofHours(1)) // Time-to-live of cache entries
        .disableCachingNullValues()
        .serializeValuesWith(RedisSerializationContext.SerializationPair
            .fromSerializer(new GenericJackson2JsonRedisSerializer()));

    return RedisCacheManager.builder(connectionFactory)
        .cacheDefaults(config)
        .build();
}
```

2. Client-Side Caching:

Client-side caching employs HTTP headers to instruct the client's browser or application on how to store response data. Using headers such as `**Cache-Control**`, `**Expires**`, and `**ETag**` helps control the caching behavior on the client side.

```
Cache-Control: max-age=3600, must-revalidate
ETag: "abcd1234"
```

Leveraging Compression Techniques

Compression involves reducing the size of API responses before they are sent across the network, which speeds up the transmission, particularly important for clients with slower network connections.

1. GZIP Compression:

GZIP is commonly employed for compressing data in web communications. Web servers like Apache and Nginx, as well as application frameworks such as Spring Boot, can be configured to automatically compress API responses.

```
# Configuring GZIP in Nginx for API responses
gzip on;
gzip_types text/plain application/json;
gzip_proxied any;
```

2. Enabling Compression in Application Servers:

In Java-based applications, particularly those using Spring Boot, response compression can be enabled via simple property settings.

```
# Activating compression in Spring Boot
server.compression.enabled=true
server.compression.mime-types=application/json,application/xml,text/html,text/xml
    ,text/plain
```

Best Practices for Caching and Compression

1. Discriminative Caching:

It's essential to discern what data benefits from being cached. Static or rarely changed data is ideal for caching, while dynamic or personalized data typically should not be cached to prevent serving outdated information.

2. Strategies for Cache Invalidation:

Create effective techniques for updating or invalidating cached data when underlying data changes. This can involve strategies such as setting expiration times, employing version tags, and actively clearing caches.

3. Monitoring System Performance:

Regularly monitor the effects of caching and compression on your system's performance. Tools like Google Lighthouse and Chrome Dev Tools are useful for assessing the impact on response times and overall system load.

4. Security Precautions:

Pay attention to security implications of caching and compression, particularly when handling sensitive information. Take measures to mitigate risks such as potential data breaches facilitated by compression techniques.

Conclusion

Implementing caching and compression for API responses is a vital strategy for optimizing the performance of web services. These methods enhance the efficiency of data handling and reduce server workload, leading to an improved user interface. Properly managing these techniques, continually monitoring their impact, and adapting strategies based on security and data integrity considerations are key to harnessing their full potential while avoiding potential pitfalls.

Chapter Five

Reactive Programming with Spring Boot

Introduction to Reactive programming and its advantages

Reactive programming is a design paradigm focused on processing data streams and propagating changes, making it highly suitable for systems requiring high responsiveness, resilience, elasticity, and message-driven capabilities. This method is especially valuable for applications handling real-time data or facing intense operational demands, enhancing both system responsiveness and user interaction.

Essentials of Reactive Programming

Reactive programming involves managing asynchronous data streams that emit various types of data or events over time, including user actions or server responses. Observers subscribe to these streams and react to the incoming data in real time.

Core Components:

- Observable: This component acts as a producer in a stream, emitting data or events that observers can handle.

- Observer: These are consumers that react to and process the data or events emitted by observables.

- Subscription: This connection manages the interaction between an observable and an observer, controlling data flow and handling lifecycle events.

- Operators: These are methods or functions that allow for manipulation and transformation of data streams, enabling sophisticated data handling strategies.

Benefits of Reactive Programming

1. Enhanced Scalability and Efficiency:

The asynchronous and non-blocking characteristics of reactive programming allow for significant scalability and resource efficiency. This capability is crucial for applications with high transaction volumes or user concurrency, enabling effective performance without substantial hardware resources.

2. Effectiveness in Real-Time Applications:

Reactive programming is highly beneficial for applications that depend on the timely update of data, such as financial monitoring systems, instant messaging apps, or interactive gaming. It ensures seamless and efficient management of data streams.

3. Improved Error Handling and Resilience:

One of the standout benefits of reactive programming is its robust approach to error management. It allows individual components of an application to fail without impacting the entire system, thereby enhancing overall system reliability and uptime.

4. Simplified Code and Maintenance:

Reactive programming addresses the complexities traditionally associated with asynchronous data handling by treating data as streams. This approach simplifies operations and transformations on these data streams, leading to cleaner, more maintainable code.

Example with RxJava

RxJava, a prominent library that supports reactive programming within the Java ecosystem, provides a comprehensive toolkit for managing data streams.

```java
import io.reactivex.rxjava3.core.Observable;

public class SimpleReactiveExample {
    public static void main(String[] args) {
        // Establishing an observable stream of numbers
        Observable<Integer> numberStream = Observable.range(1, 5);

        // Transforming data within the stream and subscribing to the outputs
        numberStream.map(n -> n * n)
                .subscribe(System.out::println);
    }
}
```

In this example, an observable emits a simple sequence of integers, which are then squared and printed. This demonstrates how reactive programming facilitates easy manipulation and handling of asynchronous data streams.

Conclusion

Reactive programming is an effective paradigm for creating applications that need to manage dynamic data streams efficiently. It provides tools for enhanced responsiveness, better error resilience, and simplified code architecture, making it indispensable for modern, interactive applications. As the need for real-time processing and sophisticated interaction models in software continues to grow, the principles of reactive programming become increasingly critical. Adopting this paradigm allows developers to build applications that are not only high-performing but also more manageable and scalable, aligning with the demands of contemporary software development challenges.

Building Reactive APIs with Spring WebFlux

Spring WebFlux is engineered to support the creation of non-blocking, asynchronous web applications that effectively handle vast volumes of concurrent users and intensive data transfers while optimizing resource use. As a key component of Spring 5, WebFlux integrates reactive programming principles using the Reactive Streams API, which is adept at managing back pressure and orchestrating reactive streams efficiently.

Overview of Spring WebFlux

Spring WebFlux presents a reactive framework alternative to the traditional Spring MVC. Diverging from MVC's reliance on a servlet API and thread-per-request strategy, WebFlux adopts an event-driven model leveraging non-blocking I/O. This approach requires fewer threads to manage web requests, thus enhancing scalability and minimizing operational overhead.

Prominent Features of Spring WebFlux

- Non-blocking Operations: WebFlux facilitates fully non-blocking I/O operations, making it apt for handling

438

scenarios that involve continuous data interactions or user engagement.

- Back Pressure Handling: It incorporates the Reactive Streams API to manage data flow effectively, ensuring downstream consumers are not overwhelmed by the data influx.

- Adaptable Routing Mechanisms: WebFlux supports both traditional MVC-style annotated controllers and functional routing approaches, offering developers flexibility in how they handle web requests.

Building APIs with Spring WebFlux

To begin with Spring WebFlux, set up a Spring Boot application with the necessary dependencies for reactive programming, primarily incorporating the `**spring-boot-starter-webflux**`.

```
<dependency>
    <groupId>org.springframework.boot</groupId>
    <artifactId>spring-boot-starter-webflux</artifactId>
</dependency>
```

Crafting a Reactive API: An Example

Below is a straightforward example demonstrating the development of a reactive API using Spring WebFlux, which involves interactions with a reactive database and the setup of RESTful services.

Step 1: Data Model Definition

Imagine a basic `**Product**` entity:

```java
import org.springframework.data.annotation.Id;
import org.springframework.data.relational.core.mapping.Table;

@Table
public class Product {
    @Id
    private String id;
    private String name;
    private double price;

    // Accessors and mutators...
}
```

Step 2: Reactive Repository Creation

Spring Data supports reactive CRUD operations through simple repository interfaces:

```java
import org.springframework.data.repository.reactive.ReactiveCrudRepository;

public interface ProductRepository extends ReactiveCrudRepository<Product, String> {
}
```

Step 3: RESTful Endpoints Configuration

RESTful endpoints are set up using `@RestController`, where return types such as `Mono` or `Flux` are used to handle single or multiple items:

```java
import reactor.core.publisher.Flux;
import reactor.core.publisher.Mono;

@RestController
@RequestMapping("/products")
public class ProductController {
    private final ProductRepository repository;

    public ProductController(ProductRepository repository) {
        this.repository = repository;
    }

    @GetMapping
    public Flux<Product> fetchAllProducts() {
        return repository.findAll();
    }

    @GetMapping("/{id}")
    public Mono<Product> fetchProductById(@PathVariable String id) {
        return repository.findById(id);
    }

    @PostMapping
    public Mono<Product> addNewProduct(@RequestBody Product product) {
        return repository.save(product);
    }
}
```

Benefits of Using Spring WebFlux

- Scalability: The event-driven and non-blocking model of WebFlux enhances the ability to scale under heavy loads.

- Resource Conservation: Reduced thread usage significantly lowers the demand for computational resources, beneficial in cost-sensitive environments.

- Responsive User Interactions: WebFlux is especially suited for applications requiring real-time updates, providing timely responses and fostering dynamic user interactions.

441

Conclusion

Spring WebFlux is a powerful framework for developing reactive APIs that meet contemporary needs for performance, scalability, and resource efficiency. By applying reactive programming principles, developers can forge resilient, responsive applications well-suited to today's interactive and real-time web environments. As the web development landscape continues to evolve toward more complex and interactive functionalities, becoming proficient in Spring WebFlux is increasingly essential for developers looking to advance in the field and lead in technological innovations.

Backpressure and its management in Reactive Streams

Backpressure is a pivotal concept in reactive programming, serving as a crucial mechanism to regulate data flow between data producers (publishers) and consumers (subscribers). This control ensures that data-consuming processes do not become overwhelmed by data-producing processes, thereby maintaining system stability and preventing performance degradation. Reactive Streams, embraced by libraries like Java's Project Reactor and RxJava, establish guidelines for asynchronous data stream processing with built-in support for backpressure.

The Essence of Backpressure

Backpressure operates as a control mechanism where subscribers inform publishers how much data they can handle without being overwhelmed. This strategy prevents scenarios where a fast-producing source can overload a slower-consuming destination, potentially causing system crashes or reduced efficiency. Managing backpressure effectively is essential for the smooth functioning and reliability of reactive systems.

The Function of Reactive Streams in Backpressure

Reactive Streams provide a framework for constructing non-blocking, backpressure-aware components that efficiently orchestrate data flows within asynchronous systems. The architecture includes several core components:

- `Publisher`: Emits data to its subscribers.

- `Subscriber`: Processes data received from a publisher.

- `Subscription`: Acts as the conduit between a subscriber and a publisher, managing data transactions and enabling the cancellation of the flow.

- `Processor`: Serves both as a subscriber and a publisher, facilitating data transformation and propagation.

Implementing Backpressure Through Reactive Streams

In Reactive Streams, backpressure is implemented by allowing subscribers to explicitly request a certain amount of data from publishers. This feature empowers subscribers to regulate data inflow based on their current processing capacity, preventing potential overloads.

Illustration with Project Reactor

Below is a practical example utilizing Project Reactor to demonstrate backpressure management:

```java
import reactor.core.publisher.Flux;
import reactor.core.scheduler.Schedulers;

public class BackpressureHandling {
    public static void main(String[] args) {
        Flux.range(1, 100)  // Publisher generates a series of numbers
            .onBackpressureBuffer()  // Backpressure strategy to buffer excess data
            .publishOn(Schedulers.boundedElastic())  // Processing on a bounded elastic
                scheduler
            .subscribe(
                data -> {
                    try {
                        Thread.sleep(100);  // Mimics a delay in processing
                        System.out.println("Data processed: " + data);
                    } catch (InterruptedException e) {
                        Thread.currentThread().interrupt();
                    }
                },
                error -> System.err.println("Error occurred: " + error),
                () -> System.out.println("Processing complete")
            );
    }
}
```

This code segment employs the `.onBackpressureBuffer()` method to buffer data when immediate processing isn't possible, thus protecting the subscriber from becoming overwhelmed by the incoming data flow.

Strategies for Managing Backpressure

Several strategies exist within Reactive Streams to manage backpressure effectively:

- Buffering: Temporarily stores messages that haven't been processed yet.

- Dropping: Discards messages when incoming rates exceed the processing capacity.

444

- Latest: Maintains only the newest message, removing previous ones.

- Error: Issues an error signal if the subscriber cannot process the data quickly enough.

The choice of strategy should align with specific application demands, considering factors like data importance and available system resources.

Advantages of Proficient Backpressure Management

Adequately managing backpressure is vital for developing robust reactive systems. It prevents resource depletion, keeps applications responsive under diverse load conditions, and ensures asynchronous operations are balanced. Additionally, it bolsters system resilience, allowing applications to handle extreme scenarios more gracefully.

Conclusion

Backpressure is a fundamental feature within the Reactive Streams specification, enabling efficient and stable data handling in asynchronous and event-driven architectures. By applying effective backpressure techniques, developers can enhance both the performance and reliability of their applications, ensuring that systems remain responsive and capable of dynamically managing varying data volumes. Mastery of backpressure is crucial for developers aiming to optimize modern software applications' performance and scalability.

Chapter Six

Database Performance Optimization

Advanced JPA and Hibernate tuning techniques

Enhancing the efficiency of Java Persistence API (JPA) and Hibernate, its widely-used counterpart, demands a profound comprehension of their nuances and the backend database system. While JPA and Hibernate offer convenient abstractions over database interactions, incorrect usage or inefficient configurations can lead to performance hurdles. Advanced tuning methods provide remedies to tackle these issues and optimize the efficacy of database operations.

Refining Entity Mapping

Streamlining entity mapping is pivotal in augmenting JPA and Hibernate performance. An optimization tactic involves employing lazy loading for entity associations, particularly for relationships with substantial datasets. This approach fetches associated entities only when required, reducing unnecessary database queries and minimizing memory usage. Moreover, meticulously selecting between eager and lazy loading strategies, based on application necessities and access patterns, can notably influence performance.

Query Enhancement

Enhancing JPA and Hibernate queries is crucial for refining database performance. Techniques such as query batching, caching, and pagination aid in minimizing database round trips and curtailing query execution duration. Batch fetching, for instance, permits fetching multiple entities in a solitary database query, diminishing the overhead of repeated fetch operations. Similarly, caching query outcomes or entities can enhance response times by obviating redundant database accesses.

Database Schema Streamlining

Adequate database schema design and optimization are fundamental for effective JPA and Hibernate performance. Indexing frequently queried columns, evading superfluous joins, and denormalizing data when applicable can result in significant performance enhancements. Furthermore, leveraging database-specific functionalities such as stored procedures and database triggers can enhance performance by transferring computation from the application to the database server.

Connection Pooling and Transaction Management

Configuring connection pooling and transaction management settings is indispensable for optimizing JPA and Hibernate performance. Connection pooling assists in managing database connections efficiently, diminishing connection overhead, and enhancing scalability. Similarly, fine-tuning transaction isolation levels and batch processing configurations can alleviate contention issues and boost database throughput.

Monitoring and Profiling

Regular monitoring and profiling of JPA and Hibernate applications are vital for pinpointing performance bottlenecks and refining resource usage. Tools such as Hibernate Profiler and JPA performance monitoring libraries offer insights into database interactions, query execution times, and object-relational mapping overhead. By scrutinizing performance metrics and identifying areas for enhancement, developers can fine-tune their applications for optimal performance.

Advanced Hibernate Attributes

Hibernate offers numerous advanced features and optimizations to further enrich performance. Features like second-level caching, optimistic locking, and custom SQL query execution provide precise control over database interactions and concurrency management. Furthermore, leveraging Hibernate-specific annotations and configuration options can optimize entity mappings and query execution strategies for specific scenarios.

Conclusion

Enhancing JPA and Hibernate performance necessitates a holistic grasp of their features, configurations, and the underlying database systems. By employing advanced tuning methods such as entity mapping refinement, query optimization, database schema streamlining, connection pooling, and transaction management, developers can substantially boost the performance and scalability of their applications. Routine monitoring, profiling, and utilization of advanced Hibernate attributes further contribute to maximizing performance and ensuring efficient utilization of database resources.

Optimizing query performance and managing transactions

Enhancing the efficiency of database queries and managing transactions proficiently are crucial aspects of optimizing software applications. Within the domain of Java Persistence API (JPA) and Hibernate, adopting advanced techniques to improve query performance and handle transactions adeptly can significantly enhance application scalability and effectiveness. Let's delve into some advanced strategies for refining query performance and managing transactions skillfully.

Strategies for Enhancing Query Performance

1. Optimization Techniques:

- Strategic Indexing: Implementing indexes on frequently accessed columns can speed up query execution by facilitating quicker data retrieval from the database.

- Refined Query Methods: Utilizing query rewriting, caching, and hints can optimize query execution plans and minimize resource usage.

2. Fetching Strategies:

- Selective Loading: Employing lazy loading ensures related entities are retrieved only when required, reducing the overhead of fetching unnecessary data.

- Timely Loading: When eager loading is necessary, ensure selective loading to prevent the retrieval of extensive datasets.

3. Batch Operations:

- Consolidated Transactions: Bundling multiple database operations into batches reduces the number of database trips, optimizing performance.

- Bulk Transactions: Leveraging bulk operations available in JPA and Hibernate for large-scale data manipulations enhances performance significantly.

Transaction Management Best Practices

1. Transactional Control:

- Optimal Transaction Definition: Clearly defining transaction boundaries balances granularity and coarseness, optimizing database resource usage.

- Isolation Level Selection: Choose isolation levels based on concurrency requirements to maintain data consistency without sacrificing performance.

2. Connection Handling:

- Efficient Pooling: Implement connection pooling to manage database connections efficiently and mitigate connection overhead.

- Timely Release: Release connections promptly after usage to prevent resource depletion and ensure availability for subsequent requests.

3. Transaction Propagation:

- Propagation Strategies: Leverage different transaction propagation attributes provided by JPA and Hibernate to control transactional flow across method calls effectively.

Monitoring and Profiling Performance

1. Performance Surveillance:

- Profiling Tools: Utilize database profiling tools to monitor query execution times, identify slow queries, and uncover areas for optimization.

- Application Analyzers: Employ application profilers to scrutinize JPA and Hibernate performance, pinpoint bottlenecks, and optimize resource allocation.

2. Query Analysis:

- Explain Plan Evaluation: Analyze database explain plans to understand query execution mechanisms and identify opportunities for optimization.

- Optimization Guidance: Use query optimization advisories provided by database management systems for actionable insights into enhancing query performance.

Conclusion

Mastering the art of optimizing query performance and transaction management in JPA and Hibernate applications is crucial for achieving superior performance and scalability. By embracing advanced query tuning methodologies, refining transaction handling approaches, and leveraging performance monitoring and profiling tools, developers can elevate their applications' efficiency and resource utilization. Continuous vigilance, analysis, and refinement of database interactions are essential for sustaining optimal performance and scalability over time.

Leveraging Spring Data repositories for performance

Enhancing the performance of applications is a vital aspect of development, particularly when handling extensive data and intricate queries. Spring Data repositories offer a potent abstraction layer for data access in Spring applications, presenting diverse features and strategies to bolster performance. Let's delve into how developers can effectively utilize Spring Data repositories to optimize application performance.

1. Utilizing Query Methods and QueryDSL:

Spring Data repositories empower developers to define query methods using method naming conventions. These methods are automatically translated into database queries, minimizing the need for manual SQL query composition and simplifying development. Moreover, developers can employ QueryDSL (Query Domain Specific Language) to dynamically craft queries programmatically, delivering increased flexibility and control over query construction.

Example:

```java
public interface ProductRepository extends JpaRepository<Product, Long> {
    List<Product> findByCategory(String category);
    List<Product> findByPriceGreaterThan(double price);
    List<Product> findByCategoryAndPriceGreaterThan(String category, double price);
}
```

2. Incorporating Pagination and Sorting:

Spring Data repositories support pagination and sorting functionality out of the box, enabling developers to retrieve data in manageable portions and specify sorting criteria. This optimization reduces the volume of data fetched from the database, thereby enhancing response times, particularly when handling extensive datasets.

Example:

```java
Page<Product> products = productRepository.findAll(PageRequest.of(pageNumber,
    pageSize, Sort.by("name")));
```

3. Leveraging Caching:

Spring Data repositories facilitate caching mechanisms such as Spring Cache Abstraction, seamlessly integrating with repositories to cache query results. By caching frequently accessed data, developers can alleviate database load and improve application performance by serving cached data rather than executing database queries repetitively.

Example:

```java
@Cacheable("products")
public List<Product> findByCategory(String category) {
    return productRepository.findByCategory(category);
}
```

4. Query Optimization:

Developers can further optimize query performance by utilizing advanced features provided by Spring Data repositories, such as QueryHints and Query Annotations. These features empower developers to tailor query behavior, optimize execution plans, and fine-tune performance parameters to suit specific use cases and requirements.

```
@QueryHints(value = @QueryHint(name = "org.hibernate.cacheable", value = "true"))
List<Product> findByCategory(String category);
```

5. Implementing Batch Operations:

Spring Data repositories facilitate batch operations for bulk data processing, allowing developers to perform operations on multiple entities efficiently. Batch operations minimize database round-trips and optimize resource utilization, resulting in improved performance and scalability.

Example:

```
@Transactional
public void deleteByCategory(String category) {
    productRepository.deleteByCategory(category);
}
```

Conclusion:

Effectively leveraging Spring Data repositories plays a pivotal role in optimizing performance in Spring applications. By harnessing query methods, pagination, sorting, caching, query optimization techniques, and batch operations, developers can streamline data access, reduce database overhead, and enhance application responsiveness. With Spring Data's robust features and abstractions, developers can focus on building resilient and efficient applications while ensuring optimal performance across diverse use cases and workloads.

Chapter Seven

Scaling Spring Boot Applications

Horizontal vs. vertical scaling strategies

In the dynamic realm of software deployment and management, mastering the art of scalability is pivotal. Scalability strategies are fundamentally categorized into two forms: horizontal and vertical scaling. Each method addresses specific operational needs and offers unique benefits and complexities, making their appropriate application critical for optimal performance management.

Horizontal Scaling: Broadening System Capacity

Horizontal scaling, also known as scaling out, increases system capacity by adding more nodes to the infrastructure. This approach does not enhance the capacity of individual machines but rather amplifies the overall system's ability to handle increased load by multiplying the number of active machines. This strategy is particularly effective in cloud-enabled environments where adding hardware can be seamlessly orchestrated.

Technical Details: Horizontal scaling is ideally suited for stateless applications—where each server handles requests independently without reliance on shared state across sessions. This independence is critical as it sidesteps the complexities related to synchronizing data across a distributed network, which can significantly impair system performance.

Spring Boot Example: Consider a scenario where a Spring Boot application needs to accommodate increased web traffic. Implementing horizontal scaling can be efficiently achieved by increasing the number of instances, all managed by a load balancer. The following Docker Compose configuration illustrates how to deploy multiple instances of a Spring Boot application to distribute the load effectively:

```
version: '3'
services:
  web:
    image: my-spring-boot-app:latest
    deploy:
      replicas: 4  # Indicates the number of server instances
    ports:
      - "8080"
    networks:
      - webnet
networks:
  webnet:
```

This configuration demonstrates the deployment strategy to distribute workload across multiple servers effectively.

Advantages of Horizontal Scaling:

- Extensible Scaling: Provides the ability to scale almost indefinitely as resource demands increase.

- Enhanced Fault Tolerance: Reduces the impact of individual node failures on the overall system performance.

- Flexible Adjustments: Allows for scalability adjustments based on real-time demand, providing high adaptability without system interruption.

Vertical Scaling: Enhancing Individual Node Capacity

Vertical scaling, or scaling up, involves enhancing the capabilities of an existing server by upgrading its hardware resources, such as CPU, RAM, or storage capacity. This method increases a server's power to support more tasks simultaneously.

Technical Details: Vertical scaling is generally simpler to implement compared to horizontal scaling as it involves upgrading existing resources. However, it is limited by the maximum potential for hardware enhancements and typically involves downtime for these upgrades.

Java Application Example: For Java-based applications, including those developed with Spring Boot, vertical scaling can be achieved by modifying JVM settings to increase memory allocation:

```
java -Xms1024m -Xmx4096m -jar my-spring-boot-app.jar
```

This command adjusts the JVM's heap settings to allow for greater memory capacity, thereby enhancing the application's performance capabilities.

Advantages of Vertical Scaling:

- Ease of Implementation: Generally easier to upgrade as it involves modifications to existing equipment.

- Cost Efficiency: More cost-effective in the short term as it does not involve complex multi-system configurations.

- Immediate Performance Enhancement: Direct upgrades to the hardware can yield swift improvements in performance metrics.

Selecting the Optimal Strategy

The choice between horizontal and vertical scaling depends on several factors, including application architecture, load variability, budgetary constraints, and strategic growth objectives. While horizontal scaling offers long-term flexibility and robustness, vertical scaling might be preferred for immediate, cost-effective performance enhancements.

Often, a hybrid approach, referred to as diagonal scaling, provides the best solution. This strategy combines initial vertical enhancements with a strategic shift towards horizontal scaling, ensuring that immediate performance needs are met while laying the groundwork for scalable future growth. This balanced approach maximizes resource utilization and maintains optimal performance across varying demand levels.

State management in distributed systems

Navigating state management within distributed systems is essential to ensure operational efficiency, reliability, and scalability. In environments where processing and data storage are decentralized across various nodes—potentially spread across different locations—managing the mutable state becomes a critical challenge. This discussion delves into the essential elements, effective techniques, and established practices for managing state in distributed architectures, highlighting common hurdles and offering practical solutions.

Defining State in Distributed Contexts

In distributed architectures, the term 'state' encompasses all the dynamic information maintained across user interactions and transactions, such as session details, configuration settings, user preferences, and historical transaction data. Unlike centralized systems, where state management can be more straightforward due to localized data storage and processing, distributed systems require synchronization of state across multiple servers and databases. This synchronization needs to address several pivotal aspects:

- Consistency: Ensuring that all nodes within the system simultaneously reflect the same state.

- Availability: Maintaining operational functionality despite any partial system failures or network disruptions.

- Partition Tolerance: Ensuring the system continues to operate effectively even when parts of it are temporarily segmented due to network partitions.

State Management Challenges

A significant challenge in distributed state management arises from the implications of the CAP Theorem, which asserts that a distributed system can provide at most two out of three guarantees: Consistency, Availability, and Partition Tolerance.

This theorem requires architects to prioritize two of these elements based on the application's operational needs.

Network delays and failures complicate state synchronization, leading to potential inconsistencies. For instance, if a node updates its state but crashes before the change is propagated to other nodes, the system must implement robust mechanisms to recover or revert to a consistent state.

Strategies for Optimal State Management

Prioritizing Statelessness

Where possible, adopting a stateless architecture can greatly simplify system design and enhance scalability. In a stateless setup, each client request contains all the information necessary for its execution, thus eliminating the need for server-side state retention. This model is particularly evident in stateless RESTful APIs, which are designed to facilitate extensive scalability of web services.

Implementing Distributed Caching

When statelessness is not feasible, distributed caching serves as an efficient alternative for state management. Distributed caches temporarily store state data and replicate it across multiple nodes, enhancing data availability and system resilience. Technologies such as Redis and Memcached are popular choices for implementing such caches. Here's an example of configuring a Redis cache within a Spring Boot application:

```
@Configuration
public class CacheConfig {

    @Bean
    public JedisConnectionFactory redisConnectionFactory() {
        return new JedisConnectionFactory();
    }

    @Bean
    public RedisTemplate<Object, Object> redisTemplate() {
        RedisTemplate<Object, Object> template = new RedisTemplate<>();
        template.setConnectionFactory(redisConnectionFactory());
        return template;
    }
}
```

This configuration facilitates seamless interaction between the application components and the Redis distributed cache, ensuring efficient and resilient data management.

Employing Consensus Protocols

To achieve consistency across distributed nodes, consensus protocols such as Raft, Paxos, or the ZAB protocol from Apache ZooKeeper are essential. These protocols help maintain agreement among nodes regarding the current state or sequence of actions, ensuring system coherence despite potential disruptions.

Embracing Eventual Consistency

For less critical applications where immediate consistency is not necessary, the eventual consistency model may be appropriate. This approach tolerates temporary state discrepancies across nodes, with the expectation that all nodes will eventually synchronize.

Recommended Practices for State Management

1. Consistent State Validation: Implement mechanisms for regular verification and reconciliation of state across all nodes to ensure ongoing consistency.

2. Transactional Integrity: Utilize transactional processes to maintain atomic operations and ensure the system remains in a consistent state during critical activities.

3. Detailed Monitoring: Establish comprehensive logging and real-time monitoring protocols to quickly detect and address any discrepancies in state management.

In conclusion, effective state management is vital for distributed systems to function reliably and efficiently. Understanding the inherent challenges and applying strategies such as statelessness, distributed caching, consensus protocols, and eventual consistency can help maintain a balance between consistency, availability, and partition tolerance. By strategically implementing these principles, distributed systems can effectively manage state, supporting complex, and highly available architectures.

Implementing and optimizing session clustering

Session clustering is a critical technique in distributed web applications, enhancing both fault tolerance and the seamless continuity of user sessions during server malfunctions or downtime. This method entails synchronizing user session data across multiple servers so that any server in the cluster can handle any request with shared session information, thus improving application reliability and scalability.

Overview of Session Clustering

Session clustering involves the replication of session state across several server instances to preserve user-specific information such as login details, shopping cart contents, and user preferences during a session. In such an environment, the synchronization of session data across servers ensures that if one server fails, another can continue the session without any data loss, maintaining a continuous user experience.

Techniques for Implementing Session Clustering

Effective implementation of session clustering requires a deep understanding of the application architecture and the specific session management techniques involved. Many web application frameworks support session clustering out of the box, which can be utilized to facilitate the implementation. For example, applications on platforms like Apache Tomcat can leverage built-in functionalities for session management across clusters.

Consider this simplified configuration example for session clustering in Apache Tomcat, added to the `**server.xml**` file:

```
<Cluster className="org.apache.catalina.ha.tcp.SimpleTcpCluster">
    <Manager className="org.apache.catalina.ha.session.DeltaManager"
             expireSessionsOnShutdown="false"
             notifyListenersOnReplication="true"/>
    <Channel className="org.apache.catalina.tribes.group.GroupChannel">
        <Receiver className="org.apache.catalina.tribes.transport.nio
            .NioReceiver"
                address="auto"
                port="4000"
                autoBind="100"
                selectorTimeout="5000"
                maxThreads="6"/>
        <Sender className="org.apache.catalina.tribes.transport
            .ReplicationTransmitter">
            <Transport className="org.apache.catalina.tribes.transport.nio
                .PooledParallelSender"/>
        </Sender>
        <Interceptor className="org.apache.catalina.tribes.group.interceptors
            .TcpFailureDetector"/>
        <Interceptor className="org.apache.catalina.tribes.group.interceptors
            .MessageDispatch15Interceptor"/>
        <Interceptor className="org.apache.catalina.tribes.group.interceptors
            .ThroughputInterceptor"/>
    </Channel>
</Cluster>
```

This configuration establishes a cluster with a TCP-based clustering mechanism, utilizing `DeltaManager` to manage session replication efficiently by transmitting only changes in session data, reducing the network load.

Strategies for Optimizing Session Clustering

While session clustering can substantially boost the resilience of an application, it is crucial to optimize this strategy to mitigate issues like excessive network load and potential data conflicts. Here are several optimization strategies:

1. Minimize Session Data: Limit the information stored in the session to essential data only. Excessive data can

465

slow down replication and increase network traffic. Non-essential information should be stored persistently or in a caching layer.

2. Employ Sticky Sessions: Use sticky sessions to reduce the need for frequent replication. By binding a user's session to a specific server and only replicating when necessary, network traffic is minimized. This can be facilitated by configuring load balancers that support session affinity.

3. Implement Asynchronous Replication: Opt for asynchronous replication of session data to improve application responsiveness. Asynchronous replication allows the application to continue operations while session data updates are being propagated, enhancing throughput and user experience.

4. Adopt Fine-Grained Replication: Instead of replicating entire session objects, replicate only the modified attributes. This selective approach reduces the data footprint and enhances the efficiency of data transfer.

5. Leverage Advanced Distributed Caching: Consider using advanced distributed caching solutions like Redis or Hazelcast. These platforms offer robust performance for managing data across distributed networks, with features like automatic data partitioning and fast replication.

Conclusion

Implementing and fine-tuning session clustering is vital for distributed applications committed to delivering a robust and uninterrupted user experience. By strategically managing session data, minimizing its footprint, and utilizing advanced technologies for data synchronization, organizations can ensure their applications remain scalable and resilient under various operational conditions. This approach not only safeguards user data integrity but also enhances overall application performance.

Chapter Eight

Microservices Performance Patterns

Design patterns for high-performance microservices

In building microservices architectures, ensuring optimal performance is a priority that requires meticulous design and thoughtful implementation strategies. Design patterns serve as key methodologies for solving frequent issues associated with microservices, such as efficiently managing service decomposition, optimizing database interactions, and facilitating effective inter-service communications. These frameworks are vital for enhancing the scalability, robustness, and manageability of microservices. This discussion highlights several critical design patterns that substantially elevate the performance of microservices infrastructures.

Patterns for Efficient Service Decomposition

1. Decomposition by Business Function

Organizing microservices based on discrete business functions facilitates focused development, deployment, and scaling of services. Each microservice is tailored to a specific operational function, like payment processing or customer support, which simplifies the architecture and minimizes overhead. This separation helps enhance service performance through isolation and dedicated handling.

Example setup:

```
services:
  payment-service:
    build: ./payment-service
    ports:
      - "9001:9001"
  support-service:
    build: ./support-service
    ports:
      - "9002:9002"
```

This Docker Compose file illustrates separate services for payment and customer support, highlighting how services can be independently managed and scaled.

2. Domain-Driven Design (DDD)

DDD shapes software designs to reflect the intricacies and behaviors of the business domain, facilitating the organization of microservices into coherent units. Services modeled around key domain entities (like Orders or Accounts) ensure clear boundaries and minimal cross-service dependencies, which streamlines performance and eases maintenance.

Patterns for Database Optimization

3. Service-Specific Databases

Allocating a unique database to each microservice prevents operational conflicts and interdependencies, allowing each service to optimize its database schema for specific tasks. This approach leads to more efficient data handling and quicker response times.

Example database configuration:

```
{
  "service": "payment-service",
  "database": {
    "type": "SQL",
    "connection": "specific_connection_string_for_payment_db"
  }
}
```

Here, a payment service uses its dedicated SQL database, ensuring that all database operations are optimized for payment processing tasks.

4. Command Query Responsibility Segregation (CQRS)

Separating the mechanisms for updating (commands) and retrieving (queries) data can significantly enhance the efficiency of these operations. CQRS allows read queries to be optimized for speed and responsiveness, while write commands can be fortified for accuracy and security.

Communication Integration Patterns

5. Utilizing an API Gateway

An API Gateway serves as the primary point of contact for all client requests, routing them to the appropriate microservices. It efficiently handles common tasks such as authentication and request routing, offloading these responsibilities from individual services to boost responsiveness and streamline operations.

Example routing logic:

```javascript
const express = require('express');
const app = express();
app.all('/api/*', (req, res) => {
    // Routing logic to appropriate services
});
```

In this Express.js setup, the API Gateway manages incoming requests, ensuring they are directed to the correct services based on the API path.

6. Asynchronous Messaging for Service Communication

Implementing message queues for communication between services enables asynchronous interactions, allowing services to function independently without waiting on synchronous responses. This non-blocking communication style enhances scalability and overall service performance.

Asynchronous communication example using RabbitMQ:

```javascript
const amqp = require('amqplib/callback_api');

amqp.connect('amqp://user:pass@localhost', (error, connection) => {
  connection.createChannel((error, channel) => {
    const queue = 'serviceTasks';
    channel.assertQueue(queue, { durable: true });
    channel.consume(queue, (message) => {
      console.log("Processing task: %s", message.content.toString());
      // Task processing logic here
    }, { noAck: true });
  });
});
```

This script showcases how a service consumes messages from a RabbitMQ queue, processing them asynchronously to maintain efficiency and responsiveness.

Conclusion

Applying targeted design patterns is crucial for developing effective and scalable microservices architectures. By judiciously utilizing patterns such as Business Function Decomposition, DDD, Service-Specific Databases, CQRS, API Gateway, and Asynchronous Messaging, developers can create dynamic microservices systems that are capable of handling complex operations and high user traffic efficiently.

Isolation, partitioning, and throttling strategies

In the architecture of microservices, ensuring robust performance and system stability necessitates strategic resource management and effective control of service interactions. Isolation, partitioning, and throttling are key strategies that help build resilient and scalable microservices systems, addressing issues like service overload, latency, and cascading failures to maintain a dependable application framework.

Isolation Strategies

Isolation entails separating services and resources to prevent systemic failures from affecting the entire network. This approach increases fault tolerance and keeps services operational under varying loads or when parts of the infrastructure fail.

1. Service Instance Isolation: Placing each microservice instance in its own isolated environment (such as a virtual

machine or container) ensures that issues in one do not impact others. Container technologies like Docker and orchestration systems like Kubernetes excel in providing these isolated environments.

Example Dockerfile for an isolated service:

```
FROM ruby:2.7
WORKDIR /app
COPY . /app
RUN bundle install
EXPOSE 4000
CMD ["ruby", "server.rb"]
```

This Dockerfile outlines the setup for a Ruby application, encapsulating it in an isolated environment with its dependencies, thus enhancing its security and stability.

2. Database Isolation: Assigning each microservice its own database helps avoid conflicts and optimizes performance, as each service can manage its data independently.

Sample configuration for a microservice-specific database:

```
{
  "service": "BillingService",
  "database": {
    "type": "Cassandra",
    "connection": "specific_connection_for_billing"
  }
}
```

This configuration ensures that the Billing Service operates with its dedicated Cassandra database, isolating its operations from other services.

Partitioning Strategies

Partitioning divides the system's data or workload across multiple services or nodes, enhancing manageability and performance. This technique is crucial for reducing response times and evenly distributing system load.

1. Data Partitioning (Sharding): Splitting databases into more manageable parts, or shards, which are spread across multiple servers. This arrangement helps in handling large volumes of data more efficiently.

SQL example for data partitioning:

```
CREATE TABLE users (
    user_id INT PRIMARY KEY,
    username VARCHAR(255),
    shard_id INT GENERATED ALWAYS AS (user_id % 4)
) PARTITION BY RANGE (shard_id);
```

This SQL command sets up a partitioned **users** table with data distributed based on the modulus of `user_id`, facilitating balanced data management across shards.

2. Service Partitioning: Running multiple instances of the same service across different servers or regions distributes the workload and enhances service availability.

Example Kubernetes deployment for partitioning a service:

```
apiVersion: apps/v1
kind: Deployment
metadata:
  name: catalog-service
spec:
  replicas: 3
  selector:
    matchLabels:
      app: catalog
  template:
    metadata:
      labels:
        app: catalog
    spec:
      containers:
      - name: catalog
        image: catalog-service:1.0
        ports:
        - containerPort: 7000
```

This deployment configures three instances of the `catalog-service`, spreading its operational load to improve performance and reliability.

Throttling Strategies

Throttling controls the rate of incoming requests or data throughput to prevent overloads and ensure fair resource distribution among all users, vital for maintaining system stability during peak loads.

1. Rate Limiting: Implementing constraints on the number of requests that a user can send to a service within a specific time frame helps prevent resource hogging.

Configuration for API rate limiting:

```
server {
    location /service/ {
        limit_req zone=api_rate_limit burst=20 nodelay;
        proxy_pass http://backend;
    }
}
```

This NGINX setup restricts the rate at which requests are processed, allowing for a burst of up to 20 requests, effectively managing sudden increases in traffic.

2. Load Shedding: Proactively rejecting requests when the system's capacity is maxed out preserves service functionality and user experience.

Service code for load shedding:

```
public void onRequestReceived(Request req) {
    if (getSystemLoad() > 90) {
        rejectRequest(req, "System is at capacity, please try again later.");
    } else {
        processRequest(req);
    }
}
```

This Java method monitors the system load and rejects incoming requests when load thresholds are exceeded, helping to stabilize the service during high-demand periods.

Conclusion

Isolation, partitioning, and throttling are integral strategies in the toolkit of microservices architectures, essential for enhancing resource efficiency, managing traffic surges, and ensuring overall service durability. By adopting these strategies, developers can ensure that their microservices infrastructure remains both scalable and robust, capable of sustaining high performance under a variety of operational conditions.

Synchronous and asynchronous communication optimization

In microservices architectures, managing communication effectively is crucial for system performance and reliability. The two predominant types of communication—synchronous and asynchronous—each play vital roles but come with their own set of benefits and operational considerations. Properly optimizing these communication types is key to ensuring efficient and stable service operations.

Insights into Synchronous Communication

Synchronous communication involves a direct, immediate exchange where the requester waits for a reply before proceeding. This approach is straightforward, mirroring function calls in traditional software development and providing immediacy and simplicity.

Advantages:

- Simplicity of Integration: It is relatively easy to use and integrate, particularly for those familiar with traditional software architectures.

- Data Integrity and Immediacy: Offers real-time processing which is critical for transactions that depend on immediate data consistency.

Disadvantages:

- Inter-service Dependency: The performance of a requesting service can be hindered by the responsiveness of the service it calls, potentially introducing delays.

- Resource Efficiency Issues: Resources can be underutilized while waiting for responses, leading to inefficiencies, especially under load.

Optimization Strategies:

1. Connection Pooling: This technique reuses existing connections for multiple requests, reducing the overhead associated with opening new connections.

2. Implementing Timeouts: By establishing timeouts, services can avoid waiting indefinitely for a response, thus preventing resource wastage and potential deadlocks.

Python example demonstrating a synchronous call with a timeout:

```python
import requests

response = None
try:
    response = requests.get('https://api.example.com/data', timeout=2)
except requests.Timeout:
    print("The request timed out.")
except requests.RequestException as e:
    print("Error during the request:", e)

if response:
    print(response.json())
```

This code snippet shows how to make a synchronous HTTP request with a timeout, ensuring that the application handles delays gracefully.

Insights into Asynchronous Communication

Asynchronous communication allows a service to make a request and continue its operations without waiting for a response. This method enhances scalability and resource efficiency by decoupling services.

Advantages:

- Reduced Coupling: Services operate independently, enhancing system resilience and scalability.

- Enhanced Resource Utilization: By not blocking resources waiting for responses, services can handle more operations, improving overall throughput.

Disadvantages:

- Complexity in Management: Asynchronous operations can complicate system architecture and require more sophisticated management strategies.

- Challenges in Ensuring Consistency: Maintaining data consistency across services becomes more complex due to the lack of immediate responses.

Optimization Strategies:

1. Employing Message Queues: By using message queues, services can communicate reliably without requiring immediate responses, thus enabling effective decoupling.

2. Adopting Event-Driven Approaches: This involves triggering actions in services through events, which can help in managing complex interactions more efficiently.

Node.js example with RabbitMQ for asynchronous messaging:

```javascript
const amqp = require('amqplib/callback_api');

amqp.connect('amqp://localhost', function(error0, connection) {
    if (error0) {
        throw error0;
    }
    connection.createChannel(function(error1, channel) {
        if (error1) {
            throw error1;
        }
        const queue = 'taskQueue';
        const msg = 'Hello World!';

        channel.assertQueue(queue, {
            durable: false
        });
        channel.sendToQueue(queue, Buffer.from(msg));

        console.log(" [x] Sent %s", msg);
    });
});
```

This script sets up a simple RabbitMQ message queue where messages are sent to a queue and can be processed later, demonstrating how asynchronous communication operates independently of the sender's processes.

Conclusion

Optimizing synchronous and asynchronous communications is vital in microservices architectures to leverage their strengths while minimizing associated risks. Implementing strategies such as connection pooling and timeouts for synchronous scenarios, alongside message queues and event-driven architectures for asynchronous scenarios, ensures microservices are resilient, scalable, and efficient. These approaches allow microservices to handle diverse and dynamic workloads effectively, maintaining high performance and system reliability.

Chapter Nine

Caching Strategies

Implementing effective caching in Spring Boot

Caching is an essential optimization strategy in application development, particularly valuable in environments where reducing repetitive database queries can significantly enhance response times and system performance. Spring Boot offers robust support for caching through a straightforward setup that integrates seamlessly with popular caching technologies such as Redis, EhCache, and Caffeine. This article discusses how to effectively implement and manage caching strategies within Spring Boot applications, detailing setup configurations, essential practices, and common pitfalls to avoid.

Introduction to Caching in Spring Boot

Caching in Spring Boot aims to shorten response times by temporarily storing frequently requested data in a fast-access layer, minimizing the need for costly data retrieval processes. Spring Boot supports caching through a simple configuration setup and annotations, making it easier to enhance and manage the application performance.

Configuring Caching in Spring Boot

To initiate caching in a Spring Boot application, you must first enable it by adding the `@**EnableCaching**` annotation to a configuration class, which activates Spring Boot's caching capabilities.

Example of Activating Caching:

```
import org.springframework.context.annotation.Configuration;
import org.springframework.cache.annotation.EnableCaching;

@Configuration
@EnableCaching
public class CacheConfiguration {
}
```

This configuration snippet activates caching, preparing the application for further caching-related operations.

Selecting a Caching Provider

Spring Boot is compatible with multiple third-party caching solutions, each offering different features suited to various application needs, such as distributed operation, persistence, or in-memory caching.

1. Redis: Provides excellent support for distributed environments and includes persistence capabilities.

2. EhCache: Offers powerful in-memory caching with options for persistent storage.

3. Caffeine: Known for its high-performance in-memory caching ideal for local caching scenarios.

Example Setup for Redis in Spring Boot:

```java
import org.springframework.data.redis.connection.RedisConnectionFactory;
import org.springframework.data.redis.connection.lettuce
    .LettuceConnectionFactory;
import org.springframework.data.redis.core.RedisTemplate;
import org.springframework.context.annotation.Bean;
import org.springframework.context.annotation.Configuration;

@Configuration
public class RedisConfiguration {

    @Bean
    public RedisConnectionFactory connectionFactory() {
        return new LettuceConnectionFactory();
    }

    @Bean
    public RedisTemplate<String, Object> redisTemplate() {
        RedisTemplate<String, Object> template = new RedisTemplate<>();
        template.setConnectionFactory(connectionFactory());
        return template;
    }
}
```

This setup demonstrates configuring Redis as a cache provider using Lettuce, which is known for its scalability and asynchronous capabilities.

Using Annotations for Caching

Spring Boot simplifies caching with annotations that specify cache operations at the method level, automating cache management tasks like storing, updating, and removing entries.

- `@Cacheable`: Caches the method return value and uses it to handle subsequent invocations with the same arguments.

- `@CacheEvict`: Clears cache entries, useful for removing stale or unused data.

- `@CachePut`: Updates the cache with the result of the method call, ensuring that subsequent calls reflect the most recent data.

Example Using `@Cacheable`:

```
import org.springframework.cache.annotation.Cacheable;
import org.springframework.stereotype.Service;

@Service
public class UserService {

    @Cacheable(cacheNames = "users", key = "#userId")
    public User getUserById(String userId) {
        // Assume a method that retrieves a user by ID from the database
        return findUserById(userId);
    }
}
```

This example caches the result of `getUserById`, significantly reducing database load by serving cached data for subsequent requests with the same `userId`.

Best Practices for Effective Caching

- Implement Thoughtful Cache Eviction: Regularly define and revise policies on when cache entries should be evicted to avoid serving outdated information.

- Customize Cache Keys: Customize cache keys when default strategies do not meet the application's specific needs.

- Monitor Cache Performance: Continuously monitor cache usage and effectiveness, adjusting configurations as necessary to optimize performance.

Conclusion

Effective caching in Spring Boot can lead to significant improvements in application performance by alleviating backend pressure and enhancing user response experiences. By carefully configuring the caching mechanism, choosing the right cache provider, and employing Spring Boot's caching annotations, developers can achieve a highly efficient and scalable application architecture.

Cache configuration and eviction policies

In software development, particularly within architectures that involve heavy data transactions like microservices, efficient cache management is essential. This involves sophisticated cache configuration and the strategic use of eviction policies to enhance data retrieval speeds and overall system performance. This guide explores effective practices for setting up cache configurations and managing eviction protocols to optimize resource utilization and application responsiveness.

Essentials of Cache Configuration

Cache configuration defines the operational parameters that influence a cache's behavior within an application. Key configuration settings typically include the cache size, data retention duration, and the eviction strategy employed to manage cache capacity. Optimizing these settings is crucial for reducing reliance on slower backend data retrieval processes and improving user experience.

Choosing the right caching solution is dependent on the specific needs of the application. Popular caching systems like Redis, Memcached, and EhCache each provide unique features that cater to different scenarios, from high-speed in-memory caching to persistent disk-based storage.

Spring Boot Redis Cache Configuration Example:

```
import org.springframework.context.annotation.Bean;
import org.springframework.context.annotation.Configuration;
import org.springframework.cache.annotation.EnableCaching;
import org.springframework.data.redis.connection.RedisConnectionFactory;
import org.springframework.data.redis.cache.RedisCacheConfiguration;
import org.springframework.data.redis.cache.RedisCacheManager;
import org.springframework.data.redis.serializer.Jackson2JsonRedisSerializer;

@Configuration
@EnableCaching
public class CacheConfiguration {

    @Bean
    public RedisCacheManager cacheManager(RedisConnectionFactory
        redisConnectionFactory) {
        RedisCacheConfiguration cacheConfig = RedisCacheConfiguration
            .defaultCacheConfig()
            .entryTtl(Duration.ofHours(1))  // Define TTL for cache entries
            .serializeValuesWith(RedisSerializationContext.SerializationPair
                .fromSerializer(new Jackson2JsonRedisSerializer<>(Object.class
                )));

        return RedisCacheManager.builder(redisConnectionFactory)
            .cacheDefaults(cacheConfig)
            .build();
    }
}
```

This setup configures Redis as a caching provider in a Spring Boot application, specifying a one-hour Time to Live (TTL) for cached entries and utilizing JSON serialization for the values stored in the cache to ensure data integrity and enhance maintainability.

Implementing Eviction Policies

Eviction policies are rules that determine how and when cache entries are removed or replaced to manage memory effectively and ensure the cache does not serve outdated information. Effective eviction is key to maintaining cache efficiency and utility.

Popular eviction strategies include:

1. Least Recently Used (LRU): Prioritizes keeping recently accessed data in cache, evicting the oldest accessed items first.

2. First In, First Out (FIFO): Evicts items in the order they were added, useful where the age of the data determines its relevance.

3. Time to Live (TTL): Sets a fixed lifespan for cached data after which it is automatically removed, suitable for data with predictable expiration such as session tokens or temporary event details.

Example of Redis Connection Factory for LRU Policy:

```
@Bean
public RedisConnectionFactory redisConnectionFactory() {
    RedisStandaloneConfiguration config = new RedisStandaloneConfiguration("127.0
        .0.1", 6379);
    return new LettuceConnectionFactory(config);
}
```

While this configuration primarily establishes connection settings, Redis internally implements an LRU eviction mechanism based on its configuration parameters, effectively managing memory without explicit command in the code.

Cache Management Best Practices

- Tailor Configurations to Match Data Access Patterns: Adjust cache size, TTL, and eviction policies based on specific access patterns and load conditions.

- Monitor Cache Performance Metrics: Regular monitoring of cache hit and miss ratios, and load times should guide the tuning of cache configurations.

- Log Cache Activities: Detailed logging of cache behaviors can help diagnose issues and optimize cache performance.

Conclusion

Setting up effective cache configurations and eviction policies is fundamental to enhancing application performance in data-intensive environments. By carefully selecting caching mechanisms and configuring them to align with an application's operational demands, developers can significantly reduce data retrieval times and improve system responsiveness. Ongoing monitoring and iterative refinement based on real-world performance data ensure that caching strategies remain aligned with evolving application needs, continuing to provide optimal support as the application scales.

Using distributed caching for scalable applications

Distributed caching is a pivotal strategy for boosting the scalability and performance of applications by managing data across multiple interconnected servers. This technique significantly mitigates the load on the backend databases and decreases latency, enabling quicker data retrieval from memory rather than slower disk-based storage. This discussion delves into the mechanics of distributed caching, its advantages for high-traffic applications, and effective implementation strategies.

Fundamentals of Distributed Caching

Distributed caching involves positioning data across a network of cache servers, enhancing data retrieval times by enabling access from the closest or most optimal node. Tools such as Redis, Hazelcast, and Memcached are widely used in implementing distributed caches. These systems integrate seamlessly into various application structures, from simple web applications to complex, distributed microservices architectures.

Benefits of Distributed Caching

1. Database Load Reduction: Frequent queries and data are stored in the cache, which lowers the direct interaction with the database, conserving resources for critical operations and eliminating performance bottlenecks.

2. Accelerated Data Access: Since memory access is much faster than disk access, caching data in memory reduces

latency and improves the overall responsiveness of applications.

3. Scalability: Distributed caching supports horizontal scaling, meaning more servers can be added to the cache as the demand increases, facilitating smooth scalability as user base and data demands grow.

4. Reliability and Availability: By replicating data across multiple nodes, distributed caching ensures that even if one node fails, the application can still fetch data from other nodes, maintaining both data availability and application uptime.

Deployment Strategies for Distributed Caching

Setting up a distributed cache requires thoughtful planning regarding the configuration of cache parameters, choice of caching technology, and maintenance strategies tailored to the specific needs of the application.

Redis Configuration Example for Distributed Caching:

```
import org.springframework.data.redis.connection.RedisStandaloneConfiguration;
import org.springframework.data.redis.connection.lettuce.LettuceConnectionFactory
    ;
import org.springframework.data.redis.core.RedisTemplate;
import org.springframework.data.redis.serializer.StringRedisSerializer;

@Configuration
public class RedisCacheConfig {

    @Bean
    public LettuceConnectionFactory connectionFactory() {
        RedisStandaloneConfiguration configuration = new
            RedisStandaloneConfiguration("localhost", 6379);
        return new LettuceConnectionFactory(configuration);
    }

    @Bean
    public RedisTemplate<String, String> redisTemplate() {
        RedisTemplate<String, String> template = new RedisTemplate<>();
        template.setConnectionFactory(connectionFactory());
        template.setKeySerializer(new StringRedisSerializer());
        template.setValueSerializer(new StringRedisSerializer());
        return template;
    }
}
```

This configuration sets up Redis with the Lettuce client, which supports asynchronous, non-blocking communication in a Spring Boot environment. It details the connection setup and data serialization processes that are critical for efficient caching.

Distributed Caching Best Practices

1. Balanced Data Distribution: Ensure data is uniformly distributed across all nodes in the cache cluster to prevent any single node from becoming a bottleneck, which could degrade performance.

492

2. Dynamic Cache Invalidation: Establish a mechanism to remove outdated or less frequently accessed data, maintaining the cache's effectiveness and relevance. Utilize Time-to-Live (TTL) policies for automatic data expiry.

3. Adjusting for Data Consistency: Decide on the appropriate level of consistency needed for the application—whether strong or eventual consistency—and configure the cache accordingly to balance between accuracy and speed.

4. Monitoring and Adjustment: Continuously monitor cache metrics like hit rates, miss rates, and the overall load. Adjust settings based on these metrics to optimize performance and resource usage.

5. Enhanced Security Measures: Implement security protocols to protect sensitive data within the cache, including encryption and secure access controls.

Conclusion

Implementing distributed caching is a powerful approach to enhance application scalability and efficiency. By caching data across a network of servers, applications can reduce reliance on slow database queries, handle higher volumes of traffic, and improve the user experience with faster response times. Thoughtful implementation, ongoing monitoring, and regular adjustments are crucial to leveraging the full potential of distributed caching in any high-performance computing environment.

Chapter Ten

Security Performance Considerations

Security best practices without compromising performance

Securing software applications effectively while maintaining optimal performance is a critical challenge in contemporary software development. Integrating robust security frameworks early in the development lifecycle and adopting efficient strategies are key to safeguarding systems without reducing operational efficiency. This discussion outlines several approaches to seamlessly incorporate security practices that preserve performance.

Early Integration of Security Measures

Incorporating security from the initial stages of system design—often referred to as "security by design"—is crucial. This approach not only makes security an integral part of the architecture but also prevents the need for costly and less efficient retrofitting of security measures later.

Principles for Proactive Security Integration:

- Minimize Data Exposure: Systems should be designed to limit the exposure of sensitive data, thus minimizing the potential attack surface.

- Default to Secure Settings: Configure systems to be secure from the start, necessitating deliberate actions to reduce security, which helps prevent inadvertent vulnerabilities due to misconfiguration.

Optimizing Authentication and Authorization

Developing streamlined authentication and authorization processes is essential for securing applications without diminishing user experience or system responsiveness.

Effective Use of JWTs (JSON Web Tokens): JWTs facilitate secure interactions between parties and are particularly useful for stateless authentication across distributed systems.

```javascript
const jwt = require('jsonwebtoken');

function checkToken(req, res, next) {
    const token = req.headers.authorization?.split(' ')[1];

    if (!token) {
        return res.sendStatus(401); // Unauthorized
    }

    jwt.verify(token, process.env.SECRET_KEY, (err, decoded) => {
        if (err) {
            return res.sendStatus(403); // Forbidden
        }
        req.user = decoded;
        next();
    });
}
```

This Node.js snippet illustrates using JWT to authenticate requests, minimizing the need for database queries for user authentication and thus enhancing performance.

495

Focused Data Encryption

Implementing encryption selectively for only critical data helps maintain security without imposing unnecessary performance overheads.

Selective Encryption Approach: Only encrypt data that, if compromised, could cause significant harm, such as personal user information or financial details.

Hardware-Assisted Encryption: Modern processors often support encryption acceleration technologies like AES-NI, which can significantly speed up encryption operations without impacting overall system performance.

Adherence to Secure Coding Practices

Secure coding is fundamental for preventing common security flaws such as SQL injection and cross-site scripting (XSS), which can also optimize the application's data processing.

Preventing SQL Injection Using Safe Practices:

```python
import psycopg2

conn = psycopg2.connect("dbname=service user=appuser")
cur = conn.cursor()

# Safe query execution
cur.execute("UPDATE accounts SET balance = balance + %s WHERE account_id = %s",
    (depositAmount, accountId))
```

This Python code uses parameterized queries, effectively preventing SQL injection while optimizing query execution time by reducing the need for repeated parsing and compilation of SQL statements.

Routine Security Audits and Updates

Consistently performing security audits and updating software components are critical for mitigating emerging threats. Automating these processes ensures ongoing security maintenance without significant manual overhead.

Automated Security Tools: Utilize automated security scanning tools and dependency management solutions to regularly update and patch vulnerabilities, keeping the system secure and up-to-date efficiently.

Conclusion

Effectively balancing security and performance requires adopting security measures early in the design process, utilizing efficient authentication mechanisms, implementing targeted encryption practices, following secure coding guidelines, and continuously monitoring and updating security measures. These practices ensure that applications are not only secure from threats but also perform efficiently to meet user and business needs.

Optimizing authentication and authorization mechanisms

In the digital realm, ensuring robust security measures without detracting from system performance is critical. Effective authentication and authorization are integral in safeguarding sensitive information and managing user access efficiently. This discussion highlights advanced strategies for refining these security measures to maintain solid protection while enhancing system performance.

Overview of Authentication and Authorization

Authentication verifies a user's identity through credentials like passwords, tokens, or biometric data, ensuring they are who they claim to be. Authorization occurs after authentication, determining if the user should have access to specific resources or capabilities within the system.

Optimally designed authentication and authorization processes are essential for secure and efficient operations. Inadequate implementations can introduce security gaps and slow down the system.

Advanced Authentication Enhancements

Streamlining authentication is pivotal in securing access while minimizing impact on user experience and system load. Here are several approaches:

1. Multi-Factor Authentication (MFA): MFA strengthens security by requiring multiple proofs of identity, greatly reducing the risk of unauthorized access.

```python
# Python code for TOTP-based MFA
import pyotp
totp = pyotp.TOTP('base32secret7890')
print("Dynamic OTP:", totp.now())
```

This Python example uses TOTP to generate a dynamic one-time password, an effective way to implement MFA, enhancing security with minimal impact on performance.

2. Single Sign-On (SSO): SSO allows users to authenticate once and access multiple systems without repeated logins, reducing the authentication burden on systems.

```javascript
// SSO implementation using OAuth2 in JavaScript
app.get('/login', passport.authenticate('oauth2'));
app.get('/login/callback',
    passport.authenticate('oauth2', { failureRedirect: '/login' }),
    function(req, res) {
        // Redirect to the homepage after successful authentication
        res.redirect('/');
    }
);
```

This JavaScript setup demonstrates SSO functionality using OAuth2, streamlining user authentication across multiple services or applications.

Refined Authorization Practices

Efficient authorization setups ensure proper access control, maintaining security without unnecessary delays.

1. Role-Based Access Control (RBAC): RBAC facilitates permission management by assigning roles to users, which simplifies controlling access to resources.

```java
// Simple RBAC example in Java
if (user.getRole().equals("MANAGER")) {
    // Grant access to managerial functions
}
```

This Java code snippet utilizes RBAC to grant access based on predefined user roles, efficiently managing user permissions within the system.

2. Attribute-Based Access Control (ABAC): ABAC allows for detailed access control by evaluating various

499

attributes of users and resources to make authorization decisions.

```
// Implementing ABAC in Java
public boolean permitAccess(User user, Document document) {
    return user.getAuthorizationLevel() >= document.getSecurityLevel();
}
```

In this example, access decisions are based on comparing user and document security levels, offering a nuanced approach to authorization.

Enhancing System Performance

To optimize performance in authentication and authorization:

- Caching Decisions: By caching the outcomes of security checks, the system can quickly retrieve and apply decisions without reprocessing, speeding up access for repeat requests.

- Efficient Data Handling: Streamlining data access and storage, particularly in complex systems, can reduce the time taken to perform security checks.

Ongoing Security Management

Regular updates and continuous monitoring of security mechanisms are essential to adapt to new threats and maintain both security and performance.

Conclusion

Incorporating sophisticated authentication methods such as MFA and SSO, along with robust access control techniques like RBAC and ABAC, ensures comprehensive security across systems without degrading performance. Implementing these strategies effectively requires careful planning and regular optimization to keep pace with evolving security demands and technological advancements.

Secure, performant handling of sensitive data

Navigating the complex interplay between stringent security protocols and system performance is essential in today's data-centric environments. Organizations must manage sensitive data—ranging from personal identifiers to financial and health records—not only with compliance to regulatory standards like GDPR and HIPAA in mind but also ensuring that these security measures do not undermine system responsiveness. This discussion highlights effective methodologies for maintaining high security without compromising on system performance.

Core Security Measures for Data Protection

The safeguarding of sensitive information begins with robust security tactics that include advanced encryption, comprehensive access controls, and effective data management strategies.

Essential Security Approaches:

- Advanced Encryption: Employing AES (Advanced Encryption Standard) for encrypting data in storage and transit is crucial for shielding it from unauthorized access.

- Stringent Access Controls: Using systems like Role-Based Access Control (RBAC) and Attribute-Based Access Control (ABAC) helps ensure that only authorized users can access certain data, based on their roles or specific attributes.

- Minimizing Data Retention: Reducing the amount of sensitive data stored minimizes risk and can enhance system performance by lightening the load on data processing and storage resources.

Optimizing Security Operations for Performance

It's vital to implement security measures that do not negatively impact system performance. Several strategies can help achieve this balance:

- Efficient Encryption Processes: Making use of hardware acceleration features like AES-NI in CPUs can facilitate faster encryption and decryption activities, reducing performance overhead.

```java
import javax.crypto.Cipher;
import javax.crypto.KeyGenerator;
import javax.crypto.SecretKey;

public class AdvancedEncryption {
    public static void main(String[] args) throws Exception {
        KeyGenerator keyGenerator = KeyGenerator.getInstance("AES");
        keyGenerator.init(256); // Opt for AES-256 for robust encryption
        SecretKey key = keyGenerator.generateKey();

        Cipher cipher = Cipher.getInstance("AES/GCM/NoPadding");
        cipher.init(Cipher.ENCRYPT_MODE, key);

        String dataToEncrypt = "Highly Sensitive Information";
        byte[] encryptedData = cipher.doFinal(dataToEncrypt.getBytes());
        System.out.println("Encrypted data: " + new String(encryptedData));
    }
}
```

This Java example showcases the application of AES-256 encryption, demonstrating how using specific CPU capabilities can enhance data security efficiently.

- Smart Data Caching: Caching non-sensitive data reduces the need to frequently access and process sensitive data, thus improving performance.

Strategies for Efficient Data Storage and Retrieval

Choosing the right storage solutions and optimizing data retrieval mechanisms are key to managing sensitive data effectively.

- Enhanced Database Security Settings: Secure database configurations should enforce encrypted connections and strict access limitations. Indexing sensitive fields can improve the efficiency of query operations without sacrificing data security.

- Data Masking Implementation: Applying data masking to sensitive information in outputs ensures that full data values are not unnecessarily exposed, safeguarding privacy while retaining functionality.

```
SELECT CONCAT('XXX-XX-', SUBSTRING(ssn, 8, 4)) as MaskedSSN FROM client_data;
```

This SQL example illustrates a technique for masking sensitive data, in this case, a Social Security Number, to prevent full exposure during data handling processes.

Continual Security Review and Compliance Assurance

Regular updates to security measures and ongoing monitoring for compliance are crucial to adapt to emerging threats and changing regulations.

Conclusion

Effectively managing sensitive data with stringent security measures while ensuring system performance is achievable through the careful application of advanced encryption, efficient data handling, and regular compliance checks. By adhering to these practices, organizations can secure their data against potential threats without compromising the efficiency and effectiveness of their operations. These strategies ensure both compliance with legal standards and the maintenance of stakeholder trust in a secure, high-performing environment.

Chapter Eleven

Advanced Application Monitoring and Metrics

Custom metrics for Spring Boot applications

In today's software development landscape, effectively monitoring the performance and health of applications is indispensable. Spring Boot, widely used for its ease and efficiency in building Java applications, is particularly adept at this through its Actuator module. Custom metrics, an extension beyond Spring Boot's default metrics, enable developers to tailor monitoring to specific operational requirements, offering granular insights into application dynamics and performance.

Essentials of Metrics in Spring Boot

Spring Boot Actuator facilitates production-ready features such as monitoring via HTTP endpoints or JMX, providing several built-in metrics out of the box. However, applications often have unique monitoring needs that require customized metrics to capture specific data points crucial for their operations.

Custom metrics serve as tailor-made measurements designed to track application-specific operations, such as transaction volumes or detailed operational statistics. These metrics are pivotal for identifying unusual patterns, comprehending application trends over time, and making data-driven decisions.

Integrating Custom Metrics with Micrometer

Micrometer provides a metrics collection facade that supports numerous monitoring systems, including Prometheus, Graphite, and Dynatrace. It streamlines the integration of custom metrics in Spring Boot applications, allowing for dynamic registration and management of these metrics.

Step 1: Configuring Micrometer

To utilize Micrometer for custom metrics, include the necessary dependencies in your project's build configuration. For Maven users, this involves adding entries to the `pom.xml` file:

```xml
<dependency>
    <groupId>io.micrometer</groupId>
    <artifactId>micrometer-core</artifactId>
    <version>1.5.5</version>
</dependency>
<dependency>
    <groupId>io.micrometer</groupId>
    <artifactId>micrometer-registry-prometheus</artifactId>
    <version>1.5.5</version>
</dependency>
```

This configuration sets up Micrometer with support for Prometheus as the data monitoring system.

Step 2: Creating Custom Metrics

Custom metrics can be defined using the `MeterRegistry`. Here is how you can create a counter metric within a Spring Boot service:

506

```java
import io.micrometer.core.instrument.Counter;
import io.micrometer.core.instrument.MeterRegistry;
import org.springframework.stereotype.Service;

@Service
public class PaymentService {

    private final Counter paymentCounter;

    public PaymentService(MeterRegistry registry) {
        paymentCounter = Counter.builder("payments.completed")
                                .description("Total number of payments processed")
                                .register(registry);
    }

    public void completePayment(Payment payment) {
        paymentCounter.increment();
        // further processing logic
    }
}
```

This code snippet sets up a counter to monitor the number of payments processed, using the `**MeterRegistry**` to register this custom metric.

Step 3: Exporting Metrics

For metrics to be useful, they must be accessible for monitoring purposes. When using Prometheus, for example, metrics can be exposed through a controller endpoint:

```java
import io.micrometer.prometheus.PrometheusMeterRegistry;
import org.springframework.web.bind.annotation.GetMapping;
import org.springframework.web.bind.annotation.RestController;

@RestController
public class MetricsEndpointController {

    private final PrometheusMeterRegistry registry;

    public MetricsEndpointController(PrometheusMeterRegistry registry) {
        this.registry = registry;
    }

    @GetMapping("/metrics")
    public String exportMetrics() {
        return registry.scrape();
    }
}
```

This controller provides an endpoint for Prometheus to scrape, displaying the metrics in a format it can interpret, facilitating data visualization via tools like Grafana.

Best Practices for Custom Metrics

When deploying custom metrics, consider the following best practices to ensure they provide meaningful insights and do not negatively impact application performance:

- Measure with Purpose: Focus on metrics that provide significant insight. Excessive data can become cumbersome and detract from important findings.

- Optimize Tags Usage: While tags are helpful for detailed analysis, excessive tagging can lead to high cardinality issues, potentially degrading database performance.

- Continual Metric Evaluation: Regularly reassess and refine metrics to align with evolving application features and business objectives.

Conclusion

Custom metrics in Spring Boot, powered by Micrometer, enable developers to closely monitor specific aspects of their applications, enhancing observability and decision-making capabilities. Thoughtful implementation and continuous management of these metrics ensure they remain a valuable asset for maintaining and improving application performance and reliability.

Advanced usage of Spring Boot Actuator and Micrometer

In the competitive landscape of software development, the effective management and monitoring of applications in production are critical. Spring Boot Actuator, coupled with Micrometer, provides a robust framework for these tasks, enabling detailed insights into application health and metrics. This capability allows developers to enhance default monitoring features to meet specific needs, improving both application visibility and control.

Customizing Monitoring with Spring Boot Actuator

Spring Boot Actuator delivers essential management features that can be accessed through HTTP endpoints or JMX, covering various application aspects like metrics, health, and configurations. By extending these endpoints, developers can tailor them to monitor specific application metrics and health indicators more precisely.

Enhancing Endpoint Functionality: Developers can modify and extend Actuator endpoints to integrate additional metrics or health indicators, enhancing the monitoring capabilities specific to their application's operational context.

```java
import org.springframework.boot.actuate.health.Health;
import org.springframework.boot.actuate.health.HealthIndicator;
import org.springframework.stereotype.Component;

@Component
public class AdvancedHealthIndicator implements HealthIndicator {

    @Override
    public Health health() {
        int errorCode = performHealthCheck(); // Custom method to check health
        if (errorCode != 0) {
            return Health.down().withDetail("Error Code", errorCode).build();
        }
        return Health.up().build();
    }

    private int performHealthCheck() {
        // Custom health check logic
        return 0; // Example error code
    }
}
```

This Java code illustrates how to implement a custom health indicator that assesses a specific aspect of the application, providing tailored health information.

Detailed Metrics with Micrometer

Micrometer serves as a metrics library providing dimensional monitoring capabilities that support a wide array of monitoring systems. It enables the precise tracking of JVM, application, and custom metrics.

Custom Metrics Implementation: Custom metrics can be specifically tailored to capture unique operational data of the application, providing developers with the flexibility to track what matters most.

```java
import io.micrometer.core.instrument.MeterRegistry;
import io.micrometer.core.instrument.binder.MeterBinder;

public class CustomMetricsBinder implements MeterBinder {

    private final ApplicationComponent applicationComponent;

    public CustomMetricsBinder(ApplicationComponent applicationComponent) {
        this.applicationComponent = applicationComponent;
    }

    @Override
    public void bindTo(MeterRegistry registry) {
        registry.gauge("application.performance", applicationComponent,
            ApplicationComponent::performanceMetric);
    }
}
```

In this example, a custom gauge metric is created to monitor a specific performance metric of an application component, integrating deep insights directly into the monitoring framework.

Applying Dynamic Metric Tags: Micrometer supports the dynamic tagging of metrics, providing detailed segmentation that enhances data analysis capabilities.

```java
import io.micrometer.core.instrument.Tags;

public void processEvent(Event event) {
    MeterRegistry registry = // Obtain MeterRegistry
    Tags tags = Tags.of("event.type", event.getType(), "source", event.getSource());

    registry.counter("events.processed", tags).increment();
}
```

This segment shows how events can be tagged with their type and source, allowing for detailed tracking and analysis of processed events.

511

Integrating Actuator and Micrometer for Enhanced Monitoring

Combining Spring Boot Actuator with Micrometer enables developers to expose detailed custom metrics through Actuator's endpoints, streamlining the monitoring process.

1. Unified Metrics Exposure: Integration allows for all metrics, including custom ones defined via Micrometer, to be accessible through Actuator's endpoints.

2. Endpoint Security Measures: Securing Actuator endpoints is essential due to the sensitive nature of the data they can expose.

```
import org.springframework.security.config.annotation.web.builders.HttpSecurity;
import org.springframework.security.config.annotation.web.configuration
    .WebSecurityConfigurerAdapter;

public class ActuatorSecurityConfigurer extends WebSecurityConfigurerAdapter {

    @Override
    protected void configure(HttpSecurity http) throws Exception {
        http
            .authorizeRequests()
            .requestMatchers(EndpointRequest.toAnyEndpoint()).hasRole("ADMIN")
            .and()
            .httpBasic();
    }
}
```

This configuration ensures that Actuator endpoints are secured, requiring ADMIN role privileges to access, thus protecting sensitive application metrics and health data.

Conclusion

The sophisticated use of Spring Boot Actuator and Micrometer offers developers comprehensive tools for in-depth application monitoring and management. By customizing and leveraging the capabilities of these tools, developers can maintain high levels of application performance and reliability, ensuring that their systems are both robust and insightful in real-time operational environments.

Integrating with monitoring tools like Prometheus and Grafana

Effective application monitoring is crucial for maintaining optimal performance and reliability in today's digital environments. Prometheus and Grafana, as leading tools in the monitoring landscape, provide exceptional capabilities for tracking and visualizing operational data. This guide explores the steps for integrating these advanced tools into your applications to improve monitoring efficacy and gain deeper insights.

Insights into Prometheus and Grafana

Prometheus is an open-source solution designed for monitoring and alerting, capturing a wide variety of metrics as time-series data. It features a robust query language that enables precise data retrieval for analysis.

Grafana is a powerful visualization tool that interfaces with Prometheus among other data sources, allowing users to create detailed dashboards that display metrics through graphs, charts, and alerts. This enhances the ability to interpret large volumes of data effectively.

Integrating Prometheus for metric collection alongside Grafana for visualization offers a comprehensive monitoring framework that can transform data into actionable insights.

Configuring Prometheus for Your Application

Integrating Prometheus involves setting up your application to expose metrics in a way that Prometheus can efficiently scrape. This process is often facilitated by libraries like Micrometer in Spring Boot applications, which provide seamless compatibility with Prometheus.

1. Incorporate Required Libraries: Ensure the Micrometer Prometheus library is included in your project:

```xml
<dependency>
    <groupId>io.micrometer</groupId>
    <artifactId>micrometer-registry-prometheus</artifactId>
    <version>LATEST_VERSION</version>
</dependency>
```

2. Enable Metrics Endpoint in Spring Boot: Micrometer simplifies the exposure of metrics in Spring Boot, typically via a `/actuator/Prometheus` endpoint, enabling Prometheus to scrape data effectively:

```java
import org.springframework.context.annotation.Bean;
import org.springframework.context.annotation.Configuration;
import io.micrometer.core.instrument.MeterRegistry;

@Configuration
public class MetricConfiguration {
    @Bean
    MeterRegistryCustomizer<MeterRegistry> configureMetrics() {
        return registry -> registry.config().commonTags("app", "YOUR_APP_LABEL");
    }
}
```

This configuration snippet ensures that metrics are neatly tagged, making them easier to manage and analyze.

3. Set Prometheus to Scrape Metrics: Adjust Prometheus's settings to fetch data from your application at regular intervals:

```
scrape_configs:
  - job_name: 'application_metrics'
    scrape_interval: 10s
    static_configs:
      - targets: ['<YOUR_APP_HOST>:<YOUR_APP_PORT>']
```

This setup directs Prometheus to periodically collect metrics from your configured endpoint.

Utilizing Grafana for Data Visualization

With Prometheus configured to aggregate metrics, Grafana can be employed to visualize this data.

1. Link Grafana to Prometheus: Configure Grafana to recognize Prometheus as a data source, specifying Prometheus's URL in the Grafana settings.

2. Develop Informative Dashboards: In Grafana, construct dashboards to visualize the data collected by Prometheus. Utilize Grafana's query editor to craft queries using PromQL for tailored visual representations:

```
sum(rate(http_request_duration_seconds_count[5m])) by (route)
```

This PromQL example calculates the rate of HTTP requests per route, averaged over the last five minutes, providing insights into traffic patterns and potential issues.

515

Recommendations for Effective Integration

- Regularly Review Metrics: Keep your metrics relevant by continuously evaluating and adjusting them.

- Implement Robust Security Measures: Secure your Prometheus and Grafana setups, especially when exposed over the internet, by implementing authentication and using encrypted connections.

- Set Up Proactive Alerts: Take advantage of alerting features in Grafana and Prometheus to monitor critical metrics and respond quickly to anomalies.

Conclusion

The integration of Prometheus and Grafana into your application infrastructure offers a robust solution for monitoring that not only collects detailed operational data but also visualizes it effectively. By following the steps outlined and adhering to recommended practices, you can establish an advanced monitoring setup that enables informed decision-making and enhances application performance and stability.

Chapter Twelve

CI/CD and DevOps for Spring Boot

Automating performance testing in CI/CD pipelines

In contemporary software development, the use of Continuous Integration/Continuous Deployment (CI/CD) pipelines is fundamental for delivering quality software rapidly and consistently. Integrating performance testing within these pipelines is critical for ensuring that applications not only operate as expected but also meet predetermined performance criteria before they are deployed.

Significance of Performance Testing in CI/CD

Performance testing in CI/CD pipelines is pivotal for identifying potential regressions and performance issues early in the software development lifecycle. This approach helps mitigate risks before they impact production systems, significantly reducing the time and resources required for fixes post-deployment.

Automation of these tests guarantees that performance is evaluated consistently and thoroughly across multiple codebases and deployment environments, aligning well with agile methodologies that emphasize speed and efficiency.

Implementing Automated Performance Testing

1. Choosing the Right Tools: Selecting appropriate tools that integrate seamlessly with your CI/CD setup is the first step in automating performance testing. Tools like JMeter, Gatling, and LoadRunner are excellent for simulating user behavior and measuring various performance metrics under load.

Example with Jenkins and JMeter:

```
# Example Jenkins pipeline stage for running JMeter tests
stage('Performance Test') {
    steps {
        script {
            sh 'jmeter -n -t my_performance_test.jmx -l result_file.jtl'
        }
    }
    post {
        success {
            archiveArtifacts artifacts: 'result_file.jtl', fingerprint: true
            junit 'result_file.jtl'
        }
    }
}
```

This example shows how to configure a Jenkins pipeline to execute a JMeter test plan, save the results, and analyze them to track performance over time.

2. Setting Performance Benchmarks: Establishing baseline metrics for performance is crucial. These benchmarks are derived from historical data and provide a standard to measure against, ensuring new changes do not degrade performance.

3. Feedback Integration: Incorporating mechanisms for immediate feedback on performance test outcomes is essential. Results should trigger alerts if performance falls

518

below acceptable levels, and detailed reports should be available for in-depth analysis to facilitate prompt corrective actions.

4. Test Maintenance and Scalability: It is vital to continuously update and scale your performance tests to accommodate new application features and user scenarios. This ensures the tests remain relevant and effective at uncovering potential issues as the application evolves.

Best Practices for Performance Testing Automation

1. Test Early and Often: Incorporate performance testing early in the software development process and execute these tests frequently. Early testing helps detect issues sooner, when they are generally simpler and less expensive to resolve.

2. Ensure Broad Test Coverage: Develop performance tests that comprehensively cover various aspects of the application. Extensive coverage helps uncover how different components perform under stress and in diverse operational conditions.

3. Simulate Realistic Usage Patterns: Performance tests should closely mimic real user behavior and load conditions to ensure the results accurately reflect potential production operations. This includes using real data and user interaction patterns.

4. Continuous Monitoring and Refinement: Keep monitoring the performance impact of newly introduced features and optimizations. Regular analysis of performance data should guide continuous improvement efforts for both the application and the testing strategies.

Conclusion

Integrating automated performance testing into CI/CD pipelines is crucial for developing high-quality, robust, and efficient software. This strategic incorporation ensures performance considerations are addressed systematically throughout the development phase. As a result, organizations can achieve more reliable software deployments, enhanced product quality, and superior user satisfaction, maintaining a competitive edge in the marketplace.

Containerization and orchestration with Docker and Kubernetes

In today's technology-driven landscape, mastering containerization and orchestration is critical for streamlining application deployment and ensuring consistent performance across diverse environments. Docker and Kubernetes lead these efforts, providing robust frameworks that simplify complex application management.

Leveraging Docker for Effective Containerization

Docker is pivotal in modern development, enabling applications and their dependencies to be packaged into containers. This encapsulation ensures applications run reliably regardless of the deployment environment.

Benefits of Using Docker:

- Consistency Across Environments: Docker ensures that containers operate the same way across any system, removing common "works on my machine" issues.

- Resource Efficiency: Containers run on the same machine and share the OS kernel, significantly reducing the overhead compared to running full virtual machines.

- Isolation and Security: Each container runs in isolation, safeguarding against system failures and providing robust security.

Docker Usage Example:

```
docker run -d -p 80:80 --name mycontainer nginx
```

This command demonstrates deploying an Nginx container that maps port 80 on the host to port 80 on the container, running detached from the terminal.

Orchestrating with Kubernetes

While Docker focuses on containerization, Kubernetes excels in orchestrating these containers, particularly in distributed systems.

Foundational Concepts in Kubernetes:

- Pods: Basic units in Kubernetes that contain one or more containers that should be managed together.

- Services: Define how applications access the services provided by pods, offering a consistent interface.

- Deployments: Help manage application updates and scaling, providing a mechanism for automated rollouts and rollbacks.

521

Kubernetes Configuration Example:

```yaml
apiVersion: apps/v1
kind: Deployment
metadata:
  name: webapp-deployment
spec:
  replicas: 3
  selector:
    matchLabels:
      app: webapp
  template:
    metadata:
      labels:
        app: webapp
    spec:
      containers:
      - name: webapp
        image: nginx:1.14.2
        ports:
        - containerPort: 80
```

This script configures Kubernetes to manage three instances of a web application using the Nginx server, ensuring high availability and load distribution.

Integrating Docker with Kubernetes

Combining Docker and Kubernetes offers streamlined management of container lifecycles across various environments. Docker packages the application, while Kubernetes handles deployment and scaling, creating an efficient orchestration system.

Docker Compose vs. Kubernetes: Docker Compose is suitable for managing multiple containers on a single host, but Kubernetes scales across a cluster, providing the robustness needed for larger deployments.

Best Practices for Optimization

1. Optimal Container Construction:

    - Select verified images to enhance security.

    - Design containers to be ephemeral, reducing complexity in management.

2. Manage Configurations Effectively:

    - Employ Kubernetes ConfigMaps and Secrets for dynamic environment-specific settings.

3. Resource Specifications:

    - Clearly define the resources each container should use within Kubernetes to prevent resource contention and ensure efficient operations.

4. Implement Advanced Monitoring:

    - Use comprehensive tools such as Prometheus for system monitoring and the EFK stack for logging to maintain visibility and control over operations.

Conclusion

The synergy of Docker and Kubernetes redefines application deployment and management, offering scalable solutions that enhance both the development cycle and the operational stability of applications. Embracing these tools equips organizations with the capabilities to manage complex infrastructures efficiently and maintain a competitive edge in the rapidly evolving tech landscape.

Infrastructure as Code (IaC) for consistent environments

Infrastructure as Code (IaC) stands as a cornerstone in modern IT strategies, providing the blueprint for automating and managing infrastructure through code. This method ties closely with best practices in software development such as version control and automated testing, promoting operational efficiency and minimizing discrepancies.

The Role of IaC

The adoption of IaC across IT landscapes offers transformative benefits:

- Efficiency in Deployment: Automation through IaC allows rapid provisioning of complex infrastructures on demand.

- Enhanced Reliability: It eliminates variability by standardizing infrastructure configurations, reducing the risk of human error.

- Traceability and Control: Infrastructure changes are version-controlled and auditable, ensuring any modifications are trackable and reversible.

- Reduction in Operational Costs: IaC minimizes the labor and potential errors involved in manual configurations, leading to cost savings.

Key IaC Technologies

There are several pivotal tools in the IaC arena, each designed to address specific needs within infrastructure management:

- Terraform: Praised for its powerful declarative approach and its capacity to handle complex deployments across various providers.

- Ansible: Known for its straightforward, agentless setup in automating deployments and managing configurations.

- AWS CloudFormation: A service that integrates deeply with AWS to define and provision AWS infrastructure using a declarative template.

- Azure Resource Manager (ARM): Manages and provisions Azure resources consistently using declarative JSON templates.

Deploying Infrastructure with Terraform

Here is an example that demonstrates deploying an infrastructure component using Terraform, showcasing its practical application:

Provisioning an AWS EC2 Instance with Terraform:

```
provider "aws" {
  region = "us-west-2"
}

resource "aws_instance" "web" {
  ami           = "ami-0c55b159cbfafe1f0"
  instance_type = "t2.micro"

  tags = {
    Name = "WebServer"
  }
}
```

This Terraform script configures an EC2 instance in the AWS Oregon region, underlining the ease and precision with which infrastructure can be specified and managed.

Implementing IaC Effectively

For optimal implementation of IaC, several best practices should be followed:

1. Modularize Infrastructure Code: Organize code into discrete modules to simplify updates and enhance reuse.

2. Complete Infrastructure Codification: Ensure that all elements of your infrastructure are codified, facilitating full governance and control.

3. Integrate with CI/CD Pipelines: Regularly integrate and test your infrastructure code within CI/CD pipelines to catch issues early and reduce risks.

4. Utilize Immutable Infrastructure: Embrace a model where updates are performed by replacing resources rather than altering existing configurations, improving predictability and rollback capabilities.

Conclusion

Infrastructure as Code revolutionizes traditional approaches to IT management, aligning it with systematic, predictable, and scalable practices. By leveraging advanced tools like Terraform and Ansible, and adopting thorough modularization and testing strategies, organizations can ensure that their infrastructure meets stringent standards of reliability and efficiency. This structured approach to infrastructure management not only reduces overhead but also enhances overall service delivery, positioning businesses for future growth and adaptability.

Chapter Thirteen

Troubleshooting and Debugging High-Performance Issues

Advanced techniques for diagnosing and resolving performance bottlenecks

Performance bottlenecks can critically impair the effectiveness and response times of applications. To ensure optimal application functionality, it's essential to employ sophisticated diagnostic techniques and precise instrumentation to accurately identify and resolve these issues.

Evaluating Performance Bottlenecks

Performance bottlenecks typically manifest within specific areas of a system, limiting overall efficiency due to poor coding practices, inadequate resource allocation, or suboptimal system configurations. These issues often result in prolonged response times, diminished throughput, or heightened latency, particularly under specific load conditions.

Identifying Performance Bottlenecks

1. Profiling: This technique involves analyzing an application's resource usage in real-time to identify inefficient operations.

- Example Using Python's cProfile:

```python
import cProfile
import your_app

def initiate_profiling():
    cProfile.run('your_app.start()', 'output.prof')

if __name__ == "__main__":
    initiate_profiling()
```

This snippet illustrates using Python's cProfile to track application performance and save the results for subsequent evaluation.

2. Tracing: This approach records detailed information about application processes, crucial for dissecting behaviors in complex systems.

   - Advanced Tracing with OpenTelemetry: OpenTelemetry offers comprehensive tools and APIs for detailed tracing and metrics, enhancing analytical capabilities for application performance.

3. Load Testing: Utilizing simulated demand to assess how applications perform under stress. Tools like JMeter and LoadRunner are used to generate user traffic and evaluate application resilience.

4. Benchmarking: Comparing current application performance against established standards or previous metrics to identify performance degradation.

Addressing Performance Bottlenecks

Several strategies can be implemented to effectively mitigate identified bottlenecks:

1. Code Optimization: Improving or rewriting inefficient code sections can significantly boost performance.

   - Optimizing SQL Queries:

```sql
SELECT * FROM Orders
JOIN Customers ON Orders.CustomerID = Customers.CustomerID
WHERE Customers.Country = 'Germany'
```

This SQL optimization, by refining joins or indexing, can drastically enhance query performance.

2. Resource Enhancement: Increasing the capacity of resources such as servers or networks can alleviate bottlenecks arising from physical constraints.

3. Concurrency Enhancements: Adjusting applications to handle tasks concurrently can optimize resource usage and improve performance.

   - Enhancing Concurrency with Python's asyncio:

```python
import asyncio

async def retrieve_data():
    print("Retrieving data")
    await asyncio.sleep(2)
    print("Data ready")
    return {'data': 'loaded'}

async def perform():
    info = await retrieve_data()
    print(info)

asyncio.run(perform())
```

This example demonstrates using Python's asyncio for better performance in handling asynchronous tasks, especially in I/O-bound operations.

4. Caching Techniques: Implementing caching mechanisms to store and swiftly retrieve frequently accessed data can substantially reduce load times and lessen the burden on critical resources.

Utilizing Comprehensive Monitoring Tools

Advanced monitoring solutions like Dynatrace, New Relic, and AppDynamics offer in-depth insights into application performance, with capabilities for automated anomaly detection and detailed causal analysis. These tools are crucial for swiftly pinpointing and addressing performance discrepancies.

Conclusion

Effectively tackling performance bottlenecks requires a combination of detailed diagnostics and targeted interventions. Techniques such as profiling, tracing, load testing, and benchmarking are crucial in identifying underlying performance issues. Remedial measures, including code optimization, resource augmentation, improvements in concurrency, and strategic caching, are essential for enhancing application performance. Additionally, state-of-the-art monitoring tools play a vital role in ongoing performance optimization, ensuring applications maintain high operational standards.

Profiling Spring Boot applications and identifying memory leaks

Spring Boot facilitates the rapid development of both microservices and comprehensive software applications. However, performance issues such as memory leaks can impede their effectiveness and degrade user interactions. Thorough profiling and timely detection of memory leaks are critical to maintaining the optimal operation of Spring Boot applications.

The Importance of Profiling in Spring Boot

Profiling allows for the examination of Spring Boot applications by tracking their resource consumption and behavioral patterns. This analytical approach is essential for identifying areas of performance slowdown, excessive memory use, and inefficient code execution within an application.

1. Application Performance Monitoring (APM) Tools: Tools like AppDynamics, Dynatrace, and New Relic are pivotal in monitoring the performance of Java applications, including those built on Spring Boot. They provide real-time insights into resource usage, execution timings, and method efficiency.

2. Java Profiling Tools: For detailed JVM analysis, tools such as YourKit, VisualVM, and JProfiler are indispensable. They offer insights into critical JVM aspects like garbage collection, heap usage, and thread management, all of which are crucial for spotting performance irregularities.

Effective Profiling Techniques for Spring Boot

Profiling Spring Boot applications effectively typically includes several important practices:

1. Integration of APM Tools: Embedding APM solutions in Spring Boot applications generally involves adding specific dependencies and configuring application properties. Most APM tools utilize Java agents that integrate seamlessly with the JVM.

   - Example of APM Integration:

```xml
<!-- Maven dependency for New Relic -->
<dependency>
    <groupId>com.newrelic.agent.java</groupId>
    <artifactId>newrelic-agent</artifactId>
    <version>LATEST_VERSION</version>
</dependency>
```

Setup includes configuring the `**newrelic.yml**` and attaching it to the JVM:

```
java -javaagent:path_to_newrelic/newrelic.jar -jar your-spring-boot-app.jar
```

2. Utilizing JVM Profiling Tools: Connecting tools like VisualVM to an actively running Spring Boot application requires no code modifications. These tools enable ongoing monitoring of memory and facilitate heap dump analyses.

   - How to Connect VisualVM: Open VisualVM, locate the process ID of your Spring Boot application, and begin monitoring key performance indicators and threads.

Detecting and Addressing Memory Leaks in Spring Boot

Memory leaks in Spring Boot occur when objects that are no longer in use continue to occupy memory space in the JVM heap, potentially leading to excessive memory consumption and `OutOfMemoryError`. Identifying and managing these leaks involves:

1. Heap Dump Analysis: Tools like Eclipse Memory Analyzer (MAT) analyze heap dumps—snapshots of memory allocation in the JVM—to identify memory leaks.

   - Generating a Heap Dump: This can be achieved using `jmap`:

```
jmap -dump:live,format=b,file=heapdump.hprof <PID>
```

Replace `<PID>` with the Process ID of your application.

2. Garbage Collection Log Analysis: Enabling garbage collection logs helps identify inefficient garbage collection processes that may suggest memory leaks.

   - Setting Up GC Logging:

```
java -Xloggc:gc.log -XX:+PrintGCDetails -XX:+PrintGCTimeStamps -jar your-spring-boot-app.jar
```

This command records detailed garbage collection data, essential for pinpointing inefficient or frequent garbage collection cycles.

3. Tracking Object Retention: Profiling tools can monitor object retention in the JVM heap, highlighting classes or beans that disproportionately consume memory.

Conclusion

Profiling Spring Boot applications and swiftly identifying memory leaks are imperative for ensuring these systems run effectively. By incorporating APM tools, using JVM profiling tools, and systematically analyzing memory utilization, developers can significantly enhance the stability and performance of their Spring Boot applications. Regular and proactive profiling aids in preempting potential issues, ensuring applications consistently deliver high performance and positive user experiences.

Log analysis and tracing for deep performance insights

In modern software development, optimal application performance is critical. Techniques like log analysis and tracing are essential for providing developers and IT professionals with in-depth insights into how applications operate and perform under various conditions. By closely examining log files and tracing application executions, teams can identify and address performance issues, better understand system behavior, and mitigate potential impacts on end-users before they occur.

Overview of Log Analysis

Log analysis entails the examination of the logs generated during an application's operation. These logs, which record a wide array of events, errors, and transactions, serve as a detailed chronological account of an application's activities. When analyzed effectively, logs can uncover hidden errors, track system health, and monitor application performance. Advanced tools such as Splunk, the ELK Stack (Elasticsearch, Logstash, Kibana), and Graylog enhance the capabilities of log analysis by enabling powerful data visualization, real-time processing, and complex queries.

Core Advantages of Log Analysis:

- Error Detection: Quickly pinpoint and address errors that may not be visible through other monitoring techniques.

- Pattern Recognition: Identify trends or recurring issues over time to better understand application behavior.

- Security Monitoring: Logs provide vital information on access and system operations, aiding in security assessments and compliance reporting.

Sample Log Entry:

```
2023-05-08T12:00:00 INFO [user.service] User login successful - userID: 12345
```

This example of a log entry records a user's successful login, including the exact time and user ID, valuable for both performance monitoring and security purposes.

The Role of Tracing

Tracing tracks the journey of requests as they pass through various components of an application, particularly in distributed systems. It is essential for diagnosing how requests are handled, where delays may occur, and how components interact under load.

Insights gained from tracing include:

- Identifying Performance Bottlenecks: Determine specific points where requests slow down, which can direct focused optimization efforts.

- Understanding Service Interactions: Visualize how different services or components interact, crucial for debugging and performance tuning.

- Tracking Error Sources: Follow the progression of a request that leads to an error, simplifying the troubleshooting process.

Tracing Implementation with OpenTelemetry: OpenTelemetry offers a robust framework for collecting traces and metrics from applications, facilitating broad observability. Here's a basic example of how to implement tracing in a Java application:

```
import io.opentelemetry.api.trace.Tracer;

public class Application {
    private static final Tracer tracer = GlobalOpenTelemetry.getTracer("com
        .example.application");

    public void performAction() {
        var span = tracer.spanBuilder("performAction").startSpan();
        try (var scope = span.makeCurrent()) {
            // Perform some actions
            Thread.sleep(1000);
        } catch (InterruptedException e) {
            span.recordException(e);
        } finally {
            span.end();  // Always ensure spans are closed
        }
    }
}
```

This code snippet demonstrates creating a span to monitor the duration and success of a method, and handling exceptions within that context.

Integrating Log Analysis with Tracing

When log analysis is combined with tracing, a more complete and nuanced view of application performance and health is achieved. Logs offer granular event data, while traces provide a macro view of the event flow within application processes. This integrated approach is critical for building a comprehensive understanding of application performance, leading to quicker and more effective problem resolution.

Best Practices:

- Correlate Logs with Traces: Enhance diagnostic capabilities by including trace IDs in log entries, linking detailed event data with broader transaction flows.

- Leverage Automation: Utilize tools to perform regular and automatic analysis of logs and traces, helping to detect and address issues proactively.

- Maintain Centralized Data Management: Ensure that logging and tracing data are centralized, particularly in distributed environments, to facilitate access and analysis.

Conclusion

Log analysis and tracing are vital for gaining deep insights into application performance. These techniques help identify and resolve performance issues, provide a clear view of application interactions, and ensure systems operate efficiently and securely. By leveraging advanced tools and adhering to established best practices, development teams can enhance application reliability and user experience.

Chapter Fourteen

Designing for High Availability and Resilience

Building fault-tolerant systems with Spring Boot

In the realm of digital services, the resilience of applications is crucial. Ensuring that systems can endure and recover from component failures without losing functionality is vital. Spring Boot offers an array of features that assist developers in building such fault-tolerant systems, enabling them to maintain seamless operations even under duress.

Essential Aspects of Fault Tolerance in Spring Boot

Creating fault-tolerant applications with Spring Boot involves structuring systems to effectively handle and recover from failures, thereby ensuring continuous operation and a consistent user experience.

Enhancing Fault Tolerance in Spring Boot

1. Unified Exception Management: Leveraging Spring Boot's `@ControllerAdvice` allows developers to handle exceptions globally, maintaining system stability by managing potential errors centrally.

```
@ControllerAdvice
public class GlobalExceptionHandler {

    @ExceptionHandler(value = Exception.class)
    public ResponseEntity<Object> handleAnyException(Exception e){
        return new ResponseEntity<>("An unexpected error has occurred. Please try
            again.", HttpStatus.INTERNAL_SERVER_ERROR);
    }
}
```

This example demonstrates how global exception handling is implemented, providing a consistent response to users and helping to stabilize the application after unexpected issues.

2. Configurable Dynamic Settings: Spring Boot's `@ConfigurationProperties` and Spring Cloud Config facilitate the external management of application settings, allowing system adjustments without downtime.

3. Service Discovery Implementation: Utilizing Spring Cloud Netflix Eureka enables automatic service registration and discovery, ensuring that applications can locate and communicate with each other reliably.

```
@EnableEurekaClient
@SpringBootApplication
public class CustomerServiceApplication {

    public static void main(String[] args) {
        SpringApplication.run(CustomerServiceApplication.class, args);
    }
}
```

This configuration demonstrates how a Spring Boot application can integrate with Eureka for dynamic service discovery, crucial for operational resilience.

4. Load Balancing and Circuit Breaking: Spring Cloud LoadBalancer distributes incoming traffic across multiple instances, preventing overload. Meanwhile, implementing circuit breakers with Resilience4j prevents failures from cascading across the system.

```
@Bean
public Customizer<Resilience4JCircuitBreakerFactory> defaultCircuitBreakerSetup()
    {
    return factory -> factory.configureDefault(id -> new Resilience4jConfigBuilder
        (id)
        .circuitBreakerConfig(CircuitBreakerConfig.ofDefaults())
        .timeLimiterConfig(TimeLimiterConfig.custom().timeoutDuration(Duration
            .ofSeconds(4)).build()).build());
}
```

This setup shows how circuit breakers can protect the system by preventing a complete shutdown when part of the system fails.

5. Facilitating Asynchronous Operations: Employing `@Async` or integrating with message brokers like Kafka or RabbitMQ enables the system to perform operations independently of the main application flow, improving scalability and responsiveness.

```
@Service
public class MessagingService {

    @Async
    public void sendMessage(String message) {
        // Simulating message sending
        System.out.println("Message dispatched: " + message);
    }
}
```

This method highlights how asynchronous processing can be implemented to enhance system performance and fault tolerance by managing tasks in the background.

Conclusion

Building fault-tolerant systems with Spring Boot involves utilizing its robust capabilities to prepare for and manage failures effectively. Through comprehensive error handling, dynamic configuration, resilient service discovery, strategic load balancing, and asynchronous communication, developers can craft robust applications that assure high availability and operational continuity. These practices are instrumental in creating systems that not only withstand failures but also ensure an uninterrupted user experience.

Strategies for disaster recovery and zero-downtime deployments

In today's relentless digital service environment, ensuring uninterrupted operations and robust IT system resilience is indispensable. Adopting strategic approaches to disaster recovery and zero-downtime deployments is key to reducing the risk of service interruptions and ensuring continuous service delivery. This exposition provides an overview of advanced methods and best practices designed to fortify systems and sustain operations during both planned upgrades and unforeseen system failures.

Key Principles of Disaster Recovery

Disaster recovery plans focus on preparing for and mitigating the impacts of significant IT disruptions. This strategy encompasses robust data backup practices, automated failover systems, and swift recovery protocols to limit downtime and safeguard data integrity.

Essential aspects of disaster recovery include:

- Geographical Data Redundancy: Implementing backups in multiple locations to mitigate risks associated with localized failures.

- Automated Failover Systems: Developing systems that can automatically switch to a backup operational mode when the primary configuration encounters issues.

- Regular Recovery Drills: Conducting consistent tests of recovery procedures to confirm their effectiveness and alignment with the organization's recovery benchmarks.

Achieving Zero-Downtime Deployments

Zero-downtime deployment is crucial for industries requiring constant availability, such as online retail, where any downtime directly affects revenue and customer satisfaction. Effective strategies to achieve this include:

1. Blue-Green Deployments: Employing dual production environments allows one to serve live traffic while updates are deployed and validated on the other. After testing, traffic is seamlessly shifted to the updated environment, minimizing any impact on service.

Example: Using orchestration platforms like Kubernetes to manage these environments facilitates smooth transitions by routing traffic between them.

2. Canary Releases: This technique involves initially rolling out changes to a limited user base, expanding to the full user base once the update is verified as stable. This limits the exposure of potential defects to a controlled group, thereby minimizing overall risk.

Example: A gradual increase in traffic directed to the updated application via load balancing allows for performance observation and issue resolution without major disruptions.

3. Feature Flags: Deploying new code behind feature flags lets teams deliver changes to production without exposing them to all users, allowing more controlled and reversible feature release processes.

```
if (featureFlags.isEnabled("new-feature")) {
    // execute new feature code
} else {
    // execute existing feature code
}
```

Example: This conditional feature check allows for seamless feature management, enabling or disabling features without destabilizing the broader application.

4. Database Schema Versioning: Aligning database schema changes with application updates is vital for deployment smoothness. Versioning tools like Liquibase and Flyway manage database migrations, ensuring consistency with the application's lifecycle.

Example: Flyway integration in the deployment pipeline automates database migrations, maintaining database and application schema consistency.

Integrating Disaster Recovery with Zero-Downtime Deployment Practices

Linking disaster recovery and zero-downtime deployment strategies provides a holistic safeguard against both expected upgrades and unexpected outages. This combined approach ensures seamless integration of updates and robust preparedness for potential failures.

Integrated best practices include:

- Automated Data Backup and Multi-Location Replication: Ensuring data is automatically backed up and replicated across various locations.

- Proactive System Monitoring and Alerts: Implementing advanced monitoring systems to detect and address anomalies swiftly.

- Consistent Updates and Security Patching: Regular updates and patches enhance system security and functionality, reducing vulnerability to failures.

Conclusion

Implementing effective disaster recovery and zero-downtime deployment strategies is essential for any organization that relies on continuous digital service availability. Through strategic approaches like blue-green deployments, canary releases, feature toggles, and database versioning, organizations can ensure operational continuity and enhance service reliability. Coupled with comprehensive disaster recovery planning, these practices help maintain system resilience, ensuring continuous availability and an optimal user experience.

Circuit breakers, rate limiters, and fallback methods

In the landscape of software development, particularly within the context of microservices architecture, it is essential to maintain system resilience and manage failures effectively. Techniques such as circuit breakers, rate limiters, and fallback methods play pivotal roles in ensuring systems remain functional and responsive, even under adverse conditions. These mechanisms are designed to prevent system overloads, efficiently manage incoming requests, and provide backup operations when primary paths fail.

Circuit Breakers

The circuit breaker pattern prevents a network or service from repeatedly trying to execute an operation that's likely to fail, thus safeguarding the overall system stability. It is particularly vital in distributed systems where multiple services interact; a failure in one component should not lead to a system-wide failure.

Operational Phases of Circuit Breakers:

1. Closed State: In its normal state, requests flow freely, but failure rates are monitored. Exceeding a failure threshold triggers a transition to the open state.

2. Open State: Attempts to execute operations are automatically blocked for a set period, reducing the load on the failing service and preventing further failures.

3. Half-Open State: Allows a limited number of test requests to determine if the underlying issue has been resolved. Success leads to closing the circuit, while failure reopens it.

Implementation Example with Resilience4j:

```java
import io.github.resilience4j.circuitbreaker.CircuitBreaker;
import io.github.resilience4j.circuitbreaker.CircuitBreakerConfig;
import java.time.Duration;

public class CommunicationService {
    private CircuitBreaker circuitBreaker = CircuitBreaker.of("service",
        CircuitBreakerConfig.custom()
        .failureRateThreshold(50)
        .waitDurationInOpenState(Duration.ofMillis(1000))
        .ringBufferSizeInHalfOpenState(2)
        .ringBufferSizeInClosedState(10)
        .build());

    public String sendMessage() {
        return circuitBreaker.executeSupplier(() -> performOperation());
    }

    private String performOperation() {
        // Logic to perform operation
        return "Operation Completed";
    }
}
```

This configuration in Resilience4j sets up a circuit breaker with specific parameters to handle failures effectively.

Rate Limiters

Rate limiting is crucial for controlling the rate of traffic flow into or out of a network or application, ensuring that resources are used within their capacity limits to prevent service degradation.

Advantages of Rate Limiting:

- Mitigates API Overload: Protects APIs from receiving more traffic than they can handle.

- Controls Traffic Bursts: Helps in managing and smoothing out bursts of incoming traffic to maintain consistent service quality.

Implementation Example with Bucket4j:

```
import io.github.bucket4j.Bucket;
import io.github.bucket4j.Bucket4j;
import io.github.bucket4j.Refill;
import io.github.bucket4j.Bandwidth;
import java.time.Duration;

public class TrafficController {
    private final Bucket bucket;

    public TrafficController() {
        Bandwidth limit = Bandwidth.classic(10, Refill.greedy(10, Duration
            .ofMinutes(1)));
        this.bucket = Bucket4j.builder().addLimit(limit).build();
    }

    public boolean canProceed() {
        return bucket.tryConsume(1);
    }
}
```

This snippet shows how Bucket4j can be utilized to implement rate limiting, managing how many requests per minute are allowed.

Fallback Methods

Fallback methods provide an alternative operational path when primary service calls fail. They ensure that the application continues to deliver functionality and maintains a positive user experience during partial outages.

Example Using Hystrix for Fallback:

```
public class CustomerService {
    @HystrixCommand(fallbackMethod = "defaultCustomer")
    public Customer getCustomer(String id) {
        // logic to fetch customer details
    }

    private Customer defaultCustomer(String id) {
        // Logic for fallback customer details
        return new Customer("default");
    }
}
```

In this Hystrix example, `getCustomer` tries to retrieve customer details; if it fails, `defaultCustomer` provides a fallback customer object.

Conclusion

Employing circuit breakers, rate limiters, and fallback methods are essential for designing resilient systems that can handle unexpected load and failures gracefully. These strategies help in maintaining service continuity, managing resources efficiently, and ensuring a seamless experience for users, even during system disruptions. Integrating these patterns and techniques into software systems is crucial for businesses relying on high availability and robust performance.

Chapter Fifteen

Performance Testing and Benchmarking

Implementing comprehensive performance testing strategies

In the current technological era, optimal application performance under varying conditions is essential for success. A meticulously crafted performance testing strategy is crucial for identifying system inefficiencies, understanding performance across diverse scenarios, and ensuring that applications meet their designated performance standards. Such strategies encompass a range of advanced testing methodologies, tools, and procedures designed to thoroughly assess how a system performs.

Essentials of Performance Testing

Performance testing involves analyzing the speed, responsiveness, and stability of a system under particular workloads. It diverges from functional testing by focusing on performance issues rather than software functionality, aiming to reveal how well the system handles expected and peak user loads.

Primary Goals of Performance Testing:

- Load Testing: Observes system performance under normal conditions.

- Stress Testing: Determines system capacity by testing beyond normal operational capacity until it fails, identifying its breaking point.

- Scalability Testing: Assesses the ability of the system to scale up or down and examines the impact of these changes on performance.

- Stability Testing (Soak Testing): Confirms the system can endure expected loads for extended periods without degradation of performance or functionality.

Developing a Performance Testing Strategy

A robust performance testing strategy includes several critical stages, from setup to execution and ongoing analysis:

1. Determine Performance Metrics: Specify clear, quantifiable targets such as response time, throughput, transaction error rate, and system resource usage.

2. Select Appropriate Tools: Pick tools that align with the technology stack of the application and fulfill the testing requirements. Commonly used tools for this purpose include Apache JMeter, LoadRunner, and Gatling, which simulate varied user behaviors and measure system performance under stress.

Example using Apache JMeter:

```xml
<httpSampler>
    <method>GET</method>
    <path>/service/endpoint</path>
    <assertions>
        <responseAssertion>
            <pattern>200 OK</pattern>
            <testType>RESPONSE_CODE</testType>
        </responseAssertion>
    </assertions>
    <constantTimer delay="500" />
</httpSampler>
```

This JMeter example configures a test to monitor an API endpoint's performance by evaluating its response time and ensuring it returns a successful response code.

3. Create Realistic Test Scenarios: Formulate test cases that mimic actual user interactions with the system to ensure it can efficiently handle both common operations and potential edge cases.

4. Emulate Real-User Conditions: Test in environments that replicate the production setting, including network variations, user concurrency levels, and geographic spread.

5. Incorporate Testing into Development Pipelines: Embed performance testing into the continuous integration/continuous deployment (CI/CD) pipeline to evaluate the impact of changes continuously.

Example CI configuration:

```
stages:
  - build
  - unitTest
  - performanceTest

performanceTest:
  stage: performanceTest
  script:
    - run_performance_tests.sh
  only:
    - main
```

This configuration for a CI tool initiates performance tests on changes to the main branch, ensuring performance impacts are assessed promptly.

6. Analyze Test Outcomes Intensively: Utilize advanced data visualization tools like Grafana or Kibana to scrutinize performance test data, identifying trends and pinpointing areas requiring optimization.

Conclusion

Implementing an effective performance testing strategy is critical for delivering high-quality software capable of performing under various scenarios. By establishing precise performance metrics, utilizing suitable testing tools, designing effective test scenarios, and embedding these tests within the development lifecycle, teams can guarantee that their applications are robust, responsive, and ready to handle real-world conditions. This strategic approach not only improves software quality but also significantly enhances the user experience by ensuring reliable and efficient application performance.

Tools and frameworks for benchmarking Spring Boot applications

Benchmarking plays a pivotal role in the development cycle of Spring Boot applications, offering crucial insights that guide performance optimizations. By leveraging specialized tools and frameworks, developers can detect areas prone to performance issues, optimize their resource usage, and ensure that applications perform well under expected operational scenarios.

The Value of Benchmarking in Spring Boot

Spring Boot is engineered to expedite the development and deployment of microservices and web applications. To guarantee these applications deliver optimal performance across various environments, thorough benchmarking is indispensable. It allows developers to simulate expected loads and measure critical performance metrics, ensuring the application can handle real-world traffic and processing demands.

Top Tools and Frameworks for Benchmarking

Several tools and frameworks stand out for benchmarking Spring Boot applications, each offering distinct features for comprehensive performance analysis:

1. Apache JMeter

   - Description: Apache JMeter is an open-source tool designed for load testing and measuring performance of web applications. It supports diverse protocols and can simulate heavy loads to assess how applications respond under stress.

- Application in Spring Boot: JMeter is effective for creating intricate test plans that involve various HTTP requests to Spring Boot endpoints, useful for analyzing performance under both typical and extreme conditions.

- Example Configuration:

```xml
<!-- Sample JMeter configuration for HTTP Request testing -->
<HTTPSamplerProxy guiclass="HttpTestSampleGui" testclass="HTTPSamplerProxy">
  <stringProp name="HTTPSampler.domain">localhost</stringProp>
  <stringProp name="HTTPSampler.port">8080</stringProp>
  <stringProp name="HTTPSampler.path">/api/items</stringProp>
  <stringProp name="HTTPSampler.method">GET</stringProp>
</HTTPSamplerProxy>
```

2. Gatling

- Overview: Gatling is a powerful, Scala-based load testing tool known for its high-performance capabilities. It enables developers to script complex user behaviors and provides rich analytics to evaluate application performance.

- Usage in Spring Boot: Gatling allows for modeling of user interactions with a Spring Boot application, offering detailed insights through performance metrics and data visualization.

- Example Usage:

```
class LoadTestSimulation extends Simulation {
  val httpConf = http.baseUrl("http://localhost:8080")

  val scn = scenario("Typical User Behavior")
    .exec(http("Request Profile Data")
    .get("/profile/data"))

  setUp(
    scn.inject(atOnceUsers(100))
  ).protocols(httpConf)
}
```

3. Spring Boot Actuator

- Overview: Integrated into the Spring Boot framework, the Actuator provides management and monitoring capabilities through HTTP endpoints or JMX, offering built-in metrics and operational information.

- Implementation in Spring Boot: It allows for easy activation of performance metrics, essential for ongoing monitoring and benchmarking during development and in production.

- Setup Example:

```java
import org.springframework.boot.SpringApplication;
import org.springframework.boot.autoconfigure.SpringBootApplication;

@SpringBootApplication
public class MainApplication {
  public static void main(String[] args) {
    SpringApplication.run(MainApplication.class, args);
  }
}
```

4. VisualVM

- Overview: VisualVM is a comprehensive visual tool integrating various JDK command-line utilities for profiling Java applications, suitable for both development and production environments.

- Usage in Spring Boot: It proves invaluable for real-time monitoring of a running Spring Boot application, helping track CPU usage, memory footprint, and thread activity to pinpoint performance optimizations.

Conclusion

Choosing the right set of tools for benchmarking Spring Boot applications is essential for ensuring they are prepared to handle the demands of modern software environments. Apache JMeter, Gatling, Spring Boot Actuator, and VisualVM each offer unique functionalities that enable developers to thoroughly understand and enhance their application's performance. Regularly integrating these tools into the development process ensures Spring Boot applications are efficient, robust, and capable of delivering exceptional performance.

Analyzing and interpreting performance test results

In software development, the execution of performance tests is crucial to ensure that applications perform optimally under varied stress and user scenarios. However, the effectiveness of these tests is contingent not just on their execution but significantly on the meticulous analysis and interpretation of the results. This analysis enables development teams to make critical improvements that boost application performance, scalability, and ultimately user satisfaction.

Deciphering Performance Test Data

Data from performance tests offers a rich array of metrics such as response times, throughput, error rates, and various system resource usages. To effectively interpret this data, one must consider the test conditions, expected behaviors, and the application's operational context.

1. Response Times and Latencies: These are critical as they affect user experience directly. When analyzing response times, it's important to look beyond averages and consider percentile distributions (like the 95th and 99th percentiles) to understand the performance under peak loads.

2. Throughput: This metric, indicating the number of transactions or requests processed per unit of time, is essential for assessing the application's capacity and identifying performance degradation points.

3. Resource Utilization: Monitoring resources like CPU, memory, and disk I/O is vital for identifying performance bottlenecks. These metrics help trace issues back to potential inefficiencies or infrastructural limitations.

Tools and Techniques for Analysis

A variety of tools can assist in the visual and analytical examination of performance test data. Platforms like Grafana and Prometheus are instrumental for their powerful visualization capabilities that simplify data analysis.

Example of Visualizing Data with Grafana:

```
- Step 1: Configure Prometheus as the data source.
- Step 2: Design a dashboard to showcase vital metrics such as response times, error
- Step 3: Implement queries in Grafana to illustrate response time percentiles.
- Step 4: Set up alerts to notify of any metric thresholds being breached.
```

These tools enable teams to delve deeper into the metrics, identifying trends and irregularities more efficiently.

Interpreting Test Results

The interpretation of performance test results must align with business objectives and user expectations. This involves several key actions:

1. Baseline and Benchmark Comparison: It's important to measure performance against established baselines or

industry benchmarks. Significant deviations may signal performance issues or areas needing enhancement.

2. Pattern and Anomaly Detection: Identifying data patterns can help pinpoint systemic issues, like memory leaks or spikes in response times due to database bottlenecks.

3. Scalability Insight: Understanding how the application's performance metrics scale with increasing load provides critical information on its scalability and capacity needs.

4. Translating Insights into Actions: The ultimate goal of analyzing performance test data is to derive actionable insights that lead to performance optimizations, whether through code refactoring, infrastructure upgrades, or query optimization.

Best Practices

1. Ongoing Monitoring: Continually monitoring application performance post-deployment is crucial to detect and address issues that were not evident during initial testing.

2. Automate Performance Regression Tests: Automating these tests to run regularly and compare against historical performance data helps in quickly identifying regressions.

3. Collaborative Review: Engaging various stakeholders in the review process ensures a comprehensive understanding of the performance data, leading to well-rounded decision-making.

Conclusion

Thorough analysis and interpretation of performance test results are vital for proactive application performance management. By employing advanced visualization tools and adopting systematic analytical methodologies, teams can ensure their applications are not only meeting current performance standards but are also prepared to handle future demands. This ongoing process helps maintain the software's competitiveness and relevance in an ever-evolving technological landscape.

Conclusion

Recap of expert-level performance tuning and configuration techniques

In today's software development realm, achieving optimal application performance goes beyond mere resource management—it involves mastering a suite of advanced tuning and configuration strategies. These strategies are crucial for optimizing system efficiency, minimizing latency, and maintaining robust performance under heavy loads.

Overview of Advanced Performance Tuning and Configuration

Performance tuning and configuration involve a series of targeted adjustments and setups that enhance how software interacts with its hardware and network environment. These adjustments range from code refinements and server optimizations to complex database configurations and network setups, all aimed at boosting operational efficiency.

Essential Advanced Techniques for Performance Optimization

Achieving expert-level proficiency in performance tuning requires an in-depth understanding of system architecture and a strategic approach to problem-solving. Here are several high-level techniques employed by seasoned professionals:

1. Code Optimization:

    • Streamlined Algorithms: Implementing more efficient algorithms to reduce computational overhead.

- Enhanced Concurrency: Leveraging modern concurrency models to improve performance in multi-threaded applications.

Example in Java:

```java
// Example of using Java's parallel streams for enhanced data processing efficiency
List<String> optimizedData = bigDataList.parallelStream()
                            .map(data -> process(data))
                            .collect(Collectors.toList());
```

2. Database Performance Enhancements:

- Effective Indexing: Creating indexes to expedite data retrieval processes.

- Query Refinement: Enhancing SQL queries for faster execution and lower resource consumption.

SQL Example:

```sql
-- Creating an index for faster queries
CREATE INDEX ON transactions(userId);

-- Optimized SQL query
SELECT * FROM transactions WHERE userId = 'user123';
```

3. Caching Mechanisms:

- Local and Application-Level Caching: Implementing caching solutions to store frequently accessed data, thus minimizing database hits.

- Distributed Caching Solutions: Utilizing technologies like Redis or Memcached to manage caching across multiple servers effectively.

Example with Redis (Pseudo-code):

```
if (redisCache.exists(key)) {
    return redisCache.get(key);
} else {
    Object data = fetchDataFromDB(key);
    redisCache.set(key, data);
    return data;
}
```

4. Network Enhancements:

- Protocol Adjustments: Tuning network protocols for optimized data delivery.

- Sophisticated Load Balancing: Implementing advanced load balancing to distribute traffic evenly across servers.

5. Resource Management:

- Memory Optimization: Configuring memory usage to ensure efficient memory allocation.

- CPU Load Management: Setting CPU priorities to optimize processing power usage.

Linux Example Commands:

```
# Setting process priority
nice -n 5 processId

# Assigning a process to specific CPUs
taskset -cp 0,1,2 4567
```

6. Profiling and Continuous Monitoring Tools:

- Application Profiling: Using tools like VisualVM or New Relic to regularly profile the application for bottlenecks.

- Real-time Monitoring: Setting up Prometheus and Grafana for ongoing system monitoring and alerting.

Monitoring Setup Example (Pseudo-code):

```
- Configure Prometheus to collect performance metrics
- Set up a Grafana dashboard to visualize these metrics and track performance trends
```

Best Practices for Performance Tuning

- Systematic Approach: Consider the entire system when applying performance enhancements to ensure balanced improvements across all components.

- Iterative Optimization: Treat performance tuning as an iterative process—regularly analyze results, adjust configurations, and measure the impact.

- Comprehensive Documentation: Maintain meticulous records of tuning activities to track changes over time and facilitate potential rollbacks or incremental adjustments.

Conclusion

Mastering expert-level performance tuning and configuration techniques is vital for developers and system administrators tasked with managing high-performance applications. By applying sophisticated coding techniques, optimizing databases, implementing effective caching strategies, and utilizing cutting-edge tools for system monitoring and profiling, professionals can ensure their applications are not only capable of handling current demands but are also scalable for future needs. This proactive stance on performance management guarantees that applications remain efficient, responsive, and competitive in an ever-evolving technological landscape.

Emphasizing the importance of continuous performance optimization

In today's fast-paced technological environment, continuous performance optimization is essential to sustain and improve the operational effectiveness of software applications. As software grows in complexity and user expectations increase, the need for ongoing enhancements to performance becomes critical. This continuous process ensures that applications can effectively respond to evolving challenges and technological shifts, thereby maintaining high service quality.

The Necessity of Continuous Performance Optimization

Performance optimization should be viewed not as an isolated event but as a vital, ongoing part of the software development lifecycle. As applications expand, integrate with new systems, or are updated, new performance issues can emerge. By adopting a strategy of continuous optimization, organizations can address these issues promptly, ensuring robust, responsive, and efficient performance under diverse operational conditions.

1. Evolving User Expectations: Users continually expect faster and more responsive applications. Regular performance optimization is crucial for meeting and exceeding these expectations.

2. Integration of Emerging Technologies: With constant technological advancements, integrating new tools and frameworks can significantly enhance performance and capabilities.

3. Addressing Scalability Issues: As user bases grow, applications must scale effectively. Continuous optimization ensures scalability while maintaining performance integrity.

4. Avoiding Performance Decay: Software can experience gradual performance decay due to cumulative minor changes. Ongoing optimization efforts are vital to identify and rectify these declines.

Approaches to Continuous Performance Optimization

Effective continuous performance optimization involves a combination of strategies that contribute to sustained application performance improvements:

1. Profiling and Continuous Monitoring: Utilizing profiling tools and continuous monitoring solutions is essential for tracking application performance and pinpointing optimization needs.

Example with Application Performance Monitoring tools:

```
- Set up continuous monitoring with tools like New Relic.
- Establish alerts for abnormal performance metrics.
```

2. Integration of Performance Tests in CI/CD: Embedding performance testing within the CI/CD pipeline ensures that updates do not adversely impact performance, maintaining a standard across updates.

Example of CI/CD pipeline integration:

```
stages:
  - build
  - test
  - deploy
  - performance

performance:
  stage: performance
  script:
    - echo "Executing performance tests..."
    - run_performance_tests.sh
  only:
    - main
```

3. Iterative Enhancement: An iterative approach allows for consistent, incremental performance improvements, reducing the risk associated with major overhauls.

4. Data-Driven Optimization: Leveraging analytics from user behavior and system performance provides concrete data to guide optimization efforts.

Example of analytics-driven insights:

```
- Use analytics to monitor page responsiveness and adapt backend operations accordingly.
- Track user engagement to prioritize performance improvements in high-traffic areas.
```

5. **Creating Feedback Loops:** Incorporating feedback from users and real-time monitoring into the development process ensures that performance tuning addresses actual user scenarios.

Benefits of Continuous Performance Optimization

The advantages of maintaining an ongoing focus on performance optimization are profound:

- **Improved User Experience:** Regular updates to performance enhance user satisfaction and engagement, leading to higher retention rates.

- **Greater System Reliability:** By consistently addressing potential performance issues, systems become more reliable and less prone to failures.

- **Cost-Effectiveness:** Efficient resource utilization through optimized performance can significantly lower operational costs.

- **Sustained Competitive Edge:** Continuous enhancement of performance keeps an application at the forefront of technology, maintaining a competitive advantage in the market.

Conclusion

Continuous performance optimization is imperative for modern software development teams aiming to deliver superior software solutions. By embedding continuous monitoring, iterative improvements, and proactive adjustments into the development lifecycle, teams can ensure their applications not only meet current performance standards but are also well-prepared for future demands. This proactive approach is crucial in a landscape where technological advancement and user expectations are ever-increasing.

Future trends in Spring Boot and performance engineering

Spring Boot has dramatically streamlined the development and management of modern web applications, promoting simplicity without sacrificing the robustness provided by the Spring Framework. As we look ahead, certain trends are poised to influence the future trajectory of Spring Boot and performance engineering significantly, driven by the need for more dynamic, scalable, and resilient systems in a cloud-centric environment.

Future Developments in Spring Boot

Spring Boot is continuously evolving to better facilitate developers in creating efficient and effective applications. Here are some anticipated advancements in Spring Boot:

1. Increased Cloud Native Integrations: As the deployment landscape continues to favor cloud environments, deeper integration with cloud-native technologies, such as Kubernetes, is expected. Future

iterations of Spring Boot might come with enhanced features for easier cloud management and scalability.

Example Integration: Future versions could offer built-in mechanisms for more seamless scaling and management of services within Kubernetes, simplifying microservices orchestration without extensive custom configuration.

2. Expansion of Reactive Programming: The demand for applications capable of handling real-time data with high responsiveness is rising. Spring Boot's reactive programming capabilities, through the WebFlux module, are likely to become more mainstream as developers seek to address these needs.

```
@RestController
@RequestMapping("/reactive")
public class ReactiveDataController {
    @GetMapping("/stream")
    public Mono<String> streamData() {
        return Mono.just("Streamed data response");
    }
}
```

3. Enhanced Performance Monitoring Tools: To aid in continuously monitoring and optimizing performance, Spring Boot might integrate more sophisticated diagnostic tools directly, enabling developers to proactively manage and optimize application performance.

573

Emerging Trends in Performance Engineering

Performance engineering is integral to delivering software that not only functions correctly but also performs efficiently under various conditions. Emerging trends in this field include:

1. AI-Driven Performance Optimization: Leveraging AI and machine learning algorithms to automate the identification of performance bottlenecks and the application of optimizations is becoming increasingly prevalent. These technologies provide predictive insights and automated optimization strategies based on comprehensive data analysis.

Example Use Case: Future performance optimization tools may automatically analyze performance metrics and logs, suggesting or implementing enhancements to improve efficiency.

2. Performance Integration in DevOps: Integrating performance management deeply within DevOps workflows ensures that performance criteria are evaluated continually throughout the software development process.

```
stages:
  - compile
  - test
  - deploy
  - performance_analysis
  - performance_optimization

performance_optimization:
  stage: performance_optimization
  script:
    - echo "Implementing automated performance enhancements..."
    - auto_optimize.sh
```

3. Serverless Architecture Optimization: With the rise of serverless computing, optimizing performance in these environments is becoming crucial. This includes enhancing how quickly serverless functions can start and efficiently manage resource allocation.

Convergence of Spring Boot and Performance Engineering Trends

The future will likely see a merging of Spring Boot development and performance engineering practices, with a greater emphasis on creating systems that are not only capable of high performance but also highly adaptable to changing conditions.

- Performance-as-Code: Following the paradigm of infrastructure-as-code, performance settings and optimizations may start being defined directly within application codebases.

- Adaptive Performance Strategies: We might see applications that adjust their performance profiles in real-time based on live performance data, utilizing cloud scalability features dynamically to handle varying loads.

Conclusion

As we move forward, Spring Boot and performance engineering will increasingly focus on integrating advanced, intelligent solutions that simplify the development of high-performance applications while ensuring they are adaptable for future needs. This ongoing evolution will make performance optimization a more integral part of the development process, ensuring that applications are not only effective upon deployment but continue to perform optimally as they scale and evolve.

www.ingramcontent.com/pod-product-compliance
Lightning Source LLC
LaVergne TN
LVHW051347050326
832903LV00030B/2892